DISTRIBUTED MULTIMEDIA DATABASE TECHNOLOGIES
Supported *Supported* **MPEG-7** and *by* **MPEG-21**

DISTRIBUTED MULTIMEDIA DATABASE TECHNOLOGIES

Supported **MPEG-7** and *by* **MPEG-21**

Harald Kosch

CRC PRESS

Boca Raton   London   New York   Washington, D.C.

Library of Congress Cataloging-in-Publication Data

Kosch, Harald.
    Distributed multimedia database technologies supported by MPEG-7 and MPEG-21 / by Harald Kosch.
      p. cm.
    Includes bibliographical references and index.
    ISBN 0-8493-1854-8 (alk. paper)
     1. MPEG (Video coding standard) 2. Multimedia systems. 3. Distributed databases. I. Title.

    TK6680.5.K67 2003
    006.7—dc22

                                      2003055582

Visit the Auerbach Publications Web site at www.auerbach-publications.com

© 2004 by CRC Press LLC
Auerbach is an imprint of CRC Press LLC

No claim to original U.S. Government works
International Standard Book Number 0-8493-1854-8
Library of Congress Card Number 2003055582
Printed in the United States of America 1 2 3 4 5 6 7 8 9 0

Dedication

I dedicate this book to my wife Edith and daughters Klara and Marie-Sophie (who painted a lot of teddy bears on my manuscript), without whose understanding the writing of this book would not have been possible.

Preface

Imagine, you download an MP3 (Moving Picture Experts Group [MPEG] 1 Audio layer 3) file, recorded in the U.S., sung by a French singer, stored in a server in Japan, routed over the Internet through Asia and Europe, and listened to on the top of an Austrian hill on a mobile phone produced in Germany.

Isn't this astonishing that all this works? How is this possible?

The main craft behind this cooperative international success is the standardization work of different organizations (International Organization for Standardization [ISO], International Electronic Commission [IEC] and their Moving Picture Experts Group [MPEG], International Telecommunications Union [ITU], and others) that makes this possible. Their definitions of interoperable multimedia formats and their specifications of decoder architectures make it possible that the same multimedia file may be consumed everywhere and anytime. From these core technologies, new and emerging standards will help us to access multimedia by their content; for example, to show all images where a dog runs after a ball, or all videos where Greta Garbo is laughing. At the same time, we can set up a multimedia framework that enables the transparent and augmented use of multimedia resources across heterogeneous networks and terminals; for example, we may define the rights a user may exercise on our digital photo album.

Today's multimedia systems are complex self-organizing file-sharing systems (see, e.g., the popular Morpheus system). The main components of such systems are database, multimedia storage server, network, and client systems in a more and more mobile environment. However, this is not enough. New standards tie these components together. These are the new and emerging standards by the ISO/IEC JTC 1/SC 29/WG 11 MPEG, namely, the MPEG-4, MPEG-7, and MPEG-21 standards. They offer standardized technology for coding multimedia data, natural and synthetic (e.g., photography and face animation, respectively) and continuous and static (e.g., video and image, respectively), as well as for describing content (Multimedia Description Interface) and for an open multimedia framework for a fair and interoperable use of multimedia in a distributed environment. We will also point out the relationship to some of the popular multimedia formats, MP3 and MP4, which are based on the MPEG coding family.

In addition to coding and describing multiple kinds of information, it is imperative to integrate their semantic meaning into the main actors of a system adequately (and not only in the database but also in network elements, users, etc.). For example, a multimedia newspaper will include text, images, audio, and short clips. An automatic analysis tool filtering out the news, which meets the user's interest, may consume it. The presented multimedia objects are conceptually related and have to exist in conjunction with each other. Synthesizing and synchronizing the various forms of information provided by the multiple media based on user needs are very important parts of the multimedia application.

The new object-coding standard, MPEG-4, will help us to integrate these diverse media in one format, in one stream, in one description, and in one architecture. In addition, and equally important, is MPEG-7 (an international standard since 2002), which provides us with a structured metadata description for semantically rich media content. It will help us to search, select, and finally access the desired information in the immensely growing forest of available multimedia content information. The currently established MPEG-21 standard introduces an open multimedia framework for a fair and interoperable use of multimedia in a distributed environment. In this sense, it incorporates resources (e.g., MPEG-4, but not exclusively) and their description (using MPEG-7 or other multimedia description standards).

Multimedia database management systems (MMDBMSs) are the technology for content management, storage, and streaming. Furthermore, a MMDBMS must be able to handle diverse kinds of data and to store sufficient information to integrate the media stored within. In addition, to be useful, a database has to provide sophisticated mechanisms for querying, processing, retrieving, inserting, deleting, and updating data. Structured query language (SQL)/MM, the multimedia extension to SQL developed by the SC 39 of ISO/IEC, supports multimedia database storage and content-based search in a standardized way.

A multimedia system needs a mechanism to communicate with its environment, with the Internet, with the clients, and with the applications in general. MPEG-7 provides a standard multimedia metadata format for global communication, but it does not provide the framework to let the different active and passive players in a global multimedia system interact. MPEG-21 closes this gap by establishing an infrastructure for a distributed multimedia framework. Digital items are created and consumed, and users can interact with, modify, view, and communicate them. A digital item is a container for all multimedia data and content and is an interoperable unit in a distributed multimedia system, which may be handled by all players participating in the MPEG-21 agreement.

In this sense, this book describes the technologies, concepts, and tools of distributed, content-based multimedia systems. We focus on the practical uses of the standard technologies of MPEG and SQL/MM in these components and for interoperability among them (for data exchange, transactions, interaction, etc.). This book presents a vision of an open distributed multimedia framework that encompasses a single view of components in such a way that it lets these components integrate in a cooperatively working environment, which offers rich multimedia access in an increasingly mobile world.

To complicate matters, the same picture may elicit different responses from different viewers, who may use very different words to describe the picture. Therefore, in an image database the use of words or keywords may fail to be an effective way of retrieving the data desired or of classifying the images stored. Thus, one needs a metadata model of multimedia data that describes the semantics of the multimedia objects and how they are related to each other.

A picture is worth a thousand words, but how do you find it?

Finding multimedia objects by their content in a database means searching on the basis of content descriptions and similarity measures. Currently available multimedia database management systems (MMDBMSs) promise to efficiently find multimedia objects by their content. They often claim that they can manage huge quantities of multimedia data and can support many different applications.[2–5] For instance, if one investigates Oracle's Technet Network at http://technet.oracle.com for applications using multimedia data through the use of their integrated search engine and through browsing, one may find out that Oracle 9i promises to support video on demand, home shopping, geographic information systems, computer-aided design, photographic libraries, art gallery and museum management, and educational systems as well as E-applications including E-business, E-commerce, and so forth.

Less poetic: *Can I get and view this image with my mobile phone?*

A number of mechanisms have been proposed to meet the demands of multimedia delivery and presentation in the (mobile) Internet. Discrete media transport is less critical to real-timeliness, but gives only a partial view of the complete multimedia world. It is conjectured that continuous media and, in particular, video flow will make up a substantial part of future network traffic, as it is an increasingly important media type in distributed information, education, and entertainment systems.[6]

The key for the effective use of multimedia in our usage and terminal environment is to guarantee the required (by user, terminal) level of QoS. QoS support in distributed multimedia systems has been a vivid research field for many years and has led to the development of sophisticated QoS architectures that address the issue of end-to-end QoS support for multimedia communications (rather than investigating individual architectural layers). A survey is available in Aurrecoechea.[7] The relationship between content and media is yet not very clear. MPEG-21[8] is currently establishing a common multimedia framework for the resource (the media itself) and its conceptual content described by metadata.

We are still at the beginning of the development of techniques to guarantee efficiency and effectiveness in content-based multimedia systems. The premature state of these technologies is caused by the peculiar nature metadata in general and the available standards in particular. Focus is put on comparative analysis, rather than complete descriptions. Some of the standards are described in more detail in later chapters as necessary (e.g., MPEG-7 is further discussed in Chapter 2). Finally, Section 1.4 gives an overview of the remaining content of the book.

1.1 Multimedia Content: Context

Exhibit 1.3 shows an average picture.

> *It is not so much that a picture is worth a thousand words, for many fewer words can describe a still picture for most retrieval purposes, the issue has more to do with the fact that those words vary from one person to another.* *

> *A picture is worth a thousand words.*

The perceptual quality of an image differs from one viewer to another, and thus the adage is certainly true. Sometimes it is just impossible to summarize the content or the message or the characteristics of a picture in words—not to mention to do so in just a few words.

> *… the issue has more to do with the fact that those (thousands) words vary from one person to another.*

Exhibit 1.3. Average picture.

*Taken from Keister, Lucinda H., User types and queries: impact on image access systems, in *Challenges in Indexing Electronic Text and Image*, Fidel, Raya, et al., Eds. ASIS Monograph Series, Learned Information, Medford, NJ, 1994, pp. 7–22.[2]

addressed. These are media related—for instance, how to develop scaleable media compression technologies that adapt to changing usage environments—or metadata oriented—for instance, how to extract semantic features from a video (to recognize that a car is displayed in an image), how to represent usage environments for adaptation and for intellectual properties, and how to relate these metadata to the media data they describe.

Other problems are related to issues of resource distribution in a multimedia system. To realize a multimedia delivery system meeting the necessary real-time constraints, new network technologies and communication protocols must be provided to guarantee sufficient quality of service (QoS). In many cases, however, the network cannot guarantee QoS, and the multimedia resource must be adapted to the new environment. Hence, solutions for content-based adaptation have to be sought.

The use of standard technologies and description in a distributed multimedia system is imperative to guarantee an interoperable usage. We review the newest coding standard from the ISO-IEC JTC 1/SC 29/WG 11 MPEG: the MPEG-4 standard. In particular, we describe its scalable coding properties. We introduce the ISO-IEC MPEG-7 multimedia description standard, which proposes tools for describing and delivering multimedia metadata, and the ISO-IEC MPEG-21 standard, which designs an open multimedia framework. MPEG-4 focuses on the representation of media data, while MPEG-7 deals with the standardization of metadata, which describes the content of media data. MPEG-21 encompasses these two standards for a global view of the distributed multimedia system. Looking at Exhibit 1.2 again, one can say that MPEG-21 intends to regulate and direct the traffic in a distributed system in a way that provides universal, interoperable, and fair access to users in this highly heterogeneous environment.

In addition, and equally important, the book describes the current state-of-the-art distributed multimedia database technologies. Hence, we describe precise technologies for multimedia indexing and retrieval in multimedia databases and introduce the multimedia enhancement for SQL (Structured Query Language), the SQL/MM (multimedia), for supporting a structured query language and query processing system. SQL/MM is related to MPEG-7. Common characteristics and differences between the two standards are pointed out.

The remainder of this chapter gives an overview of basic elements in a distributed multimedia system. Section 1.1 deals with multimedia content indexing and retrieval. Section 1.2 presents a common view of multimedia systems and databases. Section 1.3 introduces (multi)media data and multimedia metadata and associated standards. This section discusses media coding standards—in particular, we discuss standards from the MPEG family (MPEG-1, MPEG-2, and MPEG-4). It also introduces multimedia entry tier to user requests. Normally, the Web server handles authentication issues, which may be delegated to some authentication server. At the same time, the Web server is the front end to the multimedia database. The multimedia database is the "master" of metadata, and the multimedia storage and streaming server is the "master" of the media data. Both sets of data are strongly related, and a communication protocol has to be set up among these components. There are tight protocols, as are, for instance, realizable with the Oracle products. The communication link between the server elements is, in general, bidirectional, as pointed out in Exhibit 1.2. For instance, if a user inserts a video into the media storage server, the database has to be updated with its metainformation. If the database recognizes (possibly from user input) that a video is outdated, it has to instruct the media storage server to delete it.

Using metadata in a distributed multimedia system has many advantages. It enables us to search multimedia data by content; for example, "list all video clips from an online video shop where Roger Moore plays 007." However, before multimedia data can be searched, the data have to be indexed. This means that metadata information has to be extracted from the video automatically or annotated manually.

Another use for metadata is in describing usage environment characteristics (e.g., user preferences, presentation preferences) and network and terminal constraints. This information may be used to personalize the search for content. For instance, a user is looking for all the soccer events of the weekend, but the network to the user's terminal has currently an available bandwidth of only 500 kilobits per second (kbps). Thus, the database not only has to search all videos showing the soccer events of the weekend, but it has to see whether the bandwidth requirement of the video exceeds the user's constraints. If this is the case, the database may offer alternatives; for instance, showing the key-images (key-frames) extracted from the video.

Metadata are also used for describing intellectual properties of the multimedia data. These properties may guarantee a fair use of the data in commercial applications. Finally, metadata may be employed in a distributed multimedia system to describe resource adaptation capabilities. Including such metadata prepares the stream for unforeseen situations on the delivery path to the client. This makes sense, as dynamic changes in resource availability may degrade the quality of the video and make further delivery impossible. In this context, the structure of the streamed media might also be described by metadata for an efficient adaptation in the network. For example, the metadata may include information on how to transcode the media to meet resource constraints.

To guarantee the widespread use of multimedia data and metadata in a dynamic distributed multimedia system, two problems have to be

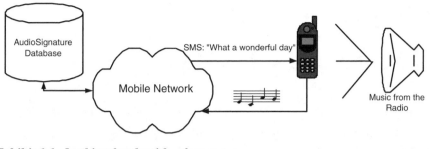

Exhibit 1.1. Looking for the title of a song.

relies on the spectral flatness properties in several frequency bands to identify the unique AudioSignature of a piece of music. The Fraunhofer Institute introduced this AudioSignature into the MPEG-7 standards, which allows not only the identification of the song but also retrieval of information on the melody, the sound timbres, recoding history, and so on.

Using multimedia metadata effectively in a distributed multimedia system requires a multimedia database for managing, storing, searching, and delivering metadata. The metadatabase needs to have knowledge about the storage location of the media data and the metadata and should match usage descriptions against media resource requirements. Exhibit 1.2 shows a possible distributed architecture and the main players in a multimedia system and database. Often referred to as N-tier architecture in the distributed database literature,[1] this system includes a Web server as an

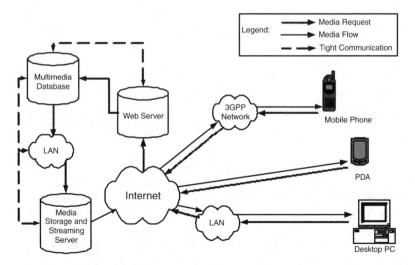

Exhibit 1.2. Components and information flow of a typical distributed multimedia system and database.

Chapter 1
Introduction

Internet multimedia communication, such as video- and audio-on-demand, video conferencing, and distance e-Learning, let us experience multimedia at the desk. Video mobile phones will, in the near future, let us create short video clips, send these videos to a partner mobile phone or to a personal database at home, and play videos that we receive from a friend. These systems are peer-to-peer: terminal clients become servers and vice versa. To realize the vision of peer-to-peer multimedia systems with heterogonous terminals, many technical problems need to be solved. These problems concern all layers of a multimedia system; for instance, the multimedia communication system, distributed control system, and storage and retrieval systems. Strongly related to this vision of peer-to-peer multimedia systems is the enhancement of a multimedia system with metadata. Metadata describe the multimedia content and could be semantic descriptions, such as which persons appear in a video clip; information on color characteristics of a video, such as the dominant color in an image; or information on how a video might be adapted if resources become rare.

The emerging International Organization for Standardization and International Electrotechnical Commission (ISO-IEC) Moving Picture Experts Group (MPEG)-7 metadata standard, proposing description schemes for multimedia, helps us to find multimedia by content. Imagine that you are listening to a radio song and you could not remember the title (see Exhibit 1.1). Using your mobile phone, you can get recorded 10 seconds of the song and then use an audio recognition service (e.g., the Music Scout service from net mobile),[*] from which you will very probably get a prompt and positive content identification via Short Message Service (SMS). How does this work?

The Fraunhofer Institute proposed an audio signature technology (integrated into Music Scout, for instance) that automatically identifies audio material through comparison with previously registered audio content.[**] More than 15,000 so-called audio fingerprints have been recorded and are ready to be searched. The search is tolerant to linear distortion (e.g., filtering and band limiting), nonlinear distortion (including the codec used: MP3 [MPEG Audio Layer-3] or MPEG-2/4, adaptive audio coding [AAC]), and

[*]http://www.net-m.de/start.uk.htm.
[**]Fraunhofer Innovation AudioID (Erlangen, Germany); see http://www.emt.iis.fraunhofer.de/PM_AudioID_Thomson.htm.

Contents

About the Author

Harald Kosch is an associate professor at the University of Klagenfurt. His domains of interest are distributed multimedia systems, multimedia databases, middleware, and Internet applications. He started research at the École Normale Supérieure in 1993 during postgraduate study and entered the Ph.D. program in 1994, obtaining his Ph.D. degree in June 1997. He actively participates in the Moving Picture Experts Group (MPEG)-7 and MPEG-21 standardization and is involved in several international research projects in the domain of distributed multimedia systems.

Acknowledgments

My thanks go to Mulugeta Libsie for constant support and for reviewing all chapters; László Böszörményi for his good examples, for correcting many errors, and for the constant encouragement. Equally, I thank Hermann Hellwagner for his corrections and improvement suggestions; Mario Döller for his proofreading and for our discussions on how to design a multimedia database; and Christian Timmerer from Klagenfurt and Jörg Heuer from Siemens CT for the common contributing work to the MPEG-7 and MPEG-21 standards.

I also thank my colleagues and friends at the Institute of Information Technology at the University Klagenfurt for their support during the writing of my habilitation thesis and this book.

of multimedia; that is, heterogeneity of the multimedia data (continuous vs. static data); higher storage, processing, and communication requirements than needed for traditional data; difficulty of semantic indexing; complex multimedia data modeling; and difficulty of adaptation to different applications and resource availabilities such as network bandwidth. To make content-based multimedia systems fully available for commercial applications, one has to consider the following topics:

1. *Retrieval and indexing.* Hardly any available content-based retrieval (CBR) techniques can answer a request like, "give me all video sequences showing Roger Moore laughing."[9,10] Video indexing schemes, based on similarity matches relying on low-level color and texture information, can only be the first step for really useful retrieval techniques.[5,11] Semantically meaningful indexing methods must be developed and linked to low-level indexing and retrieval.[12]

2. *Storage, communication, and performance.* Some multimedia data (especially video) has several orders of magnitude higher storage and network bandwidth requirements than does text (or even images).[13] Compression techniques have reached a mature level for most applications and have been standardized in various communities (e.g., the ISO-IEC MPEG [http://www.chiariglione.org/mpeg/] and ITU-T Video Coding Experts Group [VCEG; http://www.itu.int/ITU-T/]). Nevertheless, the adaptation of the digitally stored representation of the multimedia data to different applications, to different network bandwidths, and to different presentation devices is an open issue. This is, however, the key to achieving a level of performance that enables satisfactory usage of commercial applications including multimedia content.[14,15]

3. *Streaming and resource scheduling.* Continuous data (such as audio and video) needs continuous transport over the network and continuous presentation to the user. This demands resource-scheduling techniques providing guaranteed QoS at the server, as well as in the network and at the client side.[16]

4. *Authoring.* Authoring is mostly an unsolved problem.[17] There are some tools for special applications, such as video cutting, but even these have not yet reached a mature status.[18] There are some tools for annotating videos (e.g., that provided by Virage, http://www.virage.com), but there are no general tools for creating complex scenarios, such as an advertisement containing text, images, animated and natural video, and audio.

5. *Presentation.* Similar to authoring, presentation of complex scenarios not just consisting of all types of data but also requiring a set of spatial and temporal constraints on their presentation is another interesting issue.[19] In an advertisement, for example, we may be interested in presenting first a background image and music, and

then showing a video clip, which is subsequently enhanced by an animation and some blinking text. Especially interesting is the mapping of complex presentations onto widely differing devices ranging from mobile phones to high-performance workstations. Moreover, the management of presentation delivery in video servers is an open research question.[19,20]

1.2 Multimedia Systems and Databases

Multimedia systems will support media at many different levels of abstractions. Consider the following four applications: a Web-based multimedia application that manipulates images incorporated in the pages and streaming data that triggers the execution of an external viewer; a video editor that reads, writes, and manipulates video; an audio-video distribution service that distributes stored video information; and finally a multimedia search engine that finds videos in the Web that meet a certain search criteria.

At first, it appears that these multimedia applications do not have much in common. However, all of them can uniformly rely on a MMDBMS. One of the main tasks of a DBMS is to abstract the user from the details of storage access and its management and to serve as the front end to the user (i.e., to answer a content-based query, to resolve usage profiles, and to prepare the delivery of the data).

Exhibit 1.4 gives a simple architectural overview of a multimedia system with database support. The database is embedded into the multimedia system domain, located between the application domain and the device domain (computer technology, compression, storage and network). The database is integrated into the system domain through the operating system and communication components. With this architecture, the

Synchronization	Tools and Applications			Application Domain
	User Interface	Programming API	Multimedia Search Engine	Application Domain
	MM-Database System	Operating-System (Multimedia)	Communication System	System Domain
	Computer Technology			Device Domain
	Compression			Device Domain
	Storage		Network	Device Domain

Exhibit 1.4. Architectural overview of multimedia components.

above-mentioned applications can be put on the same abstraction level with respect to the DBMS and the system in general.

One of the main purposes of this book is to establish the relationship between the database, the multimedia system, and the distributed environment. This concerns multimedia coding, indexing, storage, and access, as well as delivery and consumption of multimedia content. In particular, we describe how the new standards of the ISO-IEC MPEG-7 and MPEG-21 help us to create a "big picture" of a multimedia system that ties the elements of a multimedia system (database, network, client, etc.) together. MPEG-7 provides description tools for multimedia content; MPEG-21 defines a multimedia framework that enables transparent and augmented use of multimedia resources across a wide range of networks and devices used by different communities. MPEG-21 relies on MPEG-7 for the description of the content. Both standards are open for description extensions. They provide content creators, service providers, and consumer's equal opportunities in the global system.

1.3 (Multi)Media Data and Multimedia Metadata

This section describes (multi)media data and multimedia metadata. We overview the MPEG coding family (MPEG-1, MPEG-2, MPEG-4) and then introduce multimedia metadata standards for MPEG-7 and, finally, the concepts of (multi)media data and multimedia metadata introduced in MPEG-21. Multimedia metadata models are of obvious interest for the design of content-based multimedia systems, and we refer to them throughout the book.

1.3.1 (Multi)Media Data

Given the broad use of images, audio and video data nowadays, it should not come as a surprise that much effort has been put into developing standards for codec, or coding and decoding multimedia data. Realizing that much of the multimedia data are redundant, multimedia codecs use compression algorithms to identify and use redundancy.

MPEG video compression[13] is used in many current and emerging products. It is at the heart of digital television set-top boxes, digital subscriber service, high-definition television decoders, digital video disc players, Internet video, and other applications. These applications benefit from video compression in that they now require less storage space for archived video information, less bandwidth for the transmission of the video information from one point to another, or a combination of both.

The basic idea behind MPEG video compression is to remove both spatial redundancy within a video frame and temporal redundancy between video frames. As in Joint Photographic Experts Group (JPEG), the standard for still-image compression, DCT (Discrete Cosine Transform)-based compression is used to reduce spatial redundancy. Motion compensation or estimation is used to exploit temporal redundancy. This is possible because the images in a video stream usually do not change much within small time intervals. The idea of motion compensation is to encode a video frame based on other video frames temporally close to it.

In addition to the fact that MPEG video compression works well in a wide variety of applications, a large part of its popularity is that it is defined in three finalized international standards: MPEG-1, MPEG-2, and MPEG-4.

MPEG-1[21] is the first standard (issued in 1993) by MPEG and is intended for medium-quality and medium–bit rate video and audio compression. It allows videos to be compressed by ratios in the range of 50:1 to 100:1, depending on image sequence type and desired quality. The encoded data rate is targeted at 1.5 megabits per second, for this is a reasonable transfer rate for a double-speed CD-ROM player. This rate includes audio and video. MPEG-1 video compression is based on a macroblock structure, motion compensation, and the conditional replenishment of macroblocks. MPEG-1 encodes the first frame in a video sequence in intraframe (I-frame) Each subsequent frame in a certain group of picture (e.g., 15 frames) is coded using interframe prediction (P-frame) or bidirectional prediction (B-frame). Only data from the nearest previously coded I-frame or P-frame is used for prediction of a P-frame. For a B-frame, either the previous or the next I- or P-frame or both are used. Exhibit 1.5 illustrates the principles of the MPEG-1 video compression.

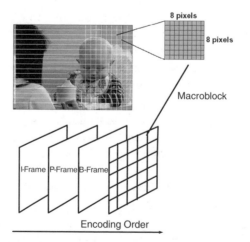

Exhibit 1.5. Principles of the MPEG-1 video compression technique.

On the encoder side, the DCT is applied to an 8×8 luminance and chrominance block, and thus, the chrominance and luminance values are transformed into the frequency domain. The dominant values (DC values) are in the upper-left corner of the resulting 8×8 block and have a special importance. They are encoded relative to the DC coefficient of the previous block (DCPM coding).

Then each of the 64 DCT coefficients is uniformly quantized. The non-zero quantized values of the remaining DCT coefficients and their locations are then zig-zag scanned and run-length entropy coded using length-code tables. The scanning of the quantized DCT two-dimensional image signal followed by variable-length code word assignment for the coefficients serves as a mapping of the two-dimensional image signal into a one-dimensional bit stream. The purpose of zig-zag scanning is to trace the low-frequency DCT coefficients (containing the most energy) before tracing the high-frequency coefficients (which are perceptually not so receivable).

MPEG-1 audio compression is based on perceptual coding schemes. It specifies three audio coding schemes, simply called Layer-1, Layer-2, and Layer-3. Encoder complexity and performance (sound quality per bit rate) progressively increase from Layer-1 to Layer-3. Each audio layer extends the features of the layer with the lower number. The simplest form is Layer-1. It has been designed mainly for the DCC (digital compact cassette), where it is used at 384 kilobits per second (kbps) (called "PASC"). Layer-2 achieves a good sound quality at bit rates down to 192 kbps, and Layer-3 has been designed for lower bit rates down to 32 kbps. A Layer-3 decoder may as well accept audio streams encoded with Layer-2 or Layer-1, whereas a Layer-2 decoder may accept only Layer-1.

MPEG video compression and audio compression are different. The audio stream flows into two independent blocks of the encoder. The mapping block of the encoder filters and creates 32 equal-width frequency sub-bands, whereas the psychoacoustics block determines a masking threshold for the audio inputs. By determining such a threshold, the psychoacoustics block can output information about noise that is imperceptible to the human ear and thereby reduce the size of the stream. Then, the audio stream is quantized to meet the actual bit rate specified by the layer used. Finally, the frame packing block assembles the actual bitstream from the output data of the other blocks, and adds header information as necessary before sending it out.

MPEG-2[22] (issued in 1994) was designed for broadcast television and other applications using interlaced images. It provides higher-picture quality than MPEG-1, but uses a higher data rate. At lower bit rates, MPEG-2 provides no advantage over MPEG-1. At higher bit rates, above about 4 megabits per second, MPEG-2 should be used in preference to MPEG-1.

Unlike MPEG-1, MPEG-2 supports interlaced television systems and vertical blanking interval signals. It is used in digital video disc videos.

The concept of I-, P-, and B-pictures is retained in MPEG-2 to achieve efficient motion prediction and to assist random access. In addition to MPEG-1, new motion-compensated field prediction modes were used to efficiently encode field pictures. The top fields and bottom fields are coded separately. Each bottom field is coded using motion-compensated interfield prediction based on the previously coded top field. The top fields are coded using motion compensation based on either the previous coded top field or the previous coded bottom field.

MPEG-2 introduces profiles for scalable coding. The intention of scalable coding is to provide interoperability between different services and to flexibly support receivers with different display capabilities. One of the important purposes of scalable coding is to provide a layered video bit stream that is amenable to prioritized transmission. Exhibit 1.6 depicts the general philosophy of a multiscale video coding scheme.

MPEG-2 syntax supports up to three different scalable layers. Signal-to-noise ratio scalability is a tool that has been primarily developed to provide graceful quality degradation of the video in prioritized transmission media. Spatial scalability has been developed to support display screens with different spatial resolutions at the receiver. Lower–spatial resolution video can be reconstructed from the base layer. The temporal scalability tool generates different video layers. The lower one (base layer) provides the basic temporal rate, and the enhancement layers are coded with temporal prediction of the lower layer. These layers, when decoded and tem-

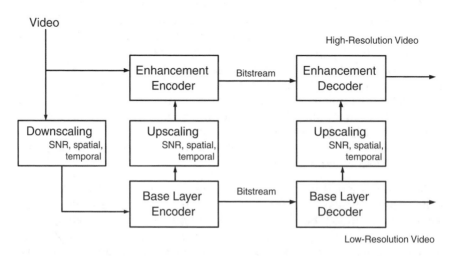

Exhibit 1.6. Scalable coding in MPEG-2.

porally multiplexed, yield full temporal resolution of the video. Stereoscopic video coding can be supported with the temporal scalability tool. A possible configuration is as follows. First, the reference video sequence is encoded in the base layer. Then, the other sequence is encoded in the enhancement layer by exploiting binocular and temporal dependencies; that is, disparity and motion estimation or compensation.

MPEG-1 and MPEG-2 use the same family of audio codecs, Layer-1, Layer-2, and Layer-3. The new audio features of MPEG-2 use lower sample rate in Layer-3 to address low–bit rate applications with limited bandwidth requirements (the bit rates extend down to 8 kbps). Furthermore, a multichannel extension for sound applications with up to five main audio channels (left, center, right, left surround, right surround) is proposed.

A non-ISO extension, called MPEG 2.5, was developed by the Fraunhofer Institute to improve the performance of MPEG-2 Audio Layer-3 at lower bit rates. This extension allows sampling rates of 8, 11.025, and 24 kHz, which is half of that used in MPEG-2. Lowering the sampling rate reduces the frequency response but allows the frequency resolution to be increased, so that the result has a significantly better quality.

The popular MP3 file format is an abbreviation for MPEG-1/2 Layer-3 and MPEG-2.5. It actually uses the MPEG 2.5 codec for small bit rates (<24 kbps). For bit rates higher than 24 kbps, it uses the MPEG-2 Layer-3 codec.

A comprehensive comparison of MPEG-2 Layer-3, MPEG 2.5, MP3, and AAC (see MPEG-4 below) is given in the MP3 overview by Brandenburg.[23]

MPEG-4[24–26] (issued in 1999) is the newest video coding standard by MPEG and goes further, from a pure pixel-based approach, that is, from coding the raw signal, to an object-based approach. It uses segmentation and a more advanced scheme of description. Object coding is for the first time implemented in JPEG-2000[20,21] (issued in 1994) and MPEG-4.[24–26] Indeed, MPEG-4 is primarily a toolbox of advanced compression algorithms for audiovisual information, and in addition, it is suitable for a variety of display devices and networks, including low–bit rate mobile networks. MPEG-4 organizes its tools into the following eight parts:

1. ISO-IEC 14496-1 (systems)
2. ISO-IEC 14496-2 (visual)
3. ISO-IEC 14496-3 (audio)
4. ISO-IEC 14496-4 (conformance)
5. ISO-IEC 14496-5 (reference software)
6. ISO-IEC 14496-6 (delivery multimedia integration framework)
7. ISO-IEC 14496-7 (optimized software for MPEG-4 tools)
8. ISO-IEC 14496-8 (carriage of MPEG-4 contents over Internet protocol networks).

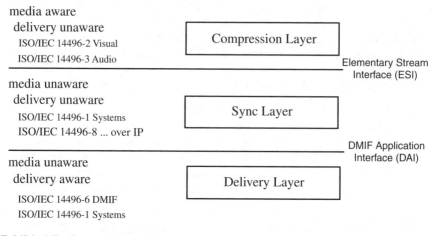

media aware
  delivery unaware
    ISO/IEC 14496-2 Visual
    ISO/IEC 14496-3 Audio

media unaware
  delivery unaware
    ISO/IEC 14496-1 Systems
    ISO/IEC 14496-8 ... over IP

media unaware
  delivery aware
    ISO/IEC 14496-6 DMIF
    ISO/IEC 14496-1 Systems

Compression Layer

Elementary Stream
Interface (ESI)

Sync Layer

DMIF Application
Interface (DAI)

Delivery Layer

Exhibit 1.7. General organization of MPEG-4.

These tools are organized in a hierarchical manner and operate on different interfaces. Exhibit 1.7 illustrates this organization model, which comprises the compression layer, the sync layer, and the delivery layer. The compression layer is media aware and delivery unaware, the sync layer is media unaware and delivery unaware, and the delivery layer is media unaware and delivery aware.

The compression layer does media encoding and decoding of elementary streams, the sync layer manages elementary streams and their synchronization and hierarchical relations, and the deliver layer ensures transparent access to MPEG-4 content irrespective of the delivery technology used. The following paragraphs briefly describe the main features supported by the MPEG-4 tools. Note also that not all the features of the MPEG-4 toolbox will be implemented in a single application. This is determined by levels and profiles, to be discussed below.

MPEG-4 is object oriented:[*] An MPEG-4 video is a composition of a number of stream objects that build together a complex scene. The temporal and spatial dependencies between the objects have to be described with a description following the BIFS (binary format for scene description).

MPEG-4 Systems provides the functionality to merge the objects (natural or synthetic) and render the product in a single scene. Elementary streams can be adapted (e.g., one object is dropped) or mixed with stored and streaming media. MPEG-4 allows for the creation of a scene consisting of objects originating from different locations. Exhibit 1.8 shows an application example of the object-scalability provided in MPEG-4. The objects that are representing videos are called video objects, or VOs. They may be

[*]Not in the sense of object-oriented programming or modeling thoughts.

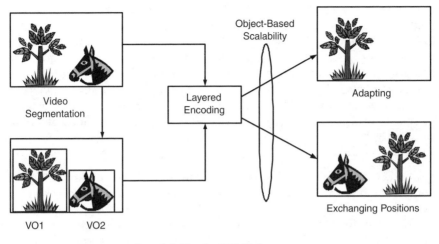

Exhibit 1.8. Object-based scalability in MPEG-4.

combined with other VOs (or audio objects and three-dimensional objects) to form a complex scene. One possible scalability option is object dropping, which may be used for adaptation purposes at the server or in the Internet. Another option is the changing of objects within a scene; for instance, transposing the positions of the two VOs in Exhibit 1.8. In addition, MPEG-4 defines the MP4 file format. This format is extremely flexible and extensible. It allows the management, exchange, authoring, and presentation of MPEG-4 media applications.

MPEG-4 Systems also provides basic support to protect and manage content. This is actually moved into the MPEG-21 intellectual property management and protection (IPMP) (MPEG-21, Part 4).

MPEG-4 Visual provides a coding algorithm that is able to produce usable media at a rate of 5 kbps and QCIF (quarter common intermediate format) resolution (176×144 pixels). This makes motion video possible on mobile devices. MPEG-4 Visual describes more than 30 profiles that define different combinations of scene resolution, bit rate, audio quality, and so forth to accommodate the different needs of different applications. To mention just two example profiles, there is the simple profile, which provides the most basic audio and video at a bit rate that scales down to 5 kbps. This profile is extremely stable and is designed to operate in exactly the same manner on all MPEG-4 decoders. The studio profile, in contrast, is used for applications involved with digital theater and is capable of bit rates in the 1 Gbps (billions of bits per second) range. Of note is that the popular DivX codec (http://www.divx-digest.com/) is based on the MPEG-4 visual coding using the simple scalable profile.

Fine granular scalability mode allows the delivery of the same MPEG-4 content at different bit rates. MPEG-4 Visual has the ability to take content intended to be experienced with a high-bandwidth connection, extract a subset of the original stream, and deliver usable content to a personal digital assistant or other mobile devices. Error correction, built into the standard, allows users to switch to lower–bit rate streams if connection degradation occurs because of lossy wireless networks or congestion. Objects in a scene may also be assigned a priority level that defines which objects will or will not be viewed during network congestion or other delivery problems.

MPEG-4 Audio offers tools for natural and synthetic audio coding. The compression is so efficient that good speech quality is achieved at 2 kbps. Synthetic music and sound are created from a rich toolset called Structured Audio. Each MPEG-4 decoder has the ability to create and process this synthetic audio making the sound quality uniform across all MPEG-4 decoders.

In this context, MPEG introduced the advanced audio coding (AAC), which is a new audio coding family based on a psychoacoustics model. Sometimes referred to as MP4, which is misleading because it coincides with the MPEG-4 file format, AAC provides significantly better quality at lower bit rates than MP3. AAC was developed under MPEG-2 and was improved for MPEG-4. Additional tools in MPEG-4 increase the effectiveness of MPEG-2 AAC at lower bit rates and add scalability and error resilience characteristics.

AAC supports a wider range of sampling rates (from 8 to 96 kHz) and up to 48 audio channels and is, thus, more powerful than MP3. Three profiles of AAC provide varying levels of complexity and scalability. MPEG-4 AAC is, therefore, designed as high-quality general audio codec for 3G (third-generation) wireless terminals. However, compared with MP3, AAC software is much more expensive to license, because the companies that hold related patents decided to keep a tighter rein on it.

The last component proposed is the Delivery Multimedia Integration Framework (DIMF). This framework provides abstraction from the transport protocol (network, broadcast, etc) and has the ability to identify delivery systems with a different QoS. DMIF also abstracts the application from the delivery type (mobile device versus wired) and handles the control interface and signaling mechanisms of the delivery system. The framework specification makes it possible to write MPEG-4 applications without in-depth knowledge of delivery systems or protocols.

1.3.1.1 Related Video Standards and Joint Efforts. There exist a handful other video standards and codecs.[14] Cinepak (http://www.cinepak.com/text.html) was developed by CTI (Compression Technologies, Inc.) to deliver high-quality compressed digital movies for the Internet and game environments.

RealNetworks (http://www.real.com) has developed codecs for audiovisual streaming applications. The codec reduces the spatial resolution and makes a thorough analysis if a frame contributes to motion and shapes and drops it if necessary. Priority is given to the encoding of the audio; that is, audio tracks are encoded first and then the video track is added. If network congestion occurs, the audio takes priority and the picture just drops a few frames to keep up. The Sure Stream feature allows the developer to create up to eight versions of the audio and video tracks. If there is network congestion during streaming, Real Player and the Real Server switch between versions to maintain image quality.

For broadcast applications, especially video conferencing, the ITU-T (http://www.itu.int/ITU-T/) standardized the H.261 (first version in 1990) and H.263 (first version in 1995) codecs. H.261 was designed to work for bit rates, which are multiples of 64 kbps (adapted to Integrated Services Digital Network connections). The H.261 coding algorithm is a hybrid of interframe prediction, transform coding, and motion compensation. Interframe prediction removes temporal redundancy. Transform coding removes the spatial redundancy. Motion vectors are used to help the codec to compensate for motion. To remove any further redundancy in the transmitted stream, variable-length coding is used. The coding algorithm of H.263 is similar to H.261; however, it was improved with respect to performance and error recovery. H.263 uses half-pixel precision for motion compensation, whereas H.261 used full-pixel precision and a loop filter. Some parts of the hierarchical structure of the stream are optional in H.263, so the codec can be configured for a lower bit rate or better error recovery. There are several optional negotiable options included to improve performance: unrestricted motion vectors, syntax-based arithmetic coding, advance prediction, and forward and backward frame prediction, which is a generalization of the concepts introduced in MPEG's P–B-frames.

MPEG and ITU-T launched in December 2001 the Joint Video Team to establish a new video coding standard. The new standard, named ISO-IEC MPEG-4 Advanced Coding (AVC-Part 10 of MPEG-4)/ITU H.264, offers significant bit-rate and quality advantages over the previous ITU/MPEG standards. To improve coding efficiency, the macroblock (see Exhibit 1.3) is broken down into smaller blocks that attempt to contain and isolate the motion. Quantization as well as entropy coding was improved. The standard is available as of autumn 2003. More technical information on MPEG-4 AVC may be found at http://www.islogic.com/products/islands/h264.html.

In addition, many different video file formats exist that must be used with a given codec. For instance, Microsoft introduced a standard for incorporating digital video under Windows by the file standard called AVI (Audio

Video Interleaved). The AVI format merely defines how the video and audio will be stored, not how they have to be encoded.

1.3.2 Multimedia Metadata

Metadata describing a multimedia resource, such as an audio or video stream, can be seen from various perspectives, based on who produces or provides the metadata:

- From the content-producer's perspective, typical metadata are bibliographical information of the resource, such as author, title, creation date, resource format, and so forth.
- From the perspective of the service providers, metadata are typically value-added descriptions (mostly in XML format) that qualify information needed for retrieval. These data include various formats, under which a resource is available, and semantic information, such as players of a soccer game. This information is necessary to enable searching with an acceptable precision in multimedia applications.
- From the perspective of the media consumer, additional metadata describing its preferences and resource availability are useful. These metadata personalize content consumption and have to be considered by the producer. Additional metadata are necessary for the delivery over the Internet or mobile networks to guarantee access to the best possible content; for example, metadata describing adaptation of the video is required when the available bandwidth decreases. One issue that needs to be addressed is whether or not an adaptation process is acceptable to the user.

To describe metadata, various research projects have developed sets of elements to facilitate the retrieval of multimedia resources.[27] Initiatives that appear likely to develop into widely used and general standards for Internet multimedia resources are the Dublin Core Standard, the Metadata Dictionary SMPTE (Society of Motion Picture and Television Engineers), MPEG-7, and MPEG-21. These four standards are general; that is, they do not target a particular industry or application domain and are supported by well-recognized organizations.

Dublin Core[28] is a Resource Description Framework–based standard that represents a metadata element set intended to facilitate the discovery of electronic resources. There have been many papers that have discussed the applicability of Dublin Core to nontextual documents such as images, audio, and video. They have primarily focused on extensions to the core elements through the use of subelements and schemes specific to audiovisual data. The core elements are title, creator, subject, published in, description, publisher, contributor, date, type, format, identifier, source, language, and rights. Dublin Core is currently used as a metadata standard in many television archives.

In this context, one has also to mention the Metadata Dictionary SMPTE. The dictionary is a big collection of registered names and data types, developed mostly for the television and video industries that form the SMPTE membership. Its hierarchical structure allows expansion and mechanisms for data formatting in television and video signals and provides a common method of implementation. Most metadata are media-specific attributes, such as timing information. Semantic annotation is, however, not possible. The SMPTE Web site contains the standards documents (http://www.smpte.org/).

MPEG-7[29] is an Extensible Markup Language (XML)-based multimedia metadata standard that proposes description elements for the multimedia processing cycle from the capture (e.g., logging descriptors), to analysis and filtering (e.g., descriptors of the MDS [Multimedia Description Schemes]), to delivery (e.g., media variation descriptors), and to interaction (e.g., user preference descriptors). MPEG-7 may, therefore, describe the metadata flow in multimedia applications more adequately than the Dublin Core Standard. There have been several attempts to extend the Dublin Core Standard to describe the multimedia processing cycle. Hunter et al.[28,30] showed that it is possible to describe both the structure and fine-grained details of video content by using the Dublin Core elements plus qualifiers. The disadvantage of this approach is that the semantic refinement of the Dublin Core through the use of qualifiers may lead to a loss of semantic interoperability. Another advantage of MPEG-7 is that it offers a system's part that allows coding of descriptions (including compression) for streaming and for associating parts of MPEG-7 descriptions to media units, which they describe. MPEG-7 is of major importance for content-based multimedia systems. Detailed information on the practical usage of this standard is given in Chapter 2.

Despite the very complete and detailed proposition of multimedia metadata descriptions in MPEG-7, the aspect of the organization of the infrastructure of a distributed multimedia system cannot be described with metadata alone. Therefore, the new MPEG-21[8] standard was initiated in 2000 to provide mechanisms for distributed multimedia systems design and associated services. A new distribution entity is proposed and validated: the Digital Item. It is used for interaction with all actors (called users in MPEG-21) in a distributed multimedia system. In particular, content management, Intellectual Property Management (IPMP), and content adaptation shall be regulated to handle different service classes. MPEG-21 shall result in an open framework for multimedia delivery and consumption, with a vision of providing content creators and service providers with equal opportunities to an open electronic market. MPEG-21 is detailed in Chapter 3.

Finally, let us notice that in addition MPEG with MPEG-7 and MPEG-21, several other consortia have created metadata schemes that describe the context, presentation, and encoding format of multimedia resources. They mainly address a partial aspect of the use of metadata in a distributed multimedia system. Broadly used standards are:

- W3C (World Wide Web Consortium) has built the Resource Description Framework–based Composite Capabilities/Preference Profiles (CC/PP) protocol.* The WAP Forum has used the CC/PP to define a User Agent Profile (UAProf) which describes the characteristics of WAP-enabled devices.
- W3C introduced the Synchronized Multimedia Integration Language (SMIL, pronounced "smile")** which enables simple authoring of interactive audiovisual presentations.
- IETF*** (Internet Engineering Task Force) has created the Protocol-Independent Content Negotiation Protocol (CONNEG), which was released in 1999.

These standards relate to different parts of MPEG; for instance CC/PP relates to the MPEG-21 Digital Item Adaptation Usage Environment, CONNEG from IETF relates to event reporting in MPEG-21, parts of SMIL relate to the MPEG-21 Digital Item Adaptation, and other parts relate to MPEG-4. Thus, MPEG integrated main concepts of standards in use and, in addition, let these concepts work cooperatively in a multimedia framework.

1.4   Purpose and Organization of the Book

This book is a research monograph, which shows a global view of modern multimedia systems. It starts with a state-of-the art description of technologies and methods and leads to visions with technical challenges. In each section, a key technology is selected and exposed in detail. Final emphasis is put in each part on the practical aspects of the techniques used. The reader will find many links to running or initiated projects in the field.

What is new in this book? You will read about the following:

- We give a comprehensive introduction to the new multimedia standards for distributed multimedia systems and their relationships.
  We describe the principles of scalable media coding in MPEG-2 and
      MPEG-4 standards.
  We introduce multimedia metadata management using MPEG-7.

---

*http://www.w3.org/Mobile/CCPP/.
**http://www.w3.org/AudioVideo/.
*** http://www.imc.org/ietf-medfree/index.html.

With MPEG-21, we show the global use of a distributed system with media and metadata as first-class citizens.

With SQL/MM, we give an overview of the structured multimedia query language.

- A detailed technical description of modern multimedia database management systems, including the following:
  Multimedia indexing and retrieval
  Multimedia data models and query languages
  Multimedia query processing
  Multimedia database products
  Relationship to MPEG-7/21 and SLQ/MM
- An overview of components and architectures of modern distributed multimedia systems including the following:
  Video servers and streaming
  Multimedia communication
  Multimedia clients
  Multimedia content adaptation
  Relationship to MPEG-4/7/21

The book is organized in six chapters. Exhibit 1.9 shows the organization of the content.

Chapter 1 introduces and focuses on the principles of multimedia data and multimedia metadata. Chapter 2 is dedicated to MPEG-7, supported with practical examples. Chapter 3 introduces MPEG-21 and gives practical use cases. From MPEG-7, we come to the description of modern multimedia database management systems in Chapter 4. Similarly, from MPEG-21 and multimedia databases, we come to distributed multimedia systems, dealt with in Chapter 5. Finally, Chapter 6 concludes the book and gives a final global view of the distributed system.

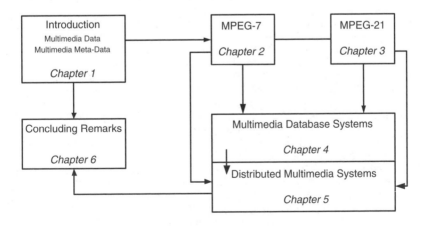

Exhibit 1.9. Organization of the book.

References

1. Özsu, M.T. and Valduriez, P., *Principles of Distributed Database Systems*, 2nd ed., Prentice-Hall, Englewood Cliffs, NJ, 1999.
2. Apers, P.M.G., Blanken, H.M., and Houtsma, M.A.W., *Multimedia Databases in Perspective*, Springer-Verlag, Heidelberg, 1997.
3. Subrahmanian, V.S., *Principles of Multimedia Database Systems*, Morgan Kaufman Press, San Francisco, January 1998.
4. Lu, G., *Multimedia Database Management Systems*, Artech House, Norwood, MA, 1999.
5. Chen, S.-C., Kashyap, R.L., and Ghafoor, A., *Semantic Models for Multimedia Database Searching and Browsing*, Kluwer Academic, Boston, 2000.
6. Xiao, X. and Ni, L.M., Internet QoS: a big picture, *IEEE Network*, 13, 8–18, 1999.
7. Aurrecoechea, C., Campbell, A.T., and Hauw, L., A survey of QoS architectures, *ACM Multimedia Syst.*, 6, 128–151, 1998.
8. Hill, K. and Bormans, J., Overview of the MPEG-21 Standard. ISO/IECJTC1/SC29/WG11 N4041 (Shanghai Meeting), October 2002, http://www.chiariglione.org/mpeg/.
9. Park, Y., Kim, P., Golshani, F., and Panchanathan, S., Concept-based visual information management with large lexical corpus, in *Proceedings of the Internation Conference on Database and Expert Applications (DEXA), Munich 2001*, Springer-Verlag, Heidelberg, pp. 350–359, LNCS 2113.
10. Li, W.-S., Selçuk Candan, K., Hirata, K., and Hara, Y., Supporting efficient multimedia database exploration, *VLDB J.*, 9, 312–326, 2001.
11. Brewer, E.A., When everything is searchable, *Comm. ACM*, 44, 53–54, 2001.
12. Zhao, R, and Grosky, W.I., Negotiating the semantic gap: from feature maps to semantic landscapes, *Pattern Recognition*, 35, 51–58, 2002.
13. Steinmetz, R., *Multimedia Technology*, 2nd ed., Springer-Verlag, Heidelberg, 2000.
14. Gecsei, J., Adaptation in distributed multimedia systems, *IEEE MultiMedia*, 4, 58–66, 1997.
15. Rejaie, R., On design of Internet multimedia streaming applications: an architectural perspective, in *Proceedings of the IEEE International Conference on Multimedia and Exhibition, New York, July 2000*, pp. 327–330.
16. Dan, A., Feldman, S.I., and Serpanos, D.N., Evolution and challenges in multimedia, *IBM J. Res. Dev.*, 24, 177–184, 1998.
17. Böszörményi, L., Hellwagner, H., and Kosch, H., Multimedia technologies for e-business systems and processes, in *Proceedings of Elektronische Geschäftsprozesse (E-Business Processes), Klagenfurt, Austria, September 2001*, IT Verlag für Informationstechnik, pp. 471–481.
18. Anderson, D.P., Device reservation in audio/video editing systems, *ACM Trans. Computer Syst.*, 15, 111–133, 1997.
19. Raymond, T.N. and Paul, S., Optimal clip ordering for multi-clip queries, *VLDB J.*, 7, 239–252, 1998.
20. Bouras, C., Kapoulas, V., Miras, D., Ouzounis, V., Spirakis, P., and Tatakis, A., On-demand hypermedia/mutimedia service using pre-orchestrated scenarios over the Internet, *Networking Inf. Syst. J.*, 2, 741–762, 1999.
21. Chiariglione, L., Short MPEG-1 description (final). ISO/IECJTC1/SC29/WG11 N MPEG96, June 1996, http://www.chiariglione.org/mpeg/.
22. Chiariglione, L., Short MPEG-2 description (final). ISO/IECJTC1/SC29/WG11 N MPEG00, October 2000, http://www.chiariglione.org/mpeg/.
23. Brandenburg, K., MP3 and AAC explained, in *Proceedings of the 17th AES International Conference on High Quality Audio Coding, Florence/Italy, 1999*.
24. Koenen, R., MPEG-4 overview. ISO/IEC JTC1/SC29/WG11 N4668, (Jeju Meeting) March 2002, http://www.chiariglione.org/mpeg/.
25. Pereira, F., Tutorial issue on the MPEG-4 standard, *Image Comm.*, 15, 2000.

26. Ebrahimi, T. and Pereira, F., *The MPEG-4 Book*, Prentice-Hall, Englewood Cliffs, NJ, 2002.

27. Hunter, J. and Armstrong, L., A comparison of schemas for video metadata representation. *Comput. Networks*, 31, 1431–1451, 1999.

28. Dublin Core Metadata Initiative, Dublin core metadata element set, version 1.1: Reference description, http://www.dublincore.org/documents/dces/, 1997.

29. Martínez, J.M., Overview of the MPEG-7 standard. ISO/IEC JTC1/SC29/WG11 N4980 (Klagenfurt Meeting), July 2002, http://www.chiariglione.org/mpeg/.

30. Hunter, J., A proposal for the Integration of Dublin Core and MPEG-7, ISO/IEC JTC1/SC29/WG11 M6500, 54th MPEG Meeting, La Baule, October 2000, http://archive.dstc.edu.au/RDU/staff/jane-hunter/m6500.zip.

Chapter 2
MPEG-7: The Multimedia Content Description Standard

2.1 Introduction

MPEG[1-4] is the ISO-IEC 15983 international standard from the Moving Picture Experts Group (MPEG) for describing multimedia content data. It provides core technologies allowing the description of audiovisual (AV) data content in multimedia environments. Audiovisual data content that has MPEG-7 data associated with it may include still pictures, graphics, three-dimensional models, audio, speech, video, and composition information about how these elements are combined in a multimedia presentation (scenarios).

MPEG-7 allows different granularity in its descriptions, offering the possibility of having different levels of discrimination. Even though the MPEG-7 description does not depend on the (coded) representation of the material, MPEG-7 can exploit the advantages provided by MPEG-4 coded content. For instance, if the material is encoded using MPEG-4, which provides the means to encode AV material as objects having certain relations in time (synchronization) and space (on the screen for video, or in the room for audio), it will be possible to attach descriptions to elements (objects) within the scene, such as audio and visual objects.

MPEG-7 data may be physically located with the associated AV material, in the same data stream or on the same multimedia database system, but the descriptions could also live somewhere else in the Internet. When the content and its descriptions are not colocated, mechanisms that link the multimedia material and their MPEG-7 descriptions are provided; these links have to work in both directions.

MPEG-7 addresses many different applications in many different environments, which means that it needs to provide a flexible and extensible framework for describing AV data. Therefore, MPEG-7 does not define a

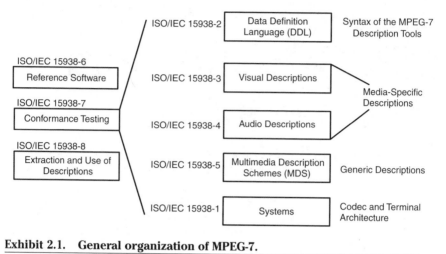

Exhibit 2.1. General organization of MPEG-7.

monolithic system for content description but rather a set of methods and tools for the different viewpoints of the description of AV content.

The MPEG-7 methods and tools are regrouped in eight parts (ISO-IEC 15938-1-8) and are organized as shown in Exhibit 2.1. The parts that are designed for creating a description and delivering it are shown on the right-hand side of the figure. The first (Part 2) is the description definition language (DDL) that is the language for defining the syntax of the MPEG-7 description tools and for defining new description schemes. The descriptive elements are defined in Parts 3 to 5, separated by the level of genericity employed. MPEG-7 Visual (Part 3) contains the description tools dealing with (only) visual descriptions. MPEG-7 Audio (Part 4) contains the description tools dealing with (only) audio descriptions. MPEG-7 Multimedia Description Schemes (MDSs, Part 5) contains the description tools dealing with generic features and multimedia descriptions. MPEG-7 Systems (Part 1) provides the binary format for encoding MPEG-7 descriptions for delivery and the terminal architecture. It is drawn as the bottom layer in Exhibit 2.1 to point out its coding and delivery character.

Parts 3 and 4 provide a lower abstraction level that may, for example, be shape, size, texture, color, movement (trajectory), and position ("where in the scene can the object be found?") for video, and key, mood, tempo, tempo changes, and position in sound space for audio. The highest level would give semantic information and may be found in Part 5, the MDS. It allows one to represent semantic content similar to, "A soccer video with the goalkeeper on the right and the ball with the player on the left." Note that intermediate levels of abstraction may also exist. In addition to semantic description tools, the MDS also provides a means for describing the creation and production processes of the content, usage, and context.[5]

Part 6, the Reference Software, encompasses the first five parts in the sense that it provides a software implementation of relevant parts of the MPEG-7 Standard with normative status and in that it is publicly available (for more details, see Section 2.9). The final two parts of MPEG-7 are Part 7, MPEG-7 Conformance Testing, which deals with guidelines and procedures for testing conformance of MPEG-7 implementations, and Part 8, MPEG-7 extraction and use of descriptions, which supplies informative material (in the form of a technical report) about the extraction and use of some of the description tools. All parts are international standard; Parts 1 to 6 were published in 2002, and the remaining parts were published in 2003.

MPEG-7 uses Extensible Markup Language (XML) as the language of choice for the textual representation of content description. XML Schema[6] has been the base for the DDL that is used for the syntactic definition of MPEG-7 description tools and that allows extensibility of description tools.

The main elements of the MPEG-7 standard are (see Exhibit 2.2):

- Description tools: Descriptors (Ds) that define the syntax and the semantics of each feature (metadata element); and description schemes (DSs) that specify the structure and semantics of the relationships between their components that may be both descriptors and description schemes.

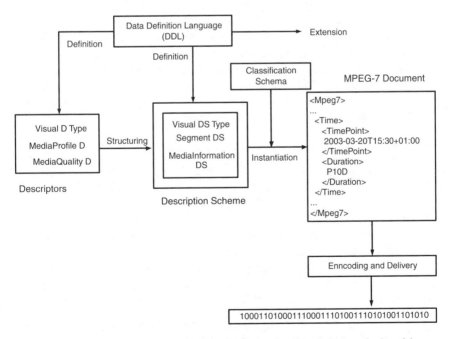

Exhibit 2.2. Main elements of the MPEG-7 standard and their relationship.

- DDL: Defines the syntax of the MPEG-7 description tools and allows the creation of new description schemes and, possibly, descriptors and the extension and modification of existing description schemes.
- Classification Schema (CS): Defines a list of typical terms used in many applications together with their meanings. For instance, it allows the definition of file formats in a standardized way. MPEG-7 provides many predefined CSs for characterizing roles, formats, and so forth. New CSs have to be registered.
- Extensibility: Supported through MPEG-7 schema extensions mechanism (new DSs and Ds).
- System tools: Support binary coded representation for efficient storage and transmission and provide the necessary transmission mechanisms.

The following sections give a practical guide for the creation and usage of MPEG-7 documents in multimedia systems and databases. Section 2.2 details possible relationships to multimedia database management systems in general. Further examples of the usage of MPEG-7 may be found throughout the book (e.g., in Chapter 4 for retrieval and indexing, in Chapter 5 for distribution). Section 2.3 introduces the principles of creating an MPEG-7 document. Section 2.4 describes the fundamentals of the DDL and provides comprehensive examples on how to use the DDL. The core Section 2.5 guides the user step-by-step to the creation of meaningful MPEG-7 documents. Important parts of the MDS are explained and their conceptual models are presented. Section 2.6 shows how MPEG-7 may be extended to deal with application-specific CSs and DSs. Section 2.7 describes how MPEG-7 documents may be encoded for delivery, and examples are given. The system part of MPEG-7 is also described here. Section 2.8 introduces the audio parts of MPEG-7. Finally, Section 2.9 introduces tools supporting the multimedia annotation process with MPEG-7.

2.2 MPEG-7 and Multimedia Database Systems

Exhibit 2.3 shows a possible use of MPEG-7 in a distributed multimedia database system. Starting from the annotation process (automatic tools or manual annotation) the MPEG-7 descriptions are generated and stored for further access. The indexing process can be supported by stored information. For example, to annotate a new soccer video, we may rely on information of the players already stored in the database to avoid multiple annotation of the same player. Note that multimedia metadata may be available before the video is available. For example, the information on location and the team players is in general available before the soccer game takes place.

The query scenario distinguishes two cases: pull and push. If we consider a pull scenario, a user submits queries to the multimedia database and will receive a set of descriptions matching the query for browsing (for

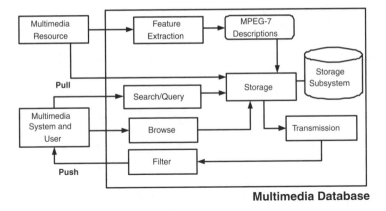

Multimedia Database

Exhibit 2.3.   Usage of MPEG-7 in a multimedia database system.

inspecting the description, for manipulating it, for retrieving the described content, etc.). Alternatively, if a streaming server is available, the user receives the media, together with the descriptions.

In a push scenario, a filter (e.g., an intelligent agent) will select descriptions from those available and perform the programmed actions afterward (e.g., switching a broadcast channel or recording the described stream). For this scenario, it is advantageous to encode and index the video in binary format for a fast-randomized access. In both scenarios, all the modules may handle descriptions coded in MPEG-7 formats (either textual or binary).

A pull scenario has been described in the introduction (Chapter 1). A user records 10 seconds of a radio song (query song) and sends it to a mobile service that relies on a multimedia database for recognition of the title and singer. The multimedia database extracts the AudioSignature of the song and generates an MPEG-7 description of the query song. This description is compared to the signatures stored in the audio database, and the most similar signature is retained. The system retrieves the title and singer information for this result signature and returns them to the user.

A typical push scenario is related to digital television broadcast enhanced with MPEG-7 information. Assume that a television viewer has expressed in MPEG-7 his or her preferences about program content (User-Preferences DS). For instance, they've requested that only sport news of a television news program be presented. In this case, the MPEG-7 descriptors in the broadcasted stream are filtered according to the MPEG-7 User-Preferences descriptions available, and only the sport news program is shown.

29

From the MPEG-7 metadata available with the broadcast stream, the user might identify additional material that is specifically of interest to them. For example, imagine a user is watching "Never Say Never Again." That user may decide to seek further information regarding that film (e.g., other films with Klaus Maria Brandauer) or simply other related data available on the Internet (e.g., price of the film's soundtrack on CD).

Many technical issues have to be addressed here. Just to mention a few: How to retrieve the features? In what format to store the MPEG-7 document? What query language to use? How to reference the media described? These issues are explored in Chapters 4 and 5.

2.3 Principles for Creating MPEG-7 Documents

The user intending to use MPEG-7 for describing the content of multimedia data must be aware of two things: the conceptual model derived from the MPEG-7 requirements and the model implementation that leads to the content descriptions and the format of the descriptors/description schemes in the MPEG-7 DDL. Exhibit 2.4 shows the relationship between the conceptual model, the DDL, and the description schemes and descriptors.

For instance, assume that a user would like to create an MPEG-7 description for a video segment (part of the video) in which several image representations of this segment are available (in the form of a mosaic view). The user decides to use the VideoSegment DS for describing the video segments and the Mosaic DS for describing the mosaic view. Exhibit 2.5 shows the conceptual model for this example in Unified Modeling Language nota-

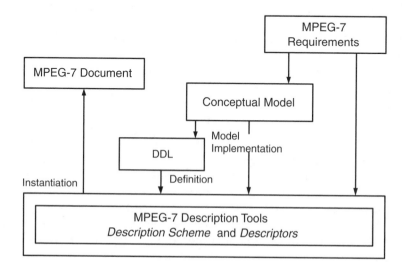

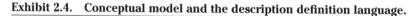

Exhibit 2.4.   Conceptual model and the description definition language.

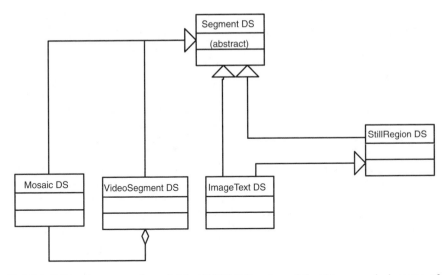

Exhibit 2.5.   Conceputal model in MPEG-7 for describing the mosaic images of a video segment.

tion (note that the complete model for describing the content of video and images is not shown here, but will be discussed later). The VideoSegment DS entity inherits from a general and abstract entity, called Segment DS. The VideoSegment entity contains means for aggregating different Mosaic DSs. The Mosaic DS Entity inherits from the StillRegion DS entity, which is used for describing the content of still images.

The MPEG-7 DDL available comprises the VideoSegmentType, which is the XML Schema representation for the VideoSegment DS. It contains an element (which may have multiple occurrences to represent the aggregation) of MosaicType that corresponds to the Mosaic DS.

2.4   MPEG-7 Description Definition Language

The MPEG-7 DDL provides the solid descriptive foundation by which users can create their own description schemes and descriptors, providing a means for representing the conceptual model. It defines the syntactic rules to express and combine description schemes and descriptors and, thus, for writing MPEG-7 documents.

The DDL is based on the XML Schema recommendations published by W3C in May 2001 (see http://www.w3.org/XML/Schema). The complete DDL may be obtained from http://m7itb.nist.gov/M7Validation.html. In the following, we will concentrate on the content descriptive parts of the descriptions and provide a step-by-step methodology for content description in MPEG-7.

Note: The DDL and MPEG-7 examples in this book use a different typesetting to be clearly identified, as shown in the following example:

```
<complexType name="VideoType">
  <sequence>
    <element name="VideoTitle" type="string"/>
  </sequence>
  <attribute name="use" type="string" default="athome"/>
</complexType>
```

MPEG-7 example:

```
<Video attribute="athome"/>
  <VideoTitle>Pisa's leaning tower</VideoTitle>
</Video>
```

2.4.1 XML Schema: Overview

The purpose of a schema is to define a class of XML documents by specifying particular constructs that constrain the structure and content of the documents. Possible constraints include elements and their content, attributes and their values, cardinalities, and datatypes. XML Schema provides a superset of the capabilities of DTDs (document type definitions).

However, because XML Schema was not designed specifically for AV content, certain MPEG-7–specific extensions are added to XML Schema. As a consequence, the DDL can be broken down into the following logical normative components:

- XML Schema structural components,
- XML Schema datatype components, and
- MPEG-7 extensions to the XML Schema.

Here we give a brief overview of XML Schema elements that are of importance for using MPEG-7 and MPEG-21 (see Chapter 3). More details and up-to-date tutorials may be obtained from the W3C XML Schema homepage at http://www.w3.org/XML/Schema.

2.4.2 XML Schema: Structures

The XML Schema: Structures (part 1 of the two-part XML Schema specification) provides facilities for describing the structure and constraining the content of XML 1.0 documents. A parser can then use them during the validation process. For instance, what elements may occur and how often, what attribute belongs to which elements, and so forth are specified.

XML Schema provides the means for defining the structure of XML documents. XML documents described by a particular schema are called instance documents and they are said to be schema valid if they comply with all constraints specified by the schema document. XML Schema includes the following main features:

- Simple and complex data types,
- Type derivation and inheritance,
- Element occurrence constraints, and
- Namespace-aware element and attribute declarations.

By using these features, it is now possible to define and enforce concise and strict rules regarding the contents of elements and attributes. For instance, one can now declare new data types or reuse and derive from existing data types.

Similar to instance documents, every schema document consists of a single root element. It includes declarations for all elements and attributes that are allowed to occur in a valid instance document.

2.4.3 Element Declaration

XML documents basically comprise a number of nested elements. Therefore, the element is one of the most important declarations in a typical schema document. The following example shows a simple schema:

```
<?xml version="1.0" encoding="ISO-8859-1?">

<schema xmlns:xsd="http://www.w3.org/2001/XMLSchema">

    <element name="Video" type="string"/>

</schema>
```

This sample schema declares one global element, namely "Video." A global element is defined as an immediate child element of the schema element, and only such elements are allowed to appear as root elements of an instance document.

2.4.4 Attribute Declaration

To add useful information to an element, it is possible to attach attributes to it. For instance, the Video element might benefit from having an additional language attribute called "lang," whose purpose is to specify the video's language. Such a declaration might look like the following:

```
<element name="Video">

  <complexType>

    <simpleContent>

      <extension base="string">
```

33

```
    <attribute name="lang" type="language" use
        ="optional"/>

  </extension>

 </simpleContent>

</complexType>

</element>
```

2.4.5 XML Schema-Type Definitions

XML Schema introduces types as a new concept within XML. It is now possible to type element declarations, which was not feasible with DTDs. This feature also makes schema documents more powerful and better suited to the task of storing instance documents into a database. Type definitions define internal schema components, which can be used in other schema components such as element or attribute declarations or other type definitions. There are two kinds of type definition components: simple types and complex types.

Simple types are used for elements that can only contain text, meaning they are not allowed to include nested elements. Attributes must always be declared with simple types, as they cannot be nested or contain subelements. Simple types can be divided into three categories: atomar or built-in types, list types, and union types, the latter two being a feature particular to XML. Atomar types are, in general, types that can be found in programming languages or database management systems, such as String or Boolean. List types separate their entries via white spaces. Union types allow a type to draw from different type spaces. For instance, a list of integer values can be defined as follows:

```
<simpleType name="integerVector">

    <list itemType="integer"/>

</simpleType>
```

It is also possible to control the range of values a simple type may have through a concept called facets. For instance, a character data type might have a maxLength facet, restricting the maximum length of a string. The following example illustrates this:

```
<simpleType name="exampleString">

  <restriction base="string">

    <maxLength value="40"/>

  </restriction>

</simpleType>
```

This new simple type is derived from the built-in string data type, but must not contain more than 40 characters.

Complex types are used for elements that may contain subelements and also have attributes. If a type declaration is embedded within an element declaration, the type is called an anonymous type instead of a named type. Named types are needed if it is necessary to share data types among multiple different elements. In the last example of the previous section, element Video has an anonymous complex type.

Complex types are created either by deriving by extension or by restriction. Deriving by extension means that the new derived type inherits all declarations of the super type. Complex types derived by restriction are a bit more complicated, as parts of the parent declaration are omitted, constraining the parent type. To tell an instance document that a derived type should be used instead of the type expected, an xsi:type attribute must be added to the respective elements.

2.4.6 Types of Element Content

There are four possible types of element content available:

- Empty,
- Simple content,
- Mixed content, and
- Any type.

Empty elements are the most restrictive form of element content, as these elements cannot contain anything. They provide information either through attributes or simply because of their position relative to other elements.

Simple content corresponds to the definition of simple types as already discussed above, whereas mixed content is basically related to mixed content elements, meaning that both character data and other elements may occur within the element's body. Include the mixed attribute to the complexType element to specify such content. The least restrictive form of element content allows including any type of content at a particular location. This can be done by using either the any element or the anyAttribute element.

2.4.7 Occurrence Constraints

A very useful feature of XML Schema is the ability to constrain the number of times an element is allowed to occur at a particular location within a document. This can be done by adding the minOccurs and maxOccurs attributes to the element. The default value for both attributes is set to 1.

2.4.8 Element Placement

There are three ways of controlling the placement of elements with XML Schema. The *sequence* element specifies that all elements must appear in exactly the same order as within the sequence. The *choice* element supports the requirement that only one element from a list of alternatives should occur. The order is of no importance here. Finally, the *all* element tells the schema processor that each of the elements contained in the list must appear in the instance document, but that they may do so in an arbitrary order.

2.4.9 XML Schema: Datatypes

The XML Schema: Datatypes (part 2 of the two-part XML Schema specification) proposes facilities for defining datatypes to be used to constrain the datatypes of elements and attributes within XML Schemas. It provides a higher degree of type checking than is available within XML 1.0 DTDs.

It provides

- A set of built-in primitive datatypes,
- A set of built-in derived datatypes, and
- Mechanisms by which users can define their own derived datatypes.

A derived datatype can be defined from a primitive datatype or another derived datatype by adding constraining facets. Precise details of the built-in datatypes and derivation mechanisms can be found in the DDL Specification, ISO-IEC 15938-2.

2.4.10 MPEG-7 Extensions to XML Schema

The following features need to be added to the XML Schema language specification to satisfy MPEG-7 specific requirements:

- Array and matrix datatypes, both fixed size and parameterized size;
- Built-in primitive time datatypes: basicTimePoint and basicDuration.

MPEG-7-specific parsers have been developed by adding validation of these additional constructs to standard XML Schema parsers. See http://m7itb.nist.gov/M7Validation.html for an overview.

2.4.11 MPEG-7 Headers: Namespaces

The description examples specified in this book assume that a schema wrapper is provided that identifies the XML Schema namespace (XML Schema) and MPEG-7 namespace:

```
<schema xmlns="http://www.w3.org/2001/XMLSchema"

    xmlns:mpeg7="urn:mpeg:mpeg7:schema:2001"

    targetNamespace="urn:mpeg:mpeg7:schema:2001"
```

```
elementFormDefault="qualified"

attributeFormDefault="unqualified">
```

The following tag is used to close the schema:

```
</schema>
```

2.4.12   MPEG-7 Headers: Documents

All MPEG-7 documents should have the following header information:

```
<?xml version="1.0" encoding="iso-8859-1?">
<Mpeg7 xmlns="urn:mpeg:mpeg7:schema:2001"
    xmlns:xsi="http://www.w3.org/2001/XMLSchema-
       instance"
    xmlns:mpeg7="urn:mpeg:mpeg7:schema:2001"
    xmlns:xml="http://www.w3.org/XML/1998/namespace"
    xsi:schemaLocation="urn:mpeg:mpeg7:schema:2001
Mpeg7-2001.xsd">

<! — Your MPEG-7 content — >

</Mpeg7>
```

You may use the online validator at http://m7itb.nist.gov/M7Validation. html to check the comformance of your MPEG-7 document to the DDL.

2.4.13   Illustrative Example of the DDL Usage

The structural elements of XML Schema are extensively used in an MPEG-7 definition. Let us consider the very important definition of time (e.g., how to specify a time point in a video or the time duration of a video segment) as an illustration to the use of these elements in MPEG-7.

The time description represents the real world time (Time datatype) as well as the time as used in the AV data (mediaTime datatype). In both cases, time instances as well as time intervals can be described.

Exhibit 2.6 illustrates the simplest way to specify a temporal instant and a temporal interval. A time instant, t1, can be defined by a lexical

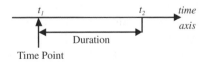
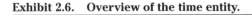

Exhibit 2.6.   Overview of the time entity.

representation using the TimePoint. An interval, [t1, t2], can be defined by its starting point, t1, (using the TimePoint) and a duration, t2 – t1.

Derived from the schema in Exhibit 2.6, the following Time datatype: TimeType is expressed in DDL:

```
<! — Definition of Time datatype — >

<complexType name="TimeType">

  <sequence>

    <choice>

       <element name="TimePoint" type="mpeg7:
          TimePointType"/>

       <element name="RelTimePoint" type="mpeg7:
          RelTimePointType"/>

       <element name="RelIncrTimePoint" type="mpeg7:
          RelIncrTimePointType"/>

    </choice>

    <choice minOccurs="0" >

       <element name="Duration" type="mpeg7:
          durationType"/>

       <element name="IncrDuration" type="mpeg7:
          IncrDurationType"/>

    </choice>

  </sequence>

</complexType>
```

For the specification of time intervals in the Time datatype, a complex type is used that is composed of two elements: the (start) time point and the duration. If only a time point is specified, the duration can be omitted, which is expressed by a sequence group element indicating that the start time must be specified in the sequence before the duration.

For the specification of the start time point, three alternatives may be used (specified by the choice element): TimePoint specifying a concrete time point; RelTimePoint, where the start time is defined as a temporal offset with respect to a reference point; and finally RelIncrTimePoint, where the start time is also defined as a temporal offset to a reference, but this time with respect to time units. We will show how TimePoint is defined; the two latter are not discussed in detail here.

The duration element is optional, which is indicated by minOccurs = "0." Two alternatives for expressing the duration are available. Duration specifies the duration of a time period according to days and daytime and is detailed later, and IncrDurationType defines the duation of a time period with respect to time units.

The TimePointType specifies a time point according to the Gregorian dates and day time and the time zone.

```
<! — Definition of TimePoint datatype — >
<simpleType name="TimePointType">
  <restriction base="mpeg7:basicTimePointType">
    <pattern value="(\-?\d+(\-\d{2}(\-\d{2})?)?)?
      (T\d{2}(:\d{2}(:\d{2}
      (:\d+)?)?)?)?(F\d+)?(\-|\+\d{2}:\d{2})?"/>
  </restriction>
</simpleType>
```

The TimePointType is a simple type with no child elements. It is a restriction of another simple type. A restriction narrows the ranges or reduces alternatives of elements or attributes. Here we narrow the range of a built-in datatype string, from which basicTimePointType is derived, by the use of the pattern element. The complex looking pattern tells us that the format of the TimePointType is YYYY-MM-DDThh:mm:ss:nnn-FNNN±hh:mm.

For instance, a time instant of December 17, 2002, at 13 hours, 20 minutes, 1 second, and 235 milliseconds would be expressed using TimePointType by 2002-12-17T13:20:01:235F1000. According to the number of decimal digits used, the number of fractions of one second are 1000, as specified in the timePointType.

The durationType specifies the duration of a time period according to days and daytime. Fractions of a second are specified according to the TimePointType. The definition of the durationType uses again a simple type.

```
<! — Definition of duration datatype — >
<simpleType name="durationType">
  <restriction base="mpeg7:basicDurationType">
    <pattern value="\-
      ?P(\d+D)?(T(\d+H)?(\d+M)?(\d+S)?(\d+N)?)?(
        \d+F)?((\-
      |\+)\d{2}:\d{2}Z)?"/>
```

```
    </restriction>
</simpleType>
```

EXAMPLE: The following example describes the time of an event that started on the October 16, 2002, at 17:00 in a country whose time zone is 1 hour ahead of GMT (or Universal time), such as Austria, and has a duration of 10 days:

```
<Time>
    <TimePoint>2002-10-16T17:00+01:00</TimePoint>
    <Duration>P10D</Duration>
</Time>
```

2.5 Step-by-Step Approach for Creating an MPEG-7 Document

This section gives a step-by-step methodology for creating an MPEG-7 document based on a practical application scenario. It covers important parts of the Multimedia Content Description Interface (Part 5 [MDS] and Part 3 [Visual]). It is not intended to cover the complete spectrum of the Multimedia Content Description Interface, which would detract the reader's attention from the practical aspect of the step-by-step approach. This approach is also helpful for creating a document relying on parts of the description interface not covered here.

The complete DDL for the Multimedia Content Description Interface may be found at http://m7itb.nist.gov/M7Validation.html (without any conceptual model). Conceptual models for most of the descriptors may be found in the MPEG-7 overview by Martínez;[1] however, without an explanation on how to create an MPEG-7 document or the DDLs. Manjunath et al.'s[4] book on MPEG-7 describes the first six parts of MPEG-7 in a comprehensive way and gives examples. In addition to these documents, we give a practical guide for the creation of MPEG-7 descriptions containing structural and visual descriptors and semantics of image and video data. The complete International Standard MPEG-7 may be found in the ISO-IEC 15938-1-8. These documents may be obtained from ISO or from a national body.

2.5.1 Example Scenario

The example scenario is the description of the content structure of a given video. It shall specify the video segments and specify for each segment its color distribution. These low-level descriptions may be used for content-based querying. Moreover, for each segment, we like to retain and describe a key frame that enables browsing functionality. Finally, the semantics of the video segment shall be described using entities such as objects, events, concepts, states, places, and time. This allows the user to search videos on the basis of their semantic content.

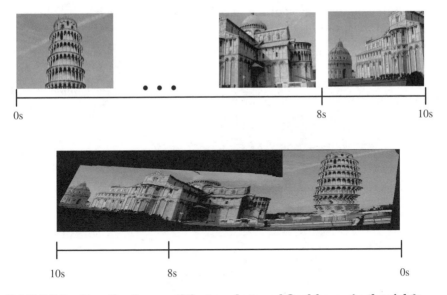

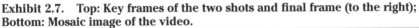

Exhibit 2.7. Top: Key frames of the two shots and final frame (to the right); Bottom: Mosaic image of the video.

The sample MPEG-1 video contains two shots from a tourist video of Pisa. The first shot scans the Pisa Leaning Tower from top to bottom, and the second one shows the palazzo besides the leaning tower. The key frames for the two shots as well as the last frame in the video are displayed in Exhibit 2.7. For a better visualization of the complete video content, Exhibit 2.7 also presents the mosaic panorama of the video, which is a very useful representation of the video.

Note that we used an in-house built segmentation tool for the segmentation of the video and for describing the visual features of the segments. Information on the video such as semantics and classification had to be added manually, because there is as of yet no support for automatic annotation. General information for supporting annotation tools may be found in Section 2.9.

2.5.2 Choosing the MPEG-7 Root Element

The first decision when writing an MPEG-7 document is to choose the appropriate root element: creating either a complete description or a description unit. A complete description is useful if one desires to describe multimedia content using the top-level types. For example, the description of an image is a complete description. A description unit is useful if one desires to describe an instance of a D or a DS. A description unit can be used to represent partial information from a complete description. For example, the description of the shape or color of an image is a description

41

unit. In our example, we want to describe a complete video; thus, we use a complete description.

The choice between a complete description and a description unit is shown in the DDL of the root element Mpeg7. If a complete description is chosen, the element Description has to be used; for a description unit, the element DescriptionUnit has to be selected.

```
<! − Definition of Mpeg7 root element − >
<element name="Mpeg7">
  <complexType>
    <complexContent>
      <extension base="mpeg7:Mpeg7Type">
        <choice>
          <element name="DescriptionUnit" type="mpeg7:
            Mpeg7BaseType"/>
          <element name="Description" type="mpeg7:
            CompleteDescriptionType" minOccurs="1"
            maxOccurs="unbounded"/>
        </choice>
      </extension>
    </complexContent>
  </complexType>
</element>
```

2.5.3 Choosing the MPEG-7 Top-Level Type

The following top-level types are used in complete descriptions to describe multimedia content and metadata related to content management. Each top-level type contains the description tools that are relevant for a particular description task, that is, for describing an image or a video.

- ContentDescriptionType (abstract): top-level type for complete description of multimedia content
  ContentEntityType: top-level type for describing multimedia content entities such as images, videos, audio, collections, and so forth
  ContentAbstractionType (abstract): top-level type for describing abstractions of multimedia content
  - SemanticDescriptionType: top-level type for describing semantics of multimedia content

- ModelDescriptionType: top-level type for describing models of multimedia content
- SummaryDescriptionType: top-level type for describing summaries of multimedia content
- ViewDescriptionType: top-level type for describing views and view decompositions of AV signals
- VariationDescriptionType: top-level type for describing variations of multimedia content

- ContentManagementType (abstract): top-level type for describing metadata related to content management

  UserDescriptionType: top-level type for describing a user of a multimedia system

  CreationDescriptionType: top-level type for describing the process of creating multimedia content

  UsageDescriptionType: top-level type for describing the usage of multimedia content

  ClassificationDescriptionType: top-level type for describing a classification scheme for multimedia content

The top-level types are organized under the type hierarchy shown in Exhibit 2.8 (note that not all concrete subtypes are shown, but typical examples are given). The CompleteDescriptionType forms the root base type of the hierarchy. The top-level types ContentDescriptionType and ContentManagementType extend CompleteDescriptionType. Similarly, the top-level types ContentEntityType and ContentAbstractionType extend ContentDescriptionType. ContentEntityType aggregates elements of type MultimediaContentType, which is the super type of VideoType, AudioType, ImageType, and so forth.

In our running example, we want to describe the complete structure and the semantics content of a video. There are two alternative ways in doing this. We may use the ContentEntityType or the ContentAbstractionType. In the first case, the semantics is embedded into the structural content descriptions of the ContentEntityType, in the other case the structural information of the video is embedded into the ContentAbstractionType. The decision of which way to take down in the type derivation hierarchy depends on the importance of the structural and semantics description part in the complete description. In our example, the structure is the anchor for our description, and we therefore rely on the ContentEntityType.

With this choice, let us create the following frame for our MPEG-7 document:

```
<Mpeg7>

    <Description xsi:type="ContentEntityType">

        . . .
```

```
</Description>

</Mpeg7>
```

Note that there is no element of type ContentDescriptionType specified in the document. ContentEntityType is introduced by "casting" the Content-DescriptionType of Description to the appropriate subtype ContentEntity-Type. This type is defined in the following DDL part:

```
<! – Definition of ContentEntity Top-level Type – >

<complexType name="ContentEntityType">

  <complexContent>

    <extension base="mpeg7:ContentDescriptionType">

      <sequence>

        <element name="MultimediaContent" type="mpeg7:
            MultimediaContentType" minOccurs="1"
            maxOccurs="unbounded"/>

      </sequence>

    </extension>

  </complexContent>

</complexType>
```

Now we have to select what AV content to describe. Following the type hierarchy shown in Exhibit 2.8, we select Video. To introduce the Video-Type, we again have again to use the xsi:type mechanism, this time for MultimediaContent (as shown in the former DDL). Hence the frame for our MPEG-7 document becomes

```
<Mpeg7>

  <Description xsi:type="ContentEntityType">

    <MultimediaContent xsi:type="VideoType">

      . . .

    </MultimediaContent>

  </Description>

</Mpeg7>
```

The complex type VideoType defines the element Video for further detailing the video content. Note that Video is of type VideoSegmentType that is a subtype of SegmentType.

```
<! – Definition of Video Content Entity – >

<complexType name="VideoType">
```

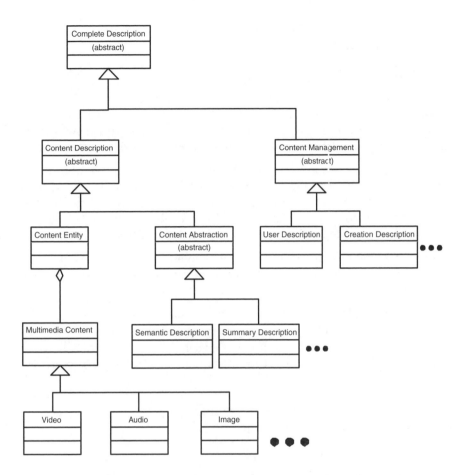

Exhibit 2.8.   Illustration of the type derivation hierarchy for top-level types.

```
<complexContent>

  <extension base="mpeg7:MultimediaContentType">

    <sequence>

      <element name="Video"type="mpeg7:
           VideoSegmentType"/>

    </sequence>

  </extension>

</complexContent>

</complexType>
```

45

2.5.4 Detailed Description of the Content with the SegmentType and Its Subtypes (Video, Audio, etc.)

The SegmentType is the root type for describing the characteristics of segments, such as creation information, media information, usage information, semantic information, text annotation, matching hints, point of view descriptions, and so forth. From the SegmentType derives the special descriptions for the different media. Exhibit 2.9a shows the principal subentities of Segment DS that are available in MPEG-7 for different media.

In our example we are interested in describing the video and its key frames, which leads to the VideoSegment DS and the StillRegion DS. To employ useful descriptions there, the elements of the main type, the SegmentType have to be studied first and then the VideoSegmentType for the video and the StillRegionType for the key frames is introduced.

Exhibit 2.9b gives an overview of the elements (and their cardinalities), which the SegmentType, VideoSegmentType, and StillRegionType provide.

2.5.5 SegmentType

The SegmentType supplies rich description elements for describing the structural media content. We shortly describe the purpose of the important elements and then point to the subsequent sections for further details.

```
<! – Definition of Segment DS – >

<complexType name="SegmentType" abstract="true">

  <complexContent>

    <extension base="mpeg7:DSType">

      <sequence>

        <choice minOccurs="0">

          <element name="MediaInformation" type=
            "mpeg7: MediaInformationType"/>

          <element name="MediaInformationRef" type=
            "mpeg7:ReferenceType"/>

          <element name="MediaLocator" type="mpeg7:
            MediaLocatorType"/>

        </choice>

      ... other elements detailed below
```

The first element to be specified is either a MediaInformation or a MediaLocator. The MediaLocator contains simple information about the location of the media, whereas the MediaInformation may unfold exact information on the property of each frame in the video, including location

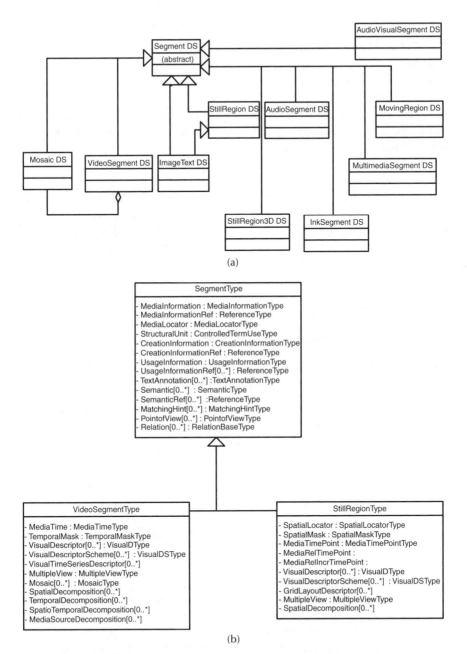

(a)

(b)

Exhibit 2.9. (a) Principal subclasses of the segment description schemes for describing multimedia content; (b) subtypes of the SegmentType and their elements.

47

information of the video. Section 2.5.1 details the usage of the MediaInformation and MediaLocator.

Note that the MediaInformation may be obtained either directly by using the element MediaInformation or by reference mechanism through the element MediaInformationRef of type ReferenceType. This distinction between direct inclusion of descriptions or referencing is drawn through the complete framework of MPEG-7, where complex descriptions are employed.

```
<element name="StructuralUnit"
  type="mpeg7:ControlledTermUseType" minOccurs="0"/>
```

The next element is the StructuralUnit. It describes the role of the segment in the context of the multimedia content. Examples of values of a StructuralUnit include "story," "scene," and "shot." The values may depend on the particular form of the multimedia content; for example, a movie or daily news report.

The type of this element is ControlledTermUseType, which may have an attribute of mpeg7:termReferenceType referring to a term in a Classification Schema. This term allows us to characterize the content as daily news report with the standardized term urn:mpeg:mpeg7:cs:GenreCS:2001:1.3.1. A Classification Schema is an important feature of MPEG-7 allowing using terms in a standardized way (see also Section 2.6).

The next element describes the creation information related to the actual segment. It may be specified directly or by reference. The Creation-Information DS contains the following information:

```
<choice minOccurs="0">
  <element name="CreationInformation" type="mpeg7:
    CreationInformationType"/>
  <element name="CreationInformationRef" type="mpeg7:
    ReferenceType"/>
</choice>
```

- Creation and production information: Information about the creation and production of the content not perceived in the content, such as author, director, characters, target audience, and so forth, and information about the creation process that may be perceived in the content, such as actors in a video, players in a concert, and so forth.
- Classification information: information related to the classification of the content, such as target audience, style, genre, rating, and so forth.

Section 2.5.2 details this description scheme.

The other important element is the usage information related to this segment. It is a well-structured and comprehensive description scheme that may be understood from the schema definition. Once again, it may be detailed directly or by reference. Briefly, the principal components are

- Rights information: information about the rights for using the multimedia content
- Usage information: information about the ways and means to use the multimedia content (e.g., edition, emission, and so forth) and the results of the usage (e.g., audience)
- Financial information: information about the financial results of the production (in the FinancialResults D within the UsageInformation DS) and of the publication (in the Financial D within each Availability DS and UsageRecord DS) of the multimedia content

```
<choice minOccurs="0">

  <element name="UsageInformation" type="mpeg7:
    UsageInformationType"/>

  <element name="UsageInformationRef" type="mpeg7:
    ReferenceType"/>

</choice>
```

The next child element is TextAnnotation. It is an important element for characterizing the content using (structured) free-text and keyword annotation. Note that only a minimum of a type concept is supplied with this annotation mechanism. For the description of semantic entities involved in a scene, the semantics tools of MPEG-7, as indicated in the next element, have to be used.

```
<element name="TextAnnotation" minOccurs="0"
    maxOccurs="unbounded">

  <complexType>

    <complexContent>

      <extension base="mpeg7:TextAnnotationType">

        <attribute name="type" use="optional">

          <simpleType>

            <union memberTypes="mpeg7:
              termReferenceType string"/>

          </simpleType>

        </attribute>

      </extension>

    </complexContent>
```

```
        </complexType>

    </element>
```

The element TextAnnotation is a complex type that extends the TextAnnotationType and adds an attribute type that indicates the type or purpose of the textual annotation (optional). It is defined as follows:

```
    <complexType name="TextAnnotationType">

        <choice minOccurs="1" maxOccurs="unbounded">

            <element name="FreeTextAnnotation" type="mpeg7:
                TextualType"/>

            <element name="StructuredAnnotation" type="mpeg7:
                StructuredAnnotationType"/>

            <element name="DependencyStructure" type="mpeg7:
                DependencyStructureType"/>

            <element name="KeywordAnnotation" type="mpeg7:
                KeywordAnnotationType"/>

        </choice>

        <attribute name="relevance" type="mpeg7:
            zeroToOneType" use="optional"/>

        <attribute name="confidence" type="mpeg7:
            zeroToOneType" use="optional"/>

        <attribute ref="xml:lang"/>

    </complexType>
```

Thus, we may employ the following means for annotating a text:

- FreeTextAnnotation: describes a free text annotation;
- StructuredAnnotation: describes a thematically structured annotation;
- DependencyStructure: describes a textual annotation with a syntactic parse-tree based on dependency structures;
- KeywordAnnotation: describes a keyword annotation.

The FreeTextAnnotation is the simplest annotation and is, therefore, frequently used. To introduce the minimum structure, one may use the other three variations; for instance, the structured annotation that supplies the following structuring frame (note that the content is not typed, but the structure):

Who: describes animate objects or beings (people and animals) or legal persons (organizations and person groups) using free text.
WhatObject: describes inanimate objects using free text.

WhatAction: describes actions using free text.

Where: describes a place using free text.

When: describes a time using free text.

Why: describes a purpose or reason using free text.

How: describes a manner using free text.

The following XML fragment shows a simple example of the FreeTextAnnotation and the StructuredAnnotation:

```
<TextAnnotation>

  <FreeTextAnnotation xml:lang="en">

    This video shows the Leaning Tower in Pisa.

  </FreeTextAnnotation>

  <StructuredAnnotation>

    <WhatObject>

      <Name xml:lang="en"> Leaning Tower </Name>

    </WhatObject>

    <WhatAction>

      <Name xml:lang="en"> Visit of the Tower </Name>

    </WhatAction>

  </StructuredAnnotation>

</TextAnnotation>
```

The Semantic element describes the semantics of the scene depicted in the segment with the help of semantic entities, like persons, events, objects, concepts, and their relationships (optional). The SemanticType is defined in Section 2.5.3. Again, one may use the direct inclusion or the reference mechanisms for the specification of the semantics.

```
<choice minOccurs="0" maxOccurs="unbounded">

  <element name="Semantic" type="mpeg7:SemanticType"/>

  <element name="SemanticRef" type="mpeg7:
      ReferenceType"/>

</choice>
```

The MatchingHint element describes the relative importance of instances of description tools in the segment DS (or parts of instances of description tools) for matching segments (optional). A segment description can include multiple MatchingHints to describe multiple matching criteria or different combinations of descriptors. An example is given below.

The PointOfView element describes the relative importance of the segment given a specific point of view (optional). Finally, the Relation element describes a relation that the segment participates in (optional). Those elements lead to more or less complicated description schemes and are not detailed here; their conceptual model may be found in the MPEG-7 overview by Martínez.[1]

```
<element name="MatchingHint" type="mpeg7:
    MatchingHintType" minOccurs="0"
    maxOccurs="unbounded"/>

<element name="PointOfView" type="mpeg7:
    PointOfViewType" minOccurs="0"
    maxOccurs="unbounded"/>

<element name="Relation" type="mpeg7:RelationType"
    minOccurs="0" maxOccurs="unbounded"/>
```

The MatchingHint may specify a subjective reliability factor of the hint values defined. The relationship of the hint to the description elements, the relative importance of which is described, is done via xpath expressions. A simple example (assuming that we may choose among different low-level color descriptors):

```
<MatchingHint reliability="0.8">

    <Hint value="0.5" xpath=".."/"../../ColorStructure"/>

    <Hint value="0.6" xpath=".."/"../../DominantColor"/>

    <Hint value="0.7" xpath=".."/"../../ColorLayout"/>

</MatchingHint>
```

The SegmentType is an abstract type, and its elements may occur in an instance document only in connection with one of its subtypes. The example scenario comprises the description of video contents and its keyframes, so the types VideoSegmentType and StillRegionType are described now.

2.5.6 VideoSegmentType

The subtypes of the SegmentType describe specific media content; the VideoSegmentType is now specific to videos. It naturally extends the SegmentType:

```
<! — Definition of VideoSegment DS — >

<complexType name="VideoSegmentType">

    <complexContent>
```

```
<extension base="mpeg7:SegmentType">
```

```
...other elements detailed below
```

The first element of the VideoSegment is the MediaTime element. It is used as a temporal locator to describe a temporally connected subinterval by specifying the start time and the duration of the video segment. It may be visualized as putting a frame (box) on the video aligned in the timeline. Section 2.5.1 gives an example. If the segment cannot be described as a single connected interval; that is, it is composed of several disconnected intervals, then the TemporalMask has to be used.

```
<choice minOccurs="0">

  <element name="MediaTime" type="mpeg7:
    MediaTimeType"/>

  <element name="TemporalMask" type="mpeg7:
    TemporalMaskType"/>

</choice>
```

The following example shows how a temporal interval consisting of two subintervals (the first being 0 to 3 seconds, and the second being 3 to 8 seconds) may be laid over the first video segment of our video (0 to 8 seconds):

```
<TemporalMask>

  <SubInterval>

    <MediaTimePoint>T00:00:00</MediaTimePoint>

    <MediaDuration>PT0M3S</MediaDuration>

  </SubInterval>

  <SubInterval>

    <MediaTimePoint>T00:00:03</MediaTimePoint>

    <MediaDuration>PT0M5S</MediaDuration>

  </SubInterval>

</TemporalMask>
```

The next child elements describe the visual features of the video segment. They are of type VisualDType or VisualDSType and may be attributed to a single frame or a sequence of frames. Typical features include color disribution, texture, and shape.

The color descriptors available as subtypes from the VisualDType are detailed in Section 2.5.4. Precise details of all VisualDescriptorType subtypes can be found in the Visual Specification, ISO-IEC 15938-3. An overview is given (without DDL) by Sikora.[7] The additional reference,

VisualTimeSeriesDescriptor, describes a temporal sequence of visual features in the video segment and is derived from the basic Visual-DescriptorTypes.

```
<choice minOccurs="0" maxOccurs="unbounded">

   <element name="VisualDescriptor" type="mpeg7:
      VisualDType"/>

   <element name="VisualDescriptionScheme" type="mpeg7:
      VisualDSType"/>

   <element name="VisualTimeSeriesDescriptor" type=
      "mpeg7:VisualTimeSeriesType"/>

</choice>
```

The MultipleView element describes visual features of a three-dimensional moving physical object depicted in the video segment as seen from one or more viewing positions or angles. The Mosaic element describes the panoramic view of a video segment (see Exhibit 2.7 for a Mosaic of the whole Pisa video).

```
<element name="MultipleView" type="mpeg7:
   MultipleViewType" minOccurs="0"/>

<element name="Mosaic" type="mpeg7:MosaicType"
   minOccurs="0" maxOccurs="unbounded"/>
```

The video segment decomposition tools, as shown below, describe the decomposition of a video segment into one or more subsegments in space, time, and media source. They all extend the SegmentDecompositionType. These tools are detailed in Section 2.5.5.

```
<choice minOccurs="0" maxOccurs="unbounded">

<element name="SpatialDecomposition" type="mpeg7:
   VideoSegmentSpatialDecompositionType"/>

<element name="TemporalDecomposition" type="mpeg7:
   VideoSegmentTemporalDecompositionType"/>

   <element name="SpatioTemporalDecomposition" type=
      "mpeg7:VideoSegmentSpatioTemporal Decomposition
      Type"/>

   <element name="MediaSourceDecomposition" type="mpeg7:
      VideoSegmentMediaSourceDecompositionType"/>

</choice>
```

2.5.7 StillRegionType

The StillRegionType is used for the descriptions of describes an image or a two-dimensional spatial region of an image or a video frame.

StillRegion3DType has to be used for three-dimensional images and differs from the StillRegionType only in the way the decomposition is specified. For the description of the key frames within a VideoSegment, we will use the StillRegionType.

First of all, the StillRegionType extends the SegmentType:

```
<complexType name="StillRegionType">
  <complexContent>
    <extension base="mpeg7:SegmentType">
...other elements detailed below
```

Then we may lay a SpatialLocator or a SpatialMask over the image to detail regions of interest:

```
<choice minOccurs="0">
  <element name="SpatialLocator" type="mpeg7:R
      egionLocatorType"/>
  <element name="SpatialMask" type="mpeg7:S
      patialMaskType"/>
</choice>
```

SpatialMasks have to be defined in terms of polygon points describing the subregion's boundary. For instance, a two-dimensional image with two disconnected subregions, identified by five polygon points:

```
<SpatialMask>
  <SubRegion>
    <Polygon>
      <Coords mpeg7:dim="2 5"> 10 15...</Coords>
    </Polygon>
  </SubRegion>
  <SubRegion>
    <Polygon>
      <Coords mpeg7:dim="2 5"> 20 30... </Coords>
    </Polygon>
  </SubRegion>
</SpatialMask>
```

As an alternative to a SpatialLocator or Mask, we may specify that the StillRegion to be described is part of a video by using the MediaTime elements as follows (this feature is useful for specifying the key frame of a VideoSegment):

```
<choice minOccurs="0">
  <element name="MediaTimePoint" type="mpeg7:
    mediaTimePointType"/>
  <element name="MediaRelTimePoint" type="mpeg7:
    MediaRelTimePointType"/>
  <element name="MediaRelIncrTimePoint" type="mpeg7:
    MediaRelIncrTimePointType"/>
</choice>
```

It follows the VisualDescriptors in the same way as for a VideoSegement. The reader is referred to Section 2.5.4 for more details.

```
<choice minOccurs="0" maxOccurs="unbounded">
  <element name="VisualDescriptor" type="mpeg7:
    VisualDType"/>
  <element name="VisualDescriptionScheme" type="mpeg7:
    VisualDSType"/>
  <element name="GridLayoutDescriptors" type="mpeg7:
    GridLayoutType"/>
</choice>
```

Finally, we have first the MultipleView element

```
<element name="MultipleView" type="mpeg7:
  MultipleViewType" minOccurs="0"/>
```

and then the specificiation of the StillRegion's subregions. The decomposition tools are detailed in Section 2.5.5.

```
<element name="SpatialDecomposition" type="mpeg7:
  StillRegionSpatialDecompositionType" minOccurs="0"
  maxOccurs="unbounded"/>
```

2.5.8 Media Description Tools

The description of the media involves a single top-level element, the MediaInformation DS. It is composed of an optional MediaIdentification D and one or several MediaProfile Ds. The MediaInformation DS is a highly structured description tool to reflect the description possibilities of the media in forms of profiles, formats, and so forth. Most of the proposed descriptors are straightforward in their meaning, and therefore, no DDL is given here. Instead, we briefly review the different components available and give a complete MediaInformation of the sample pisa.mpg video.

The MediaIdentification D contains description tools that are specific to the identification of the AV content, independent of the different available instances.

The MediaProfile D contains different description tools that allow the description of one profile of the media AV content being described. The MediaProfile D is composed of

- MediaFormat D, which contains description tools that are specific to the coding format of the media profile.
- MediaInstance D, which contains the description tools that identify and locate the media instances available for a media profile.
- MediaTranscodingHints D, which contains description tools that specify transcoding hints of the media being described. The purpose of this D is to improve quality and reduce complexity for transcoding applications. The transcoding hints can be used in video transcoding and motion estimation architectures to reduce the computational complexity. This D may be used in connection with MPEG-21 Digital Item Adaptation descriptions, as introduced in Chapter 3.
- MediaQuality D represents quality rating information of audio or visual content. It can be used to represent both subjective quality ratings and objective quality ratings.

A possible description of media information of our MPEG-1 video pisa.mpg is given below. Note that it does not yet contain the segmentation information to keep the document more readable.

The video is 10 seconds plus 13 frames long (which corresponds to 13/25ths of a second, as the frame rate is 25 frames/second; PT0H0M10S13N25F), its resolution is 240 × 320, the file size is 947.361 bytes, the frame rate is 25 Hz, the file format is MPEG-1 (CS term used urn:mpeg:mpeg7:cs:FileFormatCS:2001:3), the visual coding format is the MPEG-1 video coding format (CS term used urn:mpeg:mpeg7:cs:VisualCodingFormatCS:2001:1), and the colorDomain is used.

```
<Mpeg7>

  <Description xsi:type="ContentEntityType">

    <MultimediaContent xsi:type="VideoType">

      <Video>

        <MediaInformation>

          <MediaIdentification>

            <EntityIdentifier organization="MPEG"
                type="MPEG7ContentSetId">pisa1

          </EntityIdentifier>
```

```
      </MediaIdentification>
      <MediaProfile>
        <MediaFormat>
          <Content href="MPEG7ContentCS">
            <Name>visual</Name>
          </Content>
          <FileFormat href="urn:mpeg:mpeg7:cs:
              FileFormatCS:2001:3">
            <Name>mpg</Name>
          </FileFormat>
          <FileSize>947631</FileSize>
          <VisualCoding>
            <Format href="urn:mpeg:mpeg7:cs:
                VisualCodingFormatCS:2001:1"
                colorDomain="color"/>
            <Frame height="240" rate="25"
                width="320"/>
          </VisualCoding>
        </MediaFormat>
        <MediaInstance id="pisa">
          <InstanceIdentifier organization="MPEG"
              type="MPEG7ContentSetOnLineId">
              mpeg7/mpeg/
          </InstanceIdentifier>
          <MediaLocator>
            <MediaUri>pisa.mpg</MediaUri>
          </MediaLocator>
        </MediaInstance>
      </MediaProfile>
    </MediaInformation>
    <MediaTime>
      <MediaTimePoint>T00:00:00</MediaTimePoint>
        <MediaDuration>PT0H0M10S13N25F
        </MediaDuration>
    </MediaTime>
```

```
    </Video>

  </MultimediaContent>

 </Description>

</Mpeg7>
```

2.5.9 Creation and Production Tools

The creation and production description tools describe author-generated information about the generation and production process of the AV content. This information can usually not be extracted from the content itself. It is related to the material, but is not explicitly included in the actual content.

The description of the creation and production information has, as a top-level element, the CreationInformation DS, which is composed of one required Creation D, one optional Classification D, and several optional RelatedMaterial Ds; see the following DDL:

```
<! — Definition of CreationInformation DS — >

<complexType name="CreationInformationType">

  <complexContent>

    <extension base="mpeg7:DSType">

      <sequence>

        <element name="Creation"
            type="mpeg7:CreationType"/>

        <element name="Classification" type="mpeg7:
            ClassificationType" minOccurs="0"/>

        <element name="RelatedMaterial" type="mpeg7:
            RelatedMaterialType" minOccurs="0"
            maxOccurs="unbounded"/>

      </sequence>

    </extension>

  </complexContent>

</complexType>
```

The Creation D contains the detailed description tools related to the creation of the content, including places, dates, actions, materials, staff (technical and artistic), and organizations involved. The following elements may be declared:

```
<! — Definition of Creation DS — >

<complexType name="CreationType">
```

59

```
<complexContent>

  <extension base="mpeg7:DSType">

    <sequence>

      <element name="Title" type="mpeg7:TitleType"
          minOccurs="1" maxOccurs= "unbounded"/>

      <element name="TitleMedia" type="mpeg7:
          TitleMediaType" minOccurs="0"/>

      <element name="Abstract" type="mpeg7:
          TextAnnotationType" minOccurs="0"
          maxOccurs="unbounded"/>

      <element name="Creator" type="mpeg7:
          CreatorType" minOccurs="0"
          maxOccurs="unbounded"/>

      <element name="CreationCoordinates"
          minOccurs="0" maxOccurs= "unbounded">

        <complexType>

          <sequence>

            <element name="Location" type="mpeg7:
                PlaceType" minOccurs="0"/>

            <element name="Date" type="mpeg7:
                TimeType" minOccurs="0"/>

          </sequence>

        </complexType>

      </element>

      <element name="CreationTool" type="mpeg7:
          CreationToolType" minOccurs="0"
          maxOccurs="unbounded"/>

      <element name="CopyrightString" type="mpeg7:
          TextualType" minOccurs="0"
          maxOccurs="unbounded"/>

    </sequence>

  </extension>

</complexContent>

</complexType>
```

For instance, for the sample video pisa.mpg, the following information on the creation of the content is useful: the creator of the video is Stephan Herrmann, and he was the producer of the video. This information is specified through the CS Term urn:mpeg:mpeg7:cs:RoleCS:2001:PRO-DUCER of the RoleCS. The following MPEG-7 document contains this information (for better readability, the video information and segmentation are omitted).

```
<Mpeg7>
  <Description xsi:type="ContentEntityType">
    <MultimediaContent xsi:type="VideoType">
      <Video>
        <MediaLocator>
          <MediaUri>file://pisa.mpg</MediaUri>
        </MediaLocator>
        <CreationInformation>
          <Creation>
            <Title xml:lang="en">Pisa Video</Title>
            <Abstract>
              <FreeTextAnnotation>
                This short video shows the Pisa Leaning
                  Tower.
              </FreeTextAnnotation>
            </Abstract>
            <Creator>
              <Role href="urn:mpeg:mpeg7:cs:RoleCS:
                2001:PRODUCER">
                <Name xml:lang="en">Anchorman</Name>
              </Role>
              <Agent xsi:type="PersonType">
                <Name>
                  <GivenName>Stephan</GivenName>
                  <FamilyName>Herrmann</FamilyName>
                </Name>
              </Agent>
            </Creator>
          </Creation>
          <Classification>
```

61

```
<ParentalGuidance>
    <ParentalRating href="urn:mpeg:mpeg7:cs:
        FSKParentalRatingCS:2003:1"/>
    <Region>de</Region>
</ParentalGuidance>
</Classification>
</CreationInformation>
</Video>
</MultimediaContent>
</Description>
</Mpeg7>
```

The Classification D contains the description tools that allow the classification of the AV content. It allows the specification of user-oriented classifications (e.g., language, style, genre, etc.) and service-oriented classifications (e.g., purpose, parental guidance, market segmentation, media review, etc.).

In the previous example, we used a regional classification (for German-speaking countries) for the parental rating. The video has no violent scene; thus, it is open to the greater public, and the term urn:mpeg:mpeg7:cs:FSK-ParentalRatingCS:2003:1 has to be applied. The FSKParentalRating is not included in the predefined MPEG-7 CS list. Section 2.6 details how this new FSK rating system was introduced to MPEG-7 via its proper extension mechanism.

Finally, the RelatedMaterial D contains the description tools related to additional information about the AV content available in other materials. This could be the description of a Web page and its location; for example, the Pisa City Web homepage

```
<RelatedMaterial>
<DisseminationFormat href = "urn:mpeg:mpeg7:cs:
    DisseminationFormatCS:2001:4"/>
<MaterialType>
    <Name xml:lang = "en">Pisa City Web Page</Name>
</MaterialType>
<MediaLocator>
    <MediaUri>http://www.comune.pi.it/</MediaUri>
</MediaLocator>
</RelatedMaterial>
```

2.5.10 Visual Descriptors

MPEG-7 visual description tools consist mainly of descriptors that cover color, texture, shape, motion and face recognition. They mainly use a histogram-based approach of representation; that is, they compute a vector (histogram) of elements each representing the number of pixels (regions) in a given image, which have similar characteristics.

For example, let us suppose that we want to represent the color of an image using the RGB (red, green, and blue) color space. Each color channel is encoded using 8 bits, leading to a maximum of $256 \times 256 \times 256$ bins in a color histogram. The height of each histogram bin is computed as follows: for each discrete value from the interval $[0, 256 \times 256 \times 256]$, compute how many pixels of the given image have this color value. Obviously, such a fine representation would not be efficient in terms of space; thus, a quantization to a smaller number of bins in the histogram is required. Let us suppose that the color histogram consists of only 256 bins. Then we have to regroup three-color values to one bin value. This may be done by merging three successive values in a linear quantization to one value. For big images, the height of the bin may become quite large. Therefore, a second quantization of the height of the bin is often applied (sometimes referred as amplitude quantization, as it is applied of the amplitude [height] of the bins).

Here we will focus on a color representation of an image. Methods for shape, texture, and so forth also use similar representation techniques. An overview (without a DDL) of them may be found in the article written by Sikora;[7] the complete DDL is available in ISO-IEC 15938-3.

2.5.10.1 Color Descriptors. There are seven color descriptors available for description in MPEG-7: color space, color quantization, dominant colors, scalable color, color structure, color layout, and the group of frames (GoF) and group of pictures (GoP) color. Here we give a brief overview of these descriptors (including their DDL) and show how descriptions are created. For details on the content (without DDL), the reader is referred to Manjunath et al.[8]

2.5.10.2 Color Space Descriptor. This feature is the color space that is to be used. The following main color spaces are supported for description:

- R,G,B Color Space: three values to represent a color in terms of red, green, and blue. It is, as preferred, machine-readable color space.
- Perceptual Color Spaces available for descriptions are:
    Y,Cr,Cb Color Space: Y is the luminance, and Cb and Cr are the chrominance values of this color space.

H,S,V Color Space: HSV (hue, saturation, and value) is close to perception. The hue and saturation values clearly distinguish pure colors.

HMMD (Hue-Max-Min-Diff): Color Space is closer to a perceptually uniform color space than H,S,V Color Space.

2.5.10.3 Color Quantization Descriptor. This descriptor defines a uniform quantization of a color space. The number of bins, which the quantizer produces, is configurable such that great flexibility is provided for a wide range of applications. For a meaningful application in the context of MPEG-7, this descriptor has to be combined with dominant color descriptors; for example, to express the meaning of the values of dominant colors.

2.5.10.4 Dominant Color(s) Descriptor. This color descriptor is most suitable for representing local (object or image region) features where a small number of colors are enough to characterize the color information in the region of interest. It is also applicable on whole images; for example, flag images or color trademark images.

The DDL of dominant color is shown below. At most, eight dominant colors may be specified for one image. The most relevant elements to be specified are color quantization, used to extract a small number of representing colors in each region/image (use the ColorQuantization element together with the ColorSpace if RGB is not used); percentage of each quantized color in the region, calculated correspondingly (percentage element); spatial coherency on the entire descriptor, a single value that tells us how closely connected are the pixels having the dominant color. The Index element specifies the index of the dominant color in the selected color space as defined in ColorQuantization. The number of bits for each component is derived from the ColorQuantization element. Finally, the optional ColorVariance specifies an integer array containing the value of the variance of color values of pixels corresponding to the dominant color in the selected color space.

Note that all color descriptors extend the VisualDType to be employed in the description of a video/image as required by the VideoSegmentType and StillRegionType.

```
<complexType name="DominantColorType" final="#all">

    <complexContent>

<extension base="mpeg7:VisualDType">

    <sequence>

      <element name="ColorSpace" type="mpeg7:
          ColorSpaceType" minOccurs="0"/>
```

```
<element name="ColorQuantization" type="mpeg7:
    ColorQuantizationType" minOccurs="0"/>

<element name="SpatialCoherency" type="mpeg7:
    unsigned5"/>

<element name="Value" minOccurs="1" maxOccurs="8">

    <complexType>

    <sequence>

        <element name="Percentage"
            type="mpeg7:unsigned5"/>

        <element name="Index">

        <simpleType>

            <restriction>

            <simpleType>

            <list
            itemType="mpeg7:unsigned12"/>

            </simpleType>

            <length value="3"/>

            </restriction>

        </simpleType>

        <element name="ColorVariance"
            minOccurs="0">

            . . .

        </sequence>

        </complexType>

    </element>

    </sequence>

    </extension>

    </complexContent>

</complexType>
```

The following MPEG-7 document shows the DominantColor description for a completely red image. Note that the MPEG-7 DDL gives constraint on the coding of the values; for instance, the percentage has to be coded by mpeg7:unsigned5. A percentage value of 100% is coded to the value 31.

```
<Mpeg7>
  <Description xsi:type="ContentEntityType">
    <MultimediaContent xsi:type="ImageType">
      <Image>
        <MediaLocator>
          <MediaUri> file://red.jpg</MediaUri>
        </MediaLocator>
        <TextAnnotation>
          <FreeTextAnnotation>
            A completely red image
          </FreeTextAnnotation>
        </TextAnnotation>
        <VisualDescriptor xsi:type="DominantColorType">
          <SpatialCoherency>31</SpatialCoherency>
          <Value>
            <Percentage>31</Percentage>
            <Index>255 0 0</Index>
            <ColorVariance>1 0 0</ColorVariance>
          </Value>
        </VisualDescriptor>
      </Image>
    </MultimediaContent>
  </Description>
</Mpeg7>
```

2.5.10.5 Scalable Color Descriptor. The Scalable Color Descriptor (SCD) is a color histogram in the HSV Color Space that is encoded by a Haar transform. The Haar transformation corresponds to a low-pass filter on the histogram values obtained from counting the number of pixels that fall into a certain color range. It has been shown that a much more compact descriptor is obtained by applying this transformation without loss of retrieval accuracy.

The SCD binary representation is scalable in terms of bin numbers and bit representation of the amplitudes. It is useful for image-to-image comparison where the spatial distribution of the color is not a significant retrieval factor. Retrieval accuracy increases with the number of bits used in the representation.

The definition of the ScalableColorType is given here:

```
<complexType name="ScalableColorType" final="#all">
    <complexContent>
        <extension base="mpeg7:VisualDType">
            <sequence>
                <element name="Coeff" type="mpeg7:
                    integerVector"/>
            </sequence>
            <attribute name="numOfCoeff" use="required">
                <simpleType>
                    <restriction base="integer">
                        <enumeration value="16"/>
                        <enumeration value="32"/>
                        <enumeration value="64"/>
                        <enumeration value="128"/>
                        <enumeration value="256"/>
                    </restriction>
                </simpleType>
            </attribute>
            <attribute name="numOfBitplanesDiscarded" use=
                "required">
                <simpleType>
                    <restriction base="integer">
                        <enumeration value="0"/>
                        <enumeration value="1"/>
                        <enumeration value="2"/>
                        <enumeration value="3"/>
                        <enumeration value="4"/>
                        <enumeration value="6"/>
                        <enumeration value="8"/>
                    </restriction>
```

67

```
      </simpleType>
    </attribute>
  </extension>
  </complexContent>
</complexType>
```

In addition to the histogram values given in Coeff, two attributes have to be specified: numOfCoeff specifies the number of coefficients used in the scalable histogram representation—possible values are 16, 32, 64, 128, and 256; numOfBitplanesDiscarded specifies the number of bitplanes discarded in the scalable representation for each coefficient—possible values are 0, 1, 2, 3, 4, 6, and 8.

A complete example of a SCD is given within the context of the GoF and GoP Color Descriptor for a video, found later in this section.

2.5.10.6 Color Structure Descriptor. The Color Structure Descriptor (CSD) is a color feature descriptor that captures both color content (similar to a color histogram) and information about the structure of this content. Its main functionality is image-to-image matching where an image may consist of possibly disconnected regions.

Example 1: Consider the two images in Exhibit 2.10.

A descriptor based only on the global color distribution (e.g., the Scalable Color Descriptor) may not distinguish these two images. Thus, we need to introduce a means of describing the spatial layout (structure) of the color distribution.

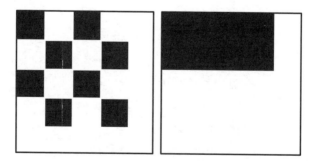

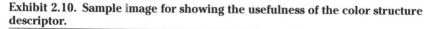

Exhibit 2.10. Sample image for showing the usefulness of the color structure descriptor.

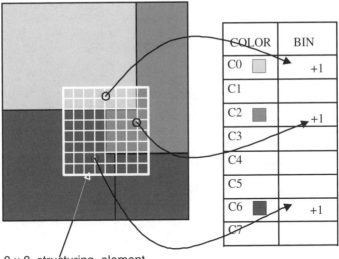

8 x 8 structuring element

Exhibit 2.11. Sample image for showing the construction process of the histogram.

The extraction method embeds color structure information into the descriptor by taking into account all colors in a structuring element of 8×8 pixels that slides over the image, instead of considering each pixel separately. Color values are represented in the double-coned HMMD Color Space, which is quantized nonuniformly into 32, 64, 128, or 256 bins (see the definition of the simpleType for the element value in the DDL below). Each bin amplitude value is represented by an 8-bit code.

Example 2: Consider the image in Exhibit 2.11. The table on the right of the image shows which bins (representing group of colors) are updated for the sample 8×8 structuring element.

The DDL of the ColorStructureType is shown below:

```
<complexType name="ColorStructureType" final="#all">
  <complexContent>
    <extension base="mpeg7:VisualDType">
      <sequence>
        <element name="Values">
          <simpleType>
            <restriction>
              <simpleType>
```

69

```
            <list itemType="mpeg7:unsigned8"/>
         </simpleType>
         <minLength value="1"/>
         <maxLength value="256"/>
      </restriction>
    </simpleType>
  </element>
 </sequence>
 <attribute name="colorQuant" type="mpeg7:
      unsigned3" use="required"/>
  </extension>
 </complexContent>
</complexType>
```

The two images from example 1 would be expressed by the following MPEG-7 documents. Note that for simplicity we use only nine values, corresponding to the nine possible positions of the structuring element in the images. For a real application, at least 32 values have to be specified. The colorQuant attribute tells us the number of bins used: 1 means 32, 2 means 64, and so on. The colorQuant value used in this example is, therefore, a dummy value.

Left image:

```
<Mpeg7>
  <Description xsi:type="ContentEntityType">
    <MultimediaContent xsi:type="ImageType">
      <Image>
        <MediaLocator>
          <MediaUri> file://left.jpg</MediaUri>
        </MediaLocator>
        <TextAnnotation>
          <FreeTextAnnotation>
            The left black and white image of Exhibit
              2.10
          </FreeTextAnnotation>
        </TextAnnotation>
```

```
<VisualDescriptor
    xsi:type="ColorStructureType"
    colorQuant="1">

  <Values> 9 0 0 0 ... 0 9 </Values>

</VisualDescriptor>

    </Image>

  </MultimediaContent>

 </Description>

</Mpeg7>
```

Right image:

```
<Mpeg7>

  <Description xsi:type="ContentEntityType">

    <MultimediaContent xsi:type="ImageType">

      <Image>

        <MediaLocator>

          <MediaUri> file://right.jpg</MediaUri>

        </MediaLocator>

        <TextAnnotation>

          <FreeTextAnnotation>

            The right black and white image of Exhibit
            2.10

          </FreeTextAnnotation>

        </TextAnnotation>

        <VisualDescriptor xsi:type=
            "ColorStructureType" colorQuant="1">

          <Values> 6 0 0 0 ... 0 7 </Values>

        </VisualDescriptor>

      </Image>

    </MultimediaContent>

  </Description>

</Mpeg7>
```

2.5.10.7 Color Layout Descriptor. The Color Layout Descriptor (CLD) represents the spatial distribution of color in an image in a compact form.

The input image is divided into 64 (8×8) blocks. The average color is used as representative for each block. Discrete cosine transform is then applied to each subpart of the image, and 63 coefficients are extracted. This compactness allows image-matching functionality with good retrieval efficiency at small computational costs. The DDL of the CLD mainly consists of the enumeration of the 63 coefficients and is not shown here.

2.5.10.8 GoF and GoP Color Descriptor. The GoF and GoP Descriptor extends the ScalableColor Descriptor (SCD) (defined earlier for still images) to color description of a video segment or a collection of still images. Two additional bits (to the SCD) allow the inclusion of information on how the color histogram was calculated (by average, median, or intersection) before the Haar transformation was applied to it.

The DDL of the GoFGoPColorType is shown below:

```
<complexType name="GoFGoPColorType" final="#all">
  <complexContent>
    <extension base="mpeg7:VisualDType">
      <sequence>
        <element name="ScalableColor" type="mpeg7:
          ScalableColorType"/>
      </sequence>
      <attribute name="aggregation" use="required">
        <simpleType>
          <restriction base="string">
            <enumeration value="Average"/>
            <enumeration value="Median"/>
            <enumeration value="Intersection"/>
          </restriction>
        </simpleType>
      </attribute>
    </extension>
  </complexContent>
</complexType>
```

The Average histogram, which refers to averaging the counter value of each bin across all frames or pictures, is equivalent to computing the aggregate color histogram of all frames and pictures with proper normalization.

The Median Histogram refers to computing the median of the counter value of each bin across all frames or pictures. The Intersection Histogram refers to computing the minimum of the counter value of each bin across all frames or pictures to capture the least common color traits of a group of images.

We will use the GoF/GoP Color Descriptor to describe the color characteristics of our sample video, pisa.mpg. We thereby use a descriptor for each segment to enable similarity matching to the segment granularity. The following is an MPEG-7 document describing the video segmentation of pisa.mpg (the StillRegions are left out for better readability, and only the GoF for the first segment is included).

```
<Mpeg7>
  <Description xsi:type="ContentEntityType">
    <MultimediaContent xsi:type="VideoType">
      <Video>
        <MediaLocator>
          <MediaUri>file://pisa.mpg</MediaUri>
        </MediaLocator>
        <TemporalDecomposition>
          <VideoSegment id="VS1">
            <TextAnnotation>
              <FreeTextAnnotation>
                Pisa Leaning Tower
              </FreeTextAnnotation>
            </TextAnnotation>
            <VisualDescriptor
                xsi:type="GoFGoPColorType"
                aggregation="Average">
              <ScalableColor numOfCoeff="4"
                  numOfBitplanesDiscarded="0">
                <Coeff>7 0 2 0 0 0 0 0 0 0 7 0 13 7 42
98 81 13 3 0 0 0 0 0 3 12 46 51 67 112 92 231 218 26 1
1 0 0 0 0 0 8 31 45 83 182 146 469 244 27 1 0 0 0 0 0 0
24 22 28 65 151 119 601 835 196 106 43 18 5 41 32 131
279 590 386 491 642 367 1387 4046 783 47 6 0 1 2 8 92
157 278 206 275 609 581 643 1666 149 3 0 0 0 0 0 6 7 4
7 21 106 204 213 649 28 0 0 0 0 0 0 0 0 0 1 14 64 1211
5436 2144 418 106 40 12 56 112 511 2381 1258 372 403 618
```

```
512 754 4879 1532 36 3 0 0 0 10 18469 8102 3961 178 50
211 311 54 683 260 0 0 0 0 0 0 0 0 0 0 0 1 12 0 51 32 0
0 0 0 0 0 0 0 0 0 0 0 0 91 275 98 19 5 2 0 1 1 4 104 43
29 31 55 49 10 79 20 0 0 0 0 0 0 442 394 13 0 0 1 0 0 0
0 0 0 0 0 0 0 0 0 0 0 0 0 0 0 0 0 0 0 0 0 0 0 0 0 0 0 0
0 0</Coeff>
```

```
                        </ScalableColor>

                    </VisualDescriptor>

                <MediaTime>

                    <MediaTimePoint>T00:00:00:0F25<
                        /MediaTimePoint>

                    <MediaIncrDuration

                        mediaTimeUnit="PT1N25F">218<
                            /MediaIncrDuration>

                </MediaTime>

            </VideoSegment>

            <VideoSegment id="VS2">

                <TextAnnotation>

                    <FreeTextAnnotation>

                        Pisa Palais

                    </FreeTextAnnotation>

                </TextAnnotation>

                <MediaTime>

                    <MediaTimePoint>T00:00:08:18F25<
                        /MediaTimePoint>

                    <MediaIncrDuration

                        mediaTimeUnit="PT1N25F">45<
                            /MediaIncrDuration>

                </MediaTime>

            </VideoSegment>

        </TemporalDecomposition>

        </Video>

    </MultimediaContent>

  </Description>

</Mpeg7>
```

2.5.11 Semantic Description Tools

For some applications, the structure of the media is only of partial use; in addition, the user is interested in the semantic of the content. For such applications, MPEG-7 provides the semantic description tools. The core type of the semantic description tools is the SemanticBase DS, which describes semantic entities in a narrative world.

The available semantic entities are shown in Exhibit 2.12 and are described here.

- The Semantic DS is the "connecting DS" to the structural DSs, for example, the Segment DS, as depicted in Exhibit 2.12. It simply extends the SemanticBag DS. The SemanticBag DS is an abstract tool that is the base of the DSs that describe a collection of semantic entities and their relation.
- The Object DS describes a perceivable or abstract object. A perceivable object is an entity that exists; that is, has temporal and spatial extent in a narrative world (e.g., "the leaning tower"). An abstract object is the result of applying abstraction to a perceivable object (e.g., "any tower"). Essentially, this generates an object template.
- The AgentObject DS extends the Object DS. It describes a person, an organization, a group of people, or personalized objects (e.g. "myself, Roger Moore").
- The Event DS describes a perceivable or abstract event. A perceivable event is a dynamic relation involving one or more objects occurring in a region in time and space of a narrative world (e.g., "myself climbing the leaning tower"). An abstract event is the result of applying abstraction to a perceivable event (e.g., "anyone climbing a tower").
- The Concept DS describes a semantic entity that cannot be described as a generalization or abstraction of a specific object, event, time place, or state. It is expressed as a property or collection of properties (e.g., "harmony"). It may refer to the media directly or to another semantic entity being described.
- The SemanticState DS describes one or more parametric attributes of a semantic entity at a given time or spatial location in the narrative world or in a given location in the media (e.g., "the tower is 50 meters high").
- Finally, SemanticPlace and SemanticTime DSs describe respectively a place and a time in a narrative world.

The conceptual aspect of a concrete description can be organized in a tree or in a graph (see Exhibit 2.13). The graph structure is defined by a set of nodes representing semantic notions and a set of edges specifying the relationship between the nodes. Edges are described by the SemanticRelation DSs.

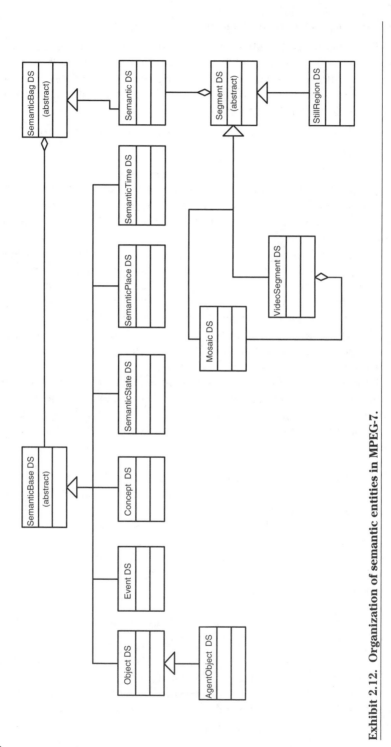

Exhibit 2.12. Organization of semantic entities in MPEG-7.

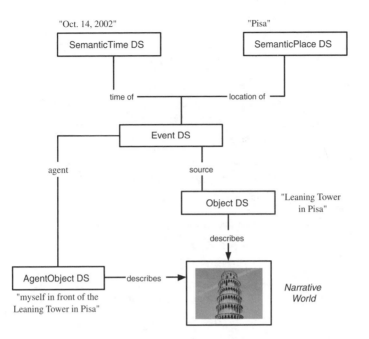

Exhibit 2.13. Semantic graph description for the running example.

2.5.11.1 Application to the Running Example. A possible conceptual aspect description for the first frame of our sample video pisa.mpg is illustrated in Exhibit 2.13. The narrative world involves myself, Harald Kosch (not shown), standing in front of the Pisa Leaning Tower and taking a picture of the tower. The semantic event is characterized by a semantic time description: "14th of October 2002" and a semantic place: "Pisa." The description of the event contains one object, the "Leaning Tower," and one person, "Harald Kosch" (myself).

The MPEG-7 document for this semantic scene graph is given below. For a better readability, only the semantic aspects are specified in the document. The semantic relations are identified by terms of a CS. A total of 82 terms are predefined. New terms are added as described in Section 2.7. Note that the SemanticPlace and SemanticTime are child elements of Event and do not require a Semantic Relation.

```
<Mpeg7>
  <Description xsi:type="ContentEntityType">
    <MultimediaContent xsi:type="ImageType">
      <Image>
        <Semantic>
```

77

```
<Label>

  <Name> Harald Kosch takes a photo of the
      Leaning Tower </Name>

</Label>

<SemanticBase xsi:type="EventType"
    id="TakingPhoto">

  <Label>

    <Name> Description of the event of taking
        a photo </Name>

  </Label>

  <Relation type="urn:mpeg:mpeg7:cs:
      SemanticRelationCS:2001:agent"

      target="#Harald"/>

  <Relation type="urn:mpeg:mpeg7:cs:
      SemanticRelationCS:2001:source"

      target="#Tower"/>

  <SemanticPlace>

    <Label>

      <Name>Pisa</Name>

    </Label>

  </SemanticPlace>

  <SemanticTime>

    <Label>

      <Name>October 14, 2002</Name>

    </Label>

  </SemanticTime>

</SemanticBase>

<SemanticBase xsi:type="ObjectType"
    id="Tower">

  <Label>

    <Name> Leaning Tower </Name>

  </Label>

</SemanticBase>
```

```
<SemanticBase xsi:type="AgentObjectType"
    id="Harald">

  <Label>

    <Name> Harald </Name>

  </Label>

    <Agent xsi:type="PersonType">

    <Name>

      <GivenName abbrev="Harry"> Harald
          </GivenName>

      <FamilyName> Kosch </FamilyName>

    </Name>

    </Agent>

  </SemanticBase>

</Semantic>

</Image>

</MultimediaContent>

</Description>

</Mpeg7>
```

2.5.12 *Media Decomposition Tools*

The Segment DS is recursive, that is, it may be subdivided into subsegments, and thus may form a hierarchy (decompositon tree). The resulting decomposition tree is used to describe the media source, the temporal, or the spatial structure of the AV content. For example, a video clip may be temporally segmented into various levels of scenes, shots, and segments. The decomposition tree may be used to generate a table of contents.

Exhibit 2.14 shows the possible decompositions for the description scheme introduced in this chapter, for example, VideoSegment DS and Still-Region DS, and derived from Segment DS. The principal decomposition mechanisms are denoted by lines and are labeled by the decomposition type (time -> temporal descomposition, space -> spatial decomposition, spaceTime -> spatial and temporal, media -> decomposition in different media tracks). The AudioVisual segment can contain both audio and visual segments. The last members in the chain of segments may be Audio, Video, and Still region.

The root type for the description of segment decomposition is the abstract SegmentDecompositionType. It defines a set of basic attributes

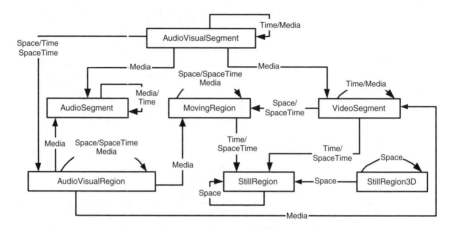

Exhibit 2.14. Multimedia decomposition in MPEG-7.

defining the type of subdivision: temporal, spatial, or spatio-temporal. They are related to the spatial and temporal subdivisions that may leave gaps and overlaps between the subsegments. The definition of the SegmentDecompostionType is given below.

```
<! — Definition of SegmentDecomposition DS — >

<complexType name="SegmentDecompositionType"
      abstract="true">

  <complexContent>

    <extension base="mpeg7:DSType">

      <attribute name="criteria" type="string"
          use="optional"/>

      <attribute name="overlap" type="boolean"
          use="optional"

          default="false"/>

      <attribute name="gap" type="boolean"
          use="optional" default="false"/>

    </extension>

  </complexContent>

</complexType>
```

From the root type, four abstract second-level types are derived: SpatialSegmentDecomposition DS, TemporalSegmentDecomposition DS, SpatioTemporalSegmentDecomposition DS, and MediaSourceSegmentDecomposition DS, describing the spatial, temporal, spatio-temporal, and media source decompositions, respectively, of segments.

The concrete tools to be employed for a given multimedia element (e.g., of type VideoSegmentType) extend these four second-level types. For instance, we have seen that in a VideoSegment, we require four types to describe any possible decomposition. In the following DDL extract, four elements are defined with the according types.

```
<choice minOccurs="0" maxOccurs="unbounded">

    <element name="SpatialDecomposition" type="mpeg7:
        VideoSegmentSpatialDecomposition- Type"/>

    <element name="TemporalDecomposition" type="mpeg7:
        VideoSegmentTemporalDecompositionType"/>

    <element name="SpatioTemporalDecomposition"
        type="mpeg7:VideoSegmentSpatioTemporal
        DecompositionType"/>

    <element name="MediaSourceDecomposition"
        type="mpeg7:VideoSegmentMediaSource
        DecompositionType"/>

</choice>
```

The instantiation of the decomposition involved in a Segment DS can be viewed as a hierarchical segmentation problem where elementary entities (region, video segment, and so forth) have to be defined and structured by inclusion relationship within a tree. In this sense, the following decomposition tree (Exhibit 2.15) may describe our sample video. We have two children segments, one for the leaning tower and one for the palais. For each segment, we retain a keyframe that gives a second level in the tree.

The following XML document translates the decomposition tree of Exhibit 2.15 into a valid MPEG-7 description. Note that MediaInformation, Visual Descriptors, and Creation and Production Information are omitted for better readability. Using a SpatioTemporalDecomposition element within the declaration of the VideoSegment specifies the key frame for each Videosegment. The key frame is a StillRegion and its position in the stream is defined relative to the beginning of the VideoSegment (i.e., Media-RelIncrTimePoint of the StillRegion to MediaTimePoint of the VideoSegment). The relative time distance is given in frames. For this, the frame rate has to be provided. This is done by specifying PT1N25F as mediaTimeUnit in the MediaRelIncrTimePoint element.

```
<Mpeg7>

    <Description xsi:type="ContentEntityType">

        <MultimediaContent xsi:type="VideoType">

            <Video>
```

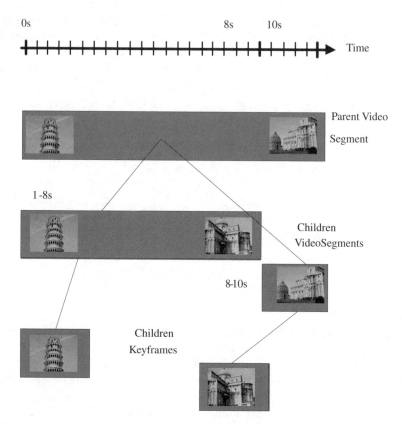

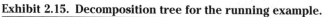

Exhibit 2.15. Decomposition tree for the running example.

```
<MediaLocator>

  <MediaUri>pisa.mpg</MediaUri>

</MediaLocator>

<TemporalDecomposition>

  <VideoSegment id="VS1">

    <TextAnnotation>

      <FreeTextAnnotation> Pisa Leaning Tower
          </FreeTextAnnotation>

    </TextAnnotation>

    <MediaTime>

      <MediaTimePoint>T00:00:00:0F25<
          /MediaTimePoint>

      <MediaIncrDuration
```

```
            mediaTimeUnit="PT1N25F">218<
                /MediaIncrDuration>

    </MediaTime>

    <SpatioTemporalDecomposition>

        <StillRegion>

            <MediaRelIncrTimePoint
                mediaTimeUnit="PT1N25F">23<
                /MediaRelIncrTimePoint>

            <SpatialDecomposition/>

        </StillRegion>

    </SpatioTemporalDecomposition>

</VideoSegment>

<VideoSegment id="VS2">

    <TextAnnotation>

        <FreeTextAnnotation> Pisa Palais
            </FreeTextAnnotation>

    </TextAnnotation>

    <MediaTime>

        <MediaTimePoint>T00:00:08:18F25<
            /MediaTimePoint>

            <MediaIncrDuration
                mediaTimeUnit="PT1N25F">45
                </MediaIncrDuration>

    </MediaTime>

    <SpatioTemporalDecomposition>

        <StillRegion>

            <MediaRelIncrTimePoint
                mediaTimeUnit="PT1N25F">32<
                /MediaRelIncrTimePoint>

            <SpatialDecomposition/>

        </StillRegion>

    </SpatioTemporalDecomposition>

</VideoSegment>

</TemporalDecomposition>

<MediaLocator>
```

```
        <MediaUri>pisa.mpg</MediaUri>

      </MediaLocator>

    </Video>

  </MultimediaContent>

 </Description>

</Mpeg7>
```

2.6 Extending the Description Schema of MPEG-7

The DDL of MPEG-7 defines the syntax of the MPEG-7 description tools. The description tools are instantiated as descriptions in textual format (XML), thanks to the DDL (based on XML Schema). Binary format of descriptions is obtained by means of the BiM defined in the Systems part (see Section 2.7).

Some applications, however, require a more detailed description framework than that proposed by MPEG-7. For instance, consider an application for the annotation of sport videos. It would be desirable to distinguish semantic entities, like players and referees, and detail their relationship and the soccer events (e.g., goal, penalty). For this purpose, MPEG-7 proposes mechanisms for the creation of specialized classification schemes. Moreover, it allows the creation of new description schemes and, possibly, descriptors. it also allows the extension and modification of existing description schemes.

The simplest extension is the creation of a new classification scheme. As stated in Section 2.1, the MPEG-7 CS defines a list of typical terms used in many applications together with their meanings. For instance, it allows the definition of the file formats in a standard way. Note that the publication of a newly created or extended CS is subject to a registration. More information on registration may be obtained from the MPEG homepage at http://www.chiariglione.org/mpeg/.

2.6.1 Creation of a New CE

Let us assume that we want to create a new CS for the parental rating specific to national standards. MPEG-7 supplies terms that are compliant to the ICRA (Internet Content Rating Association) Parental Rating Classification (http://www.icra.org/), which is an international, well-recognized classification of violence, nudity, and so forth, in multimedia material. However, most countries also support national standards for broadcasted material. For instance, the SPIO (Spitzenorganisation der Filmwirtschaft e.V.) organization (http://www.spio.de/) provides, for German-speaking countries, a CS, known as FSK, that is based on age. A total of five terms are introduced:

1. Released for general public
2. Released for persons older than 6 years of age
3. Released for persons older than 12 years of age
4. Released for persons older than 16 years of age
5. Not released for persons younger than 18 years of age

To establish the new CS, we have first to define a new identification URI (Uniform Resource Identifier). In accordance with the ICRA Rating, the URI urn:mpeg:mpeg7:cs:FSKParentalRatingCS:2003 is proposed. Second, we have to provide the domain to which this new CS applies. Obviously, it applies to the same domain as the ICRA does: "//CreationInformation/Classification/ParentalGuidance/ParentalRating."

The following XML fragment shows the declaration of the new CS identified by urn:mpeg:mpeg7:cs:FSKParentalRatingCS:2003:

```
<ClassificationScheme
uri="urn:mpeg:mpeg7:cs:FSKParentalRatingCS:2003"
domain="//CreationInformation/Classification/ParentalG
uidance/ParentalRating">

   <Header xsi:type="DescriptionMetadataType">

     <Comment>

       <FreeTextAnnotation xml:lang="en">

         Thesaurus for Parental Rating according the FSK
            of SPIO

       </FreeTextAnnotation>

     </Comment>

   </Header>

   <Term termID="1">

     <Name xml:lang="en">released for general
        public</Name>

   </Term>

   <Term termID="2">

     <Name xml:lang="en">released for persons older than
        6 years</Name>

   </Term>

   <Term termID="3">

     <Name xml:lang="en">released for persons older than
        12 years</Name>

   </Term>
```

```
<Term termID="4">

  <Name xml:lang="en">released for persons older than
    16 years</Name>

</Term>

<Term termID="5">

  <Name xml:lang="en">not released for persons
    younger than 18 years</Name>

</Term>

<Term termID="6">

  <Name xml:lang="en">not rated</Name>

</Term>

</ClassificationScheme>
```

2.6.2 *Extending Existing Descriptors and Creating New Ones*

MPEG-7 provides a standardized set of technologies for describing multi-media content. This is especially true for multimedia content such as images, video, and audio. However, for applications using specialized entities, for instance, for soccer games, a PlayerType as an extension of the PersonType might be of interest.

MPEG-7 provides in the DDL a mechanism for introducing new descriptors/description schemes without changing the definition of the DDL of each part. The proposed extensions are put into its own file, for example, named here <myMPEG-7.xsd>. The following modifications to the schema files of MPEG-7 have to be made: add the file name—<myMPEG-7.xsd>—to Mpeg7-2001.xsd by adding the line

```
<! - my own definitions - >
<include schemaLocation="./myMPEG7.xsd"/>
```

2.7   Encoding and Decoding of MPEG-7 Documents for Delivery—Binary Format for MPEG-7

MPEG-7 descriptions may in many cases be generated automatically. We have seen low-level descriptors that contain histogram-based values of size 256; a complete video may be automatically decomposed into its segments, and for each segment different low-level descriptors may be available. The resulting XML document may thus be verbose and is not suitable for consumption in a constrained and streamed environment. To overcome the lack of efficiency in this textual XML, MPEG-7 Systems defines a generic framework to facilitate the delivery and processing of MPEG-7 descriptions: the BiM (binary format for MPEG-7). It enables the streaming and compression of any XML document.

It is important to note that BiM coders and decoders can deal with any XML language. Technically, the schema definition of the XML document is processed and used to generate a binary format. This binary format has two main properties. First, because of the schema knowledge, structural redundancy (element name, attribute name, and so forth) is removed from the document. Therefore, the document structure is highly compressed (up to 98%).[9] Second, element and attribute values are encoded according to some dedicated codecs. A library of basic datatype codecs is provided by the specification (e.g., Zlib). Other codecs can be plugged easily using the type-codec mapping mechanism defined in the standard.

One of the main technical advantages of the BiM binary encoding process is that it can be guided by schema information. In BiM, the schema is known both by the encoder and the decoder. The binary format is deduced from the schema definition. Thus, there is no need to define coding tables or a specific encoding mechanism.

2.7.1 Required Software

The current version of the BiM Reference Software may be obtained from http://www.expway.fr/mpeg/bim/, though it is password protected by MPEG). An older version is included in the Reference Software available at http://www.lis.e-technik.tu-muenchen.de/research/bv/topics/mmdb/ e_mpeg7.html (see als Section 2.9). Encoding details may be found in the document ISO-IEC 15938-1.

Each document can be transmitted in one or more pieces (called access units, the minimal unit that has a time stamp for decoding). At the lowest level of granularity, each attribute value or document leaf can be modified to allow a minimal transmission in case of a minimal change in the sent document.

Example: Consider the following MPEG-7 document describing a 1.5-minute-long video with two VideoSegments: NarrationVS (the first 15 seconds) and CaptureVS.

```
<Mpeg7>
    <Description xsi:type="ContentEntityType">
        <MultimediaContent xsi:type="VideoType">
            <Video id="RootV">
                <MediaTime>
                    <MediaTimePoint>T00:00:00</MediaTimePoint>
```

```
<MediaDuration>PT1M30S</MediaDuration>
</MediaTime>
<TemporalDecomposition gap="false"
    overlap="false">
    <VideoSegment id="NarrationVS">
        <MediaTime>
            <MediaTimePoint>T00:00:00<
                /MediaTimePoint>
            <MediaDuration>PT0M15S</MediaDuration>
        </MediaTime>
    </VideoSegment>
    <VideoSegment id="CaptureVS">
        <MediaTime>
            <MediaTimePoint>T00:00:15<
                /MediaTimePoint>
            <MediaDuration>PT1M15S</MediaDuration>
        </MediaTime>
    </VideoSegment>
</TemporalDecomposition>
    </Video>
</MultimediaContent>
</Description>
</Mpeg7>
```

A possible partition of the example document is shown in Exhibit 2.16. The global information of the complete video (RootV) is put in the first access unit, and then we encode the information of the temporal decomposition and the video segments NarrationVS and CaptureVS in the second access unit. Using two access units leads to the coding scheme as depicted in Exhibit 2.16. The document is here displayed as a tree, where nodes represent the elements. For a better readability, the names of some of the elements are not shown.

The advantage of encoding a document in several pieces is that the pieces can be delivered separately to the client. It is not required for the decoder to download (and keep in memory) the entire XML file before being able to process it. This ability for separate delivery can reduce both the memory required at the terminal side and the consumed bandwidth.

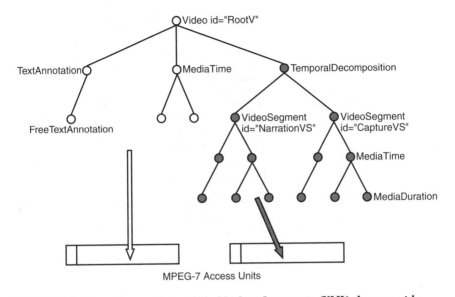

Exhibit 2.16. Encoding an Extensible Markup Language (XML) document in pieces.

2.8 Audio Part of MPEG-7

The audio part of the MPEG-7 standard relies on two basic structures: the AudioSegment DS, inherited from the Segment DS that allows defining a temporal structure of the audio signal, and a set of low-level descriptors.

The elements an AudioSegmentType provides are shown in Exhibit 2.17. They are similar to the elements of the VideoSegment that concerns the SegmentDecompostion and the definition of the time interval, but are different in the way low-level descriptors are defined. Note that a tool is proposed for combined AV content, the AudioVisualSegment DS, which in principle combines the definitions of the Video- and AudioSegment. It relies on the AudioVisualRegion DS for a description of an arbitrary spatio-temporal region of AV content.

MPEG-7 audio distinguishes two classes of structures, the generic audio description framework and the application-related tools. The first class defines generic descriptions that may be built for any signal. The descriptors include the so-called Low-Level Audio Descriptors (LLDs), the scalable series scheme, and the silence segment. The second class includes sound recognition, instrumental timbre description, spoken content descriptions, and melody description tools. These descriptors are referenced as High-Level Audio Descriptors (HLDs).

For instance, the Melody DS describes melody as a sequence of pitches or contour values, plus some information about scale, meter, beat, and key.

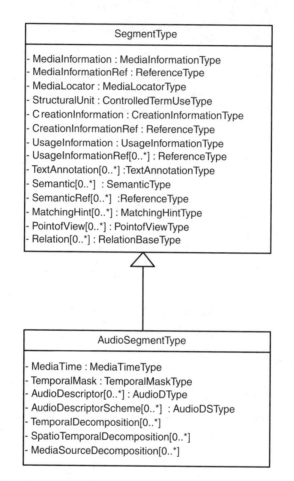

Exhibit 2.17. AudioSegementType as subtype of the SegmentType, and their elements.

The Melody DS includes tools (MelodyContour DS) for melody contour representation and tools (MelodySequence DS) for a more a complete melody representation. Both tools support matching between melodies.

Exhibit 2.18 shows a small melody containing four notes (three intervals) with a time signature of 4/4. The following MPEG-7 document extract describes the melody using the MelodyContourDS.

Exhibit 2.18. Small melody containing four notes.

```
<! — MelodyContour description of - >
<! — (3 intervals=4 notes) — >
<AudioDescriptionScheme xsi:type="MelodyType">
  <Meter>
     <Numerator>4</Numerator>
     <Denominator>4</Denominator>
  </Meter>
  <MelodyContour>
     <Contour>-2 2 -1</Contour>
     <Beat>1 1 1 1</Beat>
  </MelodyContour>
</AudioDescriptionScheme>
```

The Meter element describes the time signature, and the MelodyContour specifies the contour and the beat. The contour has as many values as there are intervals in the melody. Each value may take a value from –2 to +2 and contains the quantized interval change in cents. The beat has as many values as there are notes. The first note of a melody is labeled with its beat truncated to a whole beat. Successive notes increment the beat number according to their position relative to the first note. The MelodySequence DS avoids all quantizations and provides, therefore, a more verbose, but also more precise, description.

A simple and robust descriptor for audio retrieval is the AudioSignature DS. It summarizes the spectral flatness as unique content identifier for an audio signal. The spectral flatness expresses the deviation of the audio signal's power spectrum over frequency from a flat shape (corresponding to a noiselike or an impulselike signal). A high deviation from a flat shape may indicate the presence of tonal components. The AudioSignature DS summarizes the spectral flatness frame by frame, and the mean and variance values of the summarized flatness are retained. The spectral flatness is calculated for a number of frequency bands, which leads to a feature vector for robust matching between pairs of audio signals. AudioSignatures of two signals must have common band definitions to be compared.

Example: The AudioSignatureDS and its extraction mechanims are the base technology for the music search scenario described in Chapter 1, which is reconsidered in Section 2.2. The following audio description shows how an MPEG-7 document using the AudioSegmentType and the AudioSignatureType looks. The sample is a 3.5-second-long Wave (wav) encoded audio clip. The description was generated with the MPEG-7 Audio-Encoder provided at the Institut für Nachrichtentechnik, RWTH Aachen, and is available, for MPEG-7 developers only, at http://www.ient.rwth-aachen.de/forschung/mpeg7audio/.

```
<Mpeg7>

   <Description xsi:type="ContentEntityType">

      <MultimediaContent xsi:type="AudioType">

         <Audio xsi:type="AudioSegmentType">

            <MediaTime>

               <MediaTimePoint>T00:00:00</MediaTimePoint>

               <MediaDuration>PT3S500N1000F</MediaDuration>

            </MediaTime>

            <AudioDescriptionScheme xsi:type=
                "AudioSignatureType">

               <Flatness hiEdge="4000.0" loEdge="250.0">

                  <SeriesOfVector hopSize="PT30N1000F"
                      vectorSize="16"

                     totalNumOfSamples="96">

                        <Scaling ratio="32"
                            numOfElements="3"/>

                        <Mean mpeg7:dim="3 16">
0.730755 0.763238 0.610380 0.557224 0.630316 0.558102
0.500190 0.375704 0.459458 0.355976 0.438826 0.449985
0.661204 0.581780 0.395361 0.601645

0.756943 0.748773 0.675011 0.697741 0.648728 0.640419
0.467208 0.365971 0.376813 0.578655 0.610981 0.668466
0.727113 0.586444 0.490055 0.657457

0.741402 0.741298 0.710179 0.695944 0.678572 0.663125
0.599361 0.569031 0.578450 0.629878 0.626648 0.665652
0.749214 0.737452 0.628266 0.692530

                        </Mean>

                        <Variance mpeg7:dim="3 16">
0.039768 0.031566 0.029853 0.020935 0.032923 0.049108
0.031126 0.035234 0.045049 0.050080 0.056384 0.066359
0.019457 0.035216 0.083071 0.011095

0.039203 0.029778 0.040931 0.026889 0.040051 0.017069
0.018748 0.023640 0.020661 0.013789 0.013072 0.011485
0.016243 0.032908 0.040397 0.015138
```

```
0.041668 0.020187 0.013026 0.021801 0.032787 0.036691
0.022090 0.023869 0.016559 0.010244 0.010880 0.011096
0.014046 0.011034 0.016143 0.009134
                    </Variance>
                </SeriesOfVector>
              </Flatness>
            </AudioDescriptor>
          </Audio>
        </MultimediaContent>
      </Description>
  </Mpeg7>
```

Precise details of all AudioDescriptor(Scheme)Types can be found in the audio specification, ISO-IEC 15938-4.

2.9 MPEG-7 Supporting Tools and Reference Software

There are several tools available that support the annotation process with MPEG-7. The most complete one is the MPEG-7 Reference Software. The MPEG-7 Reference Software collected tools created during the MPEG-7 standardization process for most of the descriptors and description schemes and became part of the standard (Part 6). However, many of the tools generate XML fragments that conform only to an older version of the standard; others provide only a very limited functionality of what is proposed in the conceptual model associated to an MPEG-7 type. However, the reference software is a good starting point for any indexing and retrieval software relying on MPEG-7. Its current version can be downloaded at http://www.lis.e-technik.tu-muenchen.de/research/bv/topics/mmdb/e_mpeg7.html. This site also provides general information on the software. The reference software reached a stable version in March 2002. Many people have added their own implementations to it, based on the open framework proposed for descriptors and description schemes. Interested readers may follow the discussions on the mp7if_news group (http://groups.yahoo.com/group/mp7a_news/) set up by the MPEG-7 Alliance (see http://www.mpeg-industry.com).

Other tools support the annotation process by automatic extraction of visual features and by automatic segmentation of images and videos. Some of them propose semiautomatic creation of MPEG-7 documents, thus providing automatic low-level feature detection combined with a user-friendly interface for entering values for supplemental descriptors or description schemes.

Three commercial tools are of practical relevance. First, there is the IBM Annotation Tool (http://www.alphaworks.ibm.com/tech/videoannex), which assists in annotating video sequences with MPEG-7. Each shot in the video sequence can be annotated with static scene descriptions, key object descriptions, event descriptions, and other lexicon sets. The annotated descriptions are associated with each video shot and are stored as MPEG-7 descriptions in an XML file. It also allows customized lexicons to be created, saved, downloaded, and updated. The IBM Annotation Tool has a user-friendly interface consisting of all the necessary features for segmenting a video and classifying its content because of its lexicon, and is available on the basis of the AlphaWorks 90-Day Trial License Agreement. In addition to the IBM Annotation Tool, which proposes means for automatic segmentation, the sister tool from IBM (Multimodal Annotation [http://www.alphaworks.ibm.com/tech/multimodalannotation]) supports manual annotation of video and audio files on the basis of segmentation information obtained, for instance, from the Annotation Tool.

Second, the Ricoh MovieTool (http://www.ricoh.co.jp/src/multimedia/MovieTool/) is a tool for creating video content descriptions conforming to MPEG-7 syntax interactively. The MovieTool generates MPEG-7 descriptions based on the structure of a video. By using MovieTool, the user can create the structure while watching the video. Alternatively, MovieTool's editing functions can be used to edit the XML file, which contains the MPEG-7 description. A major advantage of using MovieTool is that the user can quickly and easily see the correspondence between the MPEG-7 descriptions and the video structure of each scene. Unfortunately, no trial version is available. The use of MovieTool requires one to agree to the terms and conditions of the support service contract, with an annual fee.

Although MovieTool generates MPEG-7 documents conformant to the standard, redundancy in the documents is high. For instance, for our pisa.mpg video, twice as many of the segments are described than are detected. These segments are dummies and do not have any useful description.

Third, the MPEG-7 Audio SpokenContent Tool by Canon generates a description file from an audio file in the wav format. The software is based on speech recognition technology being developed by Canon. It can only recognize phonemes (no words) and can only process speech signal files of limited size. Obviously, speech-recognition results depend heavily on acoustic conditions, individual speakers, and so forth. The authors tested their engine using *Wall Street Journal* data and achieved phoneme recognition rates of over 60 percent accuracy on the most likely phoneme string. More information may be obtained from http://www.cre.canon.co.uk/mpeg7asr/. Registration is obligatory for download of the software.

The Whisper Lab at the University of Wollongong developed a Web interface that runs an MPEG-7 audio low-level descriptors calculator. It calculates MPEG-7 descriptors from an audio file that is either in wav or MP3 file format and that is not longer than 1 MB. The online interface can be found at http://www.whisper.elec.uow.edu.au/mpeg7/.

Tools providing means for semantic annotation (i.e., for event, object, etc., descriptors) are actually under consideration. The actual list of available commercial tools may be found at the MPEG-7 Industrial Page at http://mpeg-industry.com/.

Recently, MPEG initiated two new MPEG-7 parts. Part 9 specifies profiles of description tools. The distinguishing feature is complexity. Part 10 specifies the schema definition across the parts of ISO/IEC 15938 and will contain a single schema across different versions. Parts 9 and 10 will be International Standard in 2004.

References

1. Martínez, J.M., Overview of the MPEG-7 Standard. ISO/IEC JTC1/SC29/WG11 N4980 (Klagenfurt Meeting), July 2002, http://www.chiariglione.org/mpeg/.
2. Koenen, R. and Pereira, F., MPEG-7 issues, *Image Comm.*, 16(1 and 2) September, 2000.
3. Chang, S.-F., Puri, A., Sikora, T., and Zhang, H., Special Issue on MPEG-7, *IEEE Trans. Circuits Syst. Video Technol.*, 11, 2001.
4. Manjunath, B.S., Salembier, P., and Sikora, T., *Introduction to MPEG-7*, John Wiley & Sons, New York, 2002.
5. van Beek, P., Benitez, A.B., Heuer, J., Martinez, J., Salembier, P., Smith, J., and Walker, T., *MPEG-7: Multimedia Description Schemes*, ISO/IEC FDIS 15938-5:2001, International Standard Document, 2001.
6. Fallside, D.C., XML Schema: W3C Recommendation. W3C Consortium, May 2001, http://www.w3.org/XML/Schema.
7. Sikora, T., The MPEG-7 visual standard for content description—an overview, *IEEE Trans. Circuits Syst. Video Technol.*, 11, 703–315, 2001.
8. Manjunath, B.S., Ohm, J.-R., Vasudevan, V.V., and Yamada, A., Color and texture descriptors, *IEEE Trans. Circuits Syst. Video Technol.*, 11, 703–315, 2001.
9. Niedermeier, U., Heuer, J., Hutter, A., Stechele, W., and Kaup, A., An MPEG-7 tool for compression and streaming of XML data, in *Proceedings of the IEEE International Conference on Multimedia and Expo*, Lausanne, Switzerland, August 26–29, IEEE CS Press, 2002, pp. 521–524.

Chapter 3
MPEG-21: The Multimedia Framework Standard

MPEG-21[1,2] is the ISO/IEC 21000 standard from the Moving Picture Experts Group (MPEG) that defines an open multimedia framework. The driving force for MPEG-21 was the current situation: Many elements exist to build an infrastructure for the delivery and consumption of multimedia content, but there exists no "big picture" to describe how these elements relate to each other.

The vision for MPEG-21 is to define an open multimedia framework that will enable transparent and augmented use of multimedia resources[*] across a wide range of networks and devices used by different communities. The intent is that the framework will cover the entire multimedia content delivery chain encompassing content creation, production, delivery, personalization, consumption, presentation, and trade.

MPEG-21 does not intend to specify the total behavior of a distributed multimedia system, but to define where standards are required in a multimedia framework. The normative methods and descriptions proposed are capable of supporting the delivery of digital content in a more interoperable and fair way than it is practiced today. For this, it is necessary to reach a shared vocabulary among the users of a distributed multimedia system. This presents a difficulty, as there are many examples of different architectures that evolve in response to a variety of models for the use of content. For instance, we have seen in the introduction (Chapter 1) that there are at least three models employed for supporting multimedia resource discovery (Dublin Core, SMPTE [Society of Motion Picture and Television Engineers], and MPEG-7). To avoid giving undue preference to one model above another, MPEG-21 proposes to describe the multimedia framework as a generic architecture. This includes first the introduction of an interoperable unit of exchange, the digital item (DI), which is a hierarchical container of resources, metadata, and other digital items. Further parts of the

[*] Resource in the MPEG-21 jargon corresponds to an identifiable media resource; that is, image, video, audio, or other media asset.

architecture are the digital item declaration (DID), which serves to declare a DI; the identification of DIs; digital rights management (DRM) and intellectual property management and protection (IPMP) of DIs; personalization of DIs; adaptation of DIs to resource constraints; and further tools for management of DIs.

The next sections detail the different parts of the MPEG-21 standard and relate them to each other to show the "big picture" of the multimedia framework. Section 3.1 gives the essential concepts of MPEG-21, introduces the structure of MPEG-21, and gives the current status of the 12 parts of MPEG-21. Section 3.2 presents the DID specification and shows a practical example. Section 3.3 introduces the IPMP and the rights expression language (REL) and data dictionary. Section 3.4 explains the elements of the digital item adaptation and gives a comprehensive example. Section 3.5 relates the various MPEG standards to each other. Finally, Section 3.6 gives examples of ongoing MPEG-21 research projects.

3.1 MPEG-21 Concepts and Structure

3.1.1 MPEG-21 Concepts

MPEG-21 is based on two essential concepts: the definition of a fundamental unit of distribution and transaction (the digital item) and the concept of users interacting with DIs. The DIs can be considered the "what" of the multimedia framework (e.g., a video collection, a music album), and the users can be considered the "who."

3.1.1.1 User Model. A user is any entity that interacts in the MPEG-21 environment or that makes use of a DI. Such users include individuals, consumers, communities, organizations, corporations, consortia, governments, and other standards bodies and initiatives around the world. Users are identified specifically by their relationship to another user for a certain interaction. A single entity may use content in many ways (publish, deliver, consume, and so on), and users may assume specific rights and responsibilities according to their interaction with other users within MPEG-21.

At its most basic level, MPEG-21 provides a framework in which one user interacts with other users and the object of that interaction is a DI. Some such interactions are creating content, providing content, archiving content, rating content, enhancing and delivering content, aggregating content, syndicating content, retail selling content, consuming content, facilitating transactions that occur from any of the above, and regulating transactions that occur from any of the above. Any of these are "uses" of MPEG-21, and the parties involved are the users.

3.1.1.2 Digital Item. The DI is the "what" of MPEG-21. Obviously, there is a need for a precise description of what constitutes such an "item." This is given in the DID, which specifies a set of abstract terms and concepts to form a useful model for defining DIs.

Example: Consider a multimedia family book. It is composed of digital photos, videos, and text documents. We would like to have a way to represent the individual digital components as a single entity, to describe the content ("myself standing in front of the Pisa Leaning Tower") of the components, and to specify the relationships among the components ("this picture was taken by Hugo"). Then, the picture itself may be included or references to it may be established. Finally, technical information required by the viewing client, such as the media format of each component, sizes of the components, and so forth, needs to be included. Finally, we like to guarantee that someone who is not a relative will not view the book. The consumption rights have to be defined.

3.1.2 MPEG-21 Structure

MPEG-21 identifies seven key architectural elements that are needed to support the multimedia delivery chain and has defined the relationships between and the operations supported by them. They are

- The DID, defining an uniform and flexible abstraction and interoperable schema for declaring DIs
- The Digital Item Identification (DII) and description, providing a framework for identification and description of a DI
- The content management and usage, providing interfaces and protocols that enable creation, manipulation, search, access, storage, delivery, and (re)use of content across its delivery and consumption chain
- The IPMP, providing means to enable DIs and their rights to be persistently and reliably managed and protected
- The terminals and networks, providing tools that enable the interoperable and transparent access to content across networks and terminals
- The content representation, defining how the media resources are represented
- The event reporting, supplying the metrics and interfaces that enable users to understand precisely the performance of all reportable events within the framework

Taking into account these seven key elements, 12 parts of MPEG-21 are currently defined (ISO/IEC 21000-1-12):

- Part 1: Vision, technologies, and strategy, covering the overview of MPEG-21
- Part 2: DID
- Part 3: DII
- Part 4: IPMP

- Part 5: REL
- Part 6: Rights data dictionary (RDD)
- Part 7: Digital item adaptation (DIA)
- Part 8: Reference software for all parts of MPEG-21
- Part 9: File format for storage and retrieval of MPEG-21 DIs
- Part 10: DI processing (DIP)
- Part 11: Persistent association tools
- Part 12: Resource delivery test bed.

Exhibit 3.1 shows the relationship among the different parts of MPEG-21.

Part 1 of the MPEG-21 standard is a technical report that describes the vision of MPEG-21, which gives an overview of the remaining parts, describes strategies for further developments, and, finally, points out the relationships and collaborations with other standardization bodies; for example, the project Mediacom 2004 issued by the ITU-T Study Group 16,* proposing a framework for the harmonized and coordinated development of global multimedia communication standards.

Part 2 of the MPEG-21 standard, the DID, specifies a set of abstract terms and concepts to form a useful model for defining DIs. It offers a representation of DIs in the form of a DID Schema (see Section 3.2).

Part 3 of the MPEG-21 standard, the DIIs, introduces tools to define unique identifiers that are used throughout MPEG-21 to name and address DIs and their parts. Note that MPEG-21 does not specify any new identification systems but standardizes the syntax of the reference to identifiers and

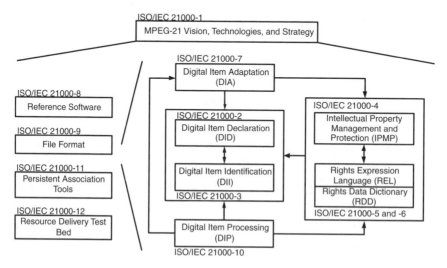

Exhibit 3.1. Parts of MPEG-21.

*http://www.itu.int/ITU-T/com16/mediacom2004/index.html.

the identification resolution process. Identification systems that may be used for DIIs are, for instance, the Digital Object Identifiers (DOIs),[*] the EAN.UCC Extensible Markup Language (XML) Schemas,[**] the identification systems used for books, and so on.

Part 4 of the MPEG-21 standard, the IPMP, enforces the rights and permissions defined on DIs. It goes hand in hand with Parts 5 and 6, the REL and the RDD. REL specifies the expression language for issuing rights for users to act on DIs. RDD forms the basis of all expressions of rights and permissions as defined by REL. Parts 4, 5, and 6 are detailed in Section 3.3.

Part 7 of the MPEG-21 standard, the DIA, refers to the terminals and networks and defines tools to support the adaptation process of a DI with respect to usage environment descriptions (see Section 3.4). It also includes descriptions for session mobility and configuration preferences with respect to the adaptation process.

Part 8 of the MPEG-21 standard is the reference software, collecting all software for descriptor generation and use as well as the implementation of the MPEG-21 tools.

Part 9 of the MPEG-21 standard defines an MPEG-21 file format that enables the DI to be efficiently stored and accessed.

Part 10 of the MPEG-21 standard, the DIP, specifies a processing architecture and a set of operations that can be used to process DIs (operations are called Digital Item Methods, or DIMs). A DIM defines an intended method for configuring, manipulating, or validating a DI.

Part 11 of the MPEG-21 standard, the persistent association tools introduce techniques that link information to identify and describe content with the content itself. Examples of these persistent tools are fingerprinting and watermarking.

Finally, Part 12 of the MPEG-21 standard, the Resource Delivery Test Bed, is a reference platform to provide a flexible and fair test environment for evaluating MPEG streaming technologies over IP (Internet Protocol) networks. The test bed has the capability of simulating different channel characteristics of various networks. As a result, new, scalable video codecs will be developed. Therefore:

- Various codecs (audio, video, scene composition) are evaluated.
- Various packetization methods and file formats are evaluated.
- Various multimedia streaming rate control and error control mechanisms to be plugged into the test bed are evaluated.
- New scalable video codecs are developed.

[*]http://www.doi.org/.
[**]http://www.ean-ucc.org/.

Parts 1 to 7 will be International Standard (ISs) in 2003. Parts 8 to 12 are currently under review and cannot yet be detailed. More information may be accessed at http://www.chiariglione.org/mpeg/.

Event reporting, as a part of the seven MPEG-21 key elements, is not yet hosted in an MPEG-21 part. Event reporting is useful, for instance, in the following situation: outgoing network congestion is detected by an intelligent router during a streaming session. The router likes to inform the streaming server of this congestion such that the server decreases on the fly the bit rate of the stream. Thus, the router generates an MPEG-21 Event Report that is delivered to the server. The server analyzes the report, and the streamed DI is adapted accordingly. In general, many different Event Reports may be triggered for different purposes on behalf of different Users when a DI is processed. Therefore, MPEG-21 suggests at the moment that it should be possible for parties responsible for the creation, production, and distribution of DIs to specify which Event Reports they require to be produced. Similar to RDD and REL, it is proposed that an event reporting dictionary and an event reporting language may need to be specified.

3.2 Digital Item Declaration

The DID specification introduces a set of abstract terms and concepts to form a model for defining DIs. In addition, the DID contains the description of the syntax and semantics of each of the DID elements and the DID Schema for its representation in XML. The DID Schema allows one to plug other description schema into a DI. For instance, a DescriptionUnit of MPEG-7, based on the Description Definition Language, may be used for descriptive elements within an item, as well as the Dublin Core, based on the Resource Description Framework.

The main elements of the DID Schema are described below, and a full DID example is given. For a complete reference of the DID Schema, please consider the ISO/IEC 21000-2 standard.

3.2.1 DID Schema

The DID Schema defines a common root element, named DIDL, within the namespace identified by the Uniform Resource Identifier urn:mpeg:mpeg21:2002:01-DIDL-NS. The declaration of the root element is given here:

```
<xsd:schema targetNamespace = "urn:mpeg:mpeg21:2002:01-
    DIDL-NS" xmlns = "urn:mpeg:mpeg21:2002:01-DIDL-NS"
    xmlns:xsd = "http://www.w3.org/2001/XMLSchema"
    version = "0.01">

<xsd:element name = "DIDL">

    <xsd:complexType>
```

```
<xsd:sequence>

  <xsd:element ref="Declarations" minOccurs="0"/>

    <xsd:choice>

      <xsd:element ref="Container"/>

      <xsd:element ref="Item"/>

    </xsd:choice>

  </xsd:sequence>

 </xsd:complexType>

</xsd:element>

 . . .

<xsd:schema>
```

The top-level element is either a container or an item; it may occur several times in an instance document.

3.2.2 *Container*

A container is a structure that allows items or other containers to be grouped. These groupings of items or containers can be used to form logical packages (for organization, transport, and exchange). The container element descriptor contains the metadata of containers. The container definition is recursive and, therefore, forms a hierarchy.

```
<xsd:element name="Container">

 <xsd:complexType>

  <xsd:sequence>

    <xsd:element ref="Descriptor" minOccurs="0"
        maxOccurs="unbounded"/>

    <xsd:choice>

      <xsd:element ref="Reference"/>

      <xsd:sequence>

        <xsd:element ref="Container" minOccurs="0"
            maxOccurs="unbounded"/>

        <xsd:element ref="Item" minOccurs="0"
            maxOccurs="unbounded"/>

      </xsd:sequence>

    </xsd:choice>

  </xsd:sequence>
```

```
            <xsd:attributeGroup ref="ID_ATTRS"/>
      </xsd:complexType>
  </xsd:element>
```

For instance, if several photo albums will be grouped together in a DI, then a container having an item declaration for each album can be used:

```
<DIDL>
 <Container>
 <Descriptor>
      <Statement mimeType = "text/plain">My Photo Albums
 in Items</Statement>
 </Descriptor>
      <Item id = "Album1">
 . . .
      </Item>
  <Item id = "Album2">
      . . .
  </Item>
 </Container>
 </DIDL>
```

In the former XML document, the Descriptor contains the metadata in the form of a statement. Alternatively, a component element containing descriptive multimedia data can be used. This could be, for instance, an image containing a set of thumbnails showing the first pages of each photo album.

The statement is a comfortable description tool that can contain any data format, including plaintext and machine-interpretable formats, for example, XML, identified by a MIME media type as defined in RFC 2045. The used MIME media type is given in the attribute mimeType.

The plaintext (mimeType = "text/plain") description "My Photo Albums In Items" used in the example above, however, gives no formatting. One may rely on MPEG-7 descriptors for a more precise description, such as

```
<DIDL>
 <Container>
 <Descriptor>
      <Statement mimeType="text/xml">
```

```
<mpeg7:Mpeg7>

  <mpeg7:DescriptionUnit xsi:type=
     "CreationInformationType">

  <mpeg7:Creation>

  <mpeg7:Title> My Photo Albums </mpeg7:Title>

     <mpeg7:Creator>

       <mpeg7:Role

  href="urn:mpeg:mpeg7:cs:RoleCS:2001:PRODUCER">

  <mpeg7:Name xml:lang="en">Anchorman<
     /mpeg7:Name>

    </mpeg7:Role>

    <mpeg7:Agent xsi:type="mpeg7:PersonType">

       <mpeg7:Name>

         <mpeg7:GivenName>Harald</mpeg7:
            GivenName>

         <mpeg7:FamilyName>Kosch</mpeg7:
            FamilyName>

       </mpeg7:Name>

     </mpeg7:Agent>

    </mpeg7:Creator>

    </mpeg7:Creation>

   </mpeg7:DescriptionUnit>

  </mpeg7:Mpeg7>

 </Statement>

</Descriptor>

<Item id="Album1">

. . .

</Item>

<Item id="Album2">

. . .

</Item>

</Container>

</DIDL>
```

3.2.3 Item

An item is a grouping of subitems or components that are bound to relevant descriptors. Descriptors contain information about the item. Items may contain choices, which allow them to be configured. Items may be conditional on predicates asserted by selections defined in the choices. Items may contain subitems if they are composed of potential subparts. Items may also contain annotations to their subparts. The definition of the element named "Item" is given in the XML-Schema here:

```
<xsd:element name="Item">

  <xsd:complexType>

    <xsd:sequence>

      <xsd:element ref="Condition" minOccurs="0"
          maxOccurs="unbounded"/>

      <xsd:element ref="Descriptor" minOccurs="0"
          maxOccurs="unbounded"/>

      <xsd:element ref="Choice" minOccurs="0"
          maxOccurs="unbounded"/>

      <xsd:choice>

        <xsd:element ref="Reference"/>

        <xsd:choice minOccurs="0"
            maxOccurs="unbounded">

          <xsd:element ref="Item"/>

          <xsd:element ref="Component"/>

        </xsd:choice>

      </xsd:choice>

      <xsd:element ref="Annotation" minOccurs="0"
          maxOccurs="unbounded"/>

    </xsd:sequence>

    <xsd:attributeGroup ref="ID_ATTRS"/>

  </xsd:complexType>

</xsd:element>
```

The main components, which appear in the declaration of an item, are the component and the descriptor. Their relationship is illustrated in Exhibit 3.2. Please note that the definition of an item is hierarchical: An item might contain other subitems. Further elements of an item are the condition, the choice, and the annotation. Let us start by describing the component.

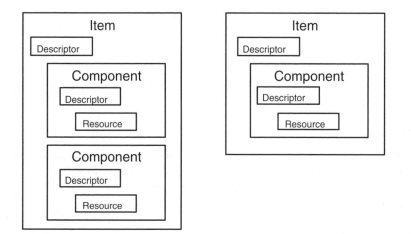

Exhibit 3.2. **Relationship of the principal elements within the digital identification declaration model.**

3.2.4 Component

A component is the binding of a resource to all of its relevant descriptors. The component's descriptors are data related to all or parts of the specific resource instance. Such descriptors will typically contain control or structural information about the resource (such as bit rate and character set). A component may also contain conditions to describe optional resources and descriptors (see below). Conditions are used in connection with choice and selection elements declared in the same DI. Finally, the component may contain an anchor. It binds a set of descriptors to a specific location within the resource.

For instance, the following component description fragment of a DID contains an anchor description for a complete mp3 file and then an anchor description for the first 10 seconds of the mp3 file [specified through the external function media_time(10s)]:

```
<Component> <Resource ref = "starmania.mp3" mimeType =
"audio/mp3"/> <Anchor> <Descriptor> <Statement mimeType
= "text/plain">

        The complete mp3 file</Statement> </Descriptor>
</Anchor> <Anchor fragment = "media_time(10s)">
<Descriptor> <Statement mimeType = "text/plain"> The
first 10s of the mp3 file

        </Statement>

        </Descriptor>

    </Anchor>

</Component>
```

Finally, the optional annotation element can be used to logically add elements to an item without actually modifying its contents. For instance, an annotation description may be added to an outer item to reference an inner item in a hierarchical-build item structure.

The operational behavior of a DI is defined through the condition element.

3.2.5 Condition

A condition describes the enclosing element as being optional and links it to the selection or selections that affect its inclusion. Multiple predicates within a condition are combined as a conjunction (an AND relationship). Any predicate can be negated within a condition. Multiple conditions associated with a given element are combined as a disjunction when determining whether to include the element.

3.2.6 Choice

A choice describes a set of related selections that can affect the configuration of an item. The selections within a choice are either exclusive (choose exactly one) or inclusive (choose any number, including all or none). A selection describes a specific decision that will affect one or more conditions somewhere within an item.

> *Example of a DID: The following example illustrates how the choice, selection, and condition elements can be used to package a deliverable resource (in this case, a video file) that is available in more than one media file format (mpeg and quicktime [QT]). The component contains, in addition to the required conditions, a descriptor in MPEG-7 for the specification of file size and file format of the corresponding resource. This also demonstrates the metadata integration capacity of the DID.*

```
<DIDL xmlns = "urn:mpeg:mpeg21:2002:01-DIDL-NS"
xmlns:xsi = "http://www.w3.org/2001/XMLSchema-instance"
xsi:schemaLocation = "urn:mpeg:mpeg21:2002:01-DIDL-NS
Mpeg21DIDL-2002.xsd">
   <Item>
     <Choice minSelections="1" maxSelections="1">
       <Descriptor>
         <Statement mimeType="text/plain">
           What video format would you prefer?
         </Statement>
       </Descriptor>
       <Selection select_id="MPEG_FORMAT">
```

```xml
    <Descriptor>

      <Statement mimeType="text/plain">I want
          MPEG</Statement>

    </Descriptor>

  </Selection>

  <Selection select_id="QT_FORMAT">

    <Descriptor>

      <Statement mimeType="text/plain">I want
          Quicktime</Statement>

    </Descriptor>

  </Selection>

</Choice>

<Component>

  <Condition require="MPEG_FORMAT"/>

  <Descriptor>

    <Statement mimeType="text/xml">

      <mpeg7:Mpeg7>

        <mpeg7:DescriptionUnit xsi:type="
            mpeg7:MediaFormatType">

          <mpeg7:Content href="MPEG7ContentCS">
              <mpeg7:Name>audiovisual</mpeg7:Name>

          </mpeg7:Content>

          <mpeg7:FileFormat

            href="urn:mpeg:mpeg7:cs:FileFormatCS:
                2001:3">

            <mpeg7:Name xml:lang="en">mpeg<
                /mpeg7:Name>

          </mpeg7:FileFormat>

          <mpeg7:FileSize>136987</mpeg7:FileSize>

        </mpeg7:DescriptionUnit>

      </mpeg7:Mpeg7>

    </Statement>

  </Descriptor>
```

```
        <Resource mimeType="video/mpeg"
            ref="video.mpeg"/>

    </Component>

    <Component>

        <Condition require="QT_FORMAT"/>

            <Descriptor>

                <Statement mimeType="text/xml">

                    <mpeg7:Mpeg7>

                        <mpeg7:DescriptionUnit xsi:type="
                            mpeg7:MediaFormatType">

                            <mpeg7:Content href="MPEG7ContentCS">

                            <mpeg7:Name>audiovisual</mpeg7:Name>

                            </mpeg7:Content>

                            <mpeg7:FileFormat
                                href="urn:mpeg: mpeg7:cs:
                                FileFormatCS:2001:16">

                            <mpeg7:Name
                                xml:lang="en">quicktime</mpeg7:
                                Name>

                            </mpeg7:FileFormat>

                            <mpeg7:FileSize>197457</mpeg7:
                                FileSize>

                        </mpeg7:DescriptionUnit>

                    </mpeg7:Mpeg7>

                </Statement>

            </Descriptor>

            <Resource mimeType="video/quicktime"
                ref="video.qt"/>

    </Component>

    </Item>

</DIDL>
```

3.3 Intellectual Property Management and Protection, Rights Expression Language, and Rights and Data Dictionary

The IPMP (ISO/IEC 21000-4) contains the expression and enforcement of rights and defines consequences and obligations that are associated with the distribution, management, and usage of DIs. To allow the multimedia systems to control the flow and use of a DI in accordance with the relevant user permissions and rights, the IPMP capabilities of DIs, terminals, peers, and users must be defined. To meet these objectives, IPMP is proposed to be a language and dictionary. The language will provide syntax for the articulation of attributes of the parties in the framework. The dictionary will provide semantic information for terms used in the articulation of the IPMP capabilities. MPEG-21 is currently evaluating proposals for the IPMP-L (language) and the IPMP-D (dictionary).

The specification of the rights for exchange and use of DIs are currently specified in the MPEG rights expressions. They are organized in a language (REL) and a dictionary (RDD); Section 3.3.1 introduces REL, and Section 3.3.2 introduces RDD.

A typical digital rights management (DRM) system using the MPEG-21 REL and RDD includes the following processes: during the creation of the DI, the licenses related to this item are specified; during the distribution of the DI, licenses are issued to users and terminals; finally, during the consumption of a DI, the terminal receives the item and its licenses that specify the rights that have been granted and the conditions under which the rights can be exercised. Section 3.3.3 gives a simple use case scenario based on MPEG-21 REL.

3.3.1 MPEG Rights Expression Language

The REL (ISO/IEC 21000-5) provides interoperable mechanisms to protect the resources and metadata and that accept the rights, conditions, and fees specified for them. To do so, REL offers means—the REL data model realized in XML Schema—for declaring rights, conditions, and obligations in identifying and associating these rights with DIs. REL can declare rights and permissions using the terms as defined in the RDD. Further, the *REL* authorization algorithm defines the authorization decision process for the question: Is a principal authorized to exercise a right against a resource?

The REL data model for rights expression consists of four basic entities and relationships among these entities. A principal is an element of the multimedia system to which rights are granted; examples are users and terminals. A resource is the object to which a principal can be granted a right; the resource may be a DI. The condition specifies the terms, conditions, and obligations under which rights can be exercised. An example is the time period for which a right may be granted. Exhibit 3.3 displays the entities and their relationships. The relationships are defined by the REL assertion grants that are specified within a license.

The REL authorization algorithm defines the authorization decision process, which is a central part of a DRM. Exhibit 3.4 gives an example. The

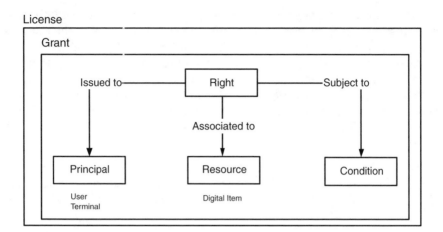

Exhibit 3.3.   The components of the Rights Expression Language data model.

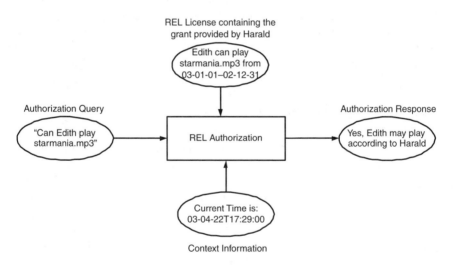

Exhibit 3.4.   Example of the Rights Expression Language authorization process.

input to this process is the authorization query: context information that is relevant for the decision making and the REL licenses. These licenses may be, for instance, delivered with the DI to be consumed. The output of the algorithms is the authorization response for the consumption of the respective resource.

3.3.2 MPEG Rights and Data Dictionary

The RDD (ISO/IEC 21000-6) comprises a set of uniquely identified terms to support the MPEG-21 REL, called a dictionary. The RDD standard provides a methodology for making the dictionary. It contains the initial group of terms—the RDD standardized terms—defined according to this method. Finally, the standard also provides extension mechanisms that will manage the ongoing work of adding a new term to the dictionary. This is similar to the principle for registrations of new CSs within MPEG-7 (see Section 2.7).

The dictionary may be seen as ontology, designed to provide a set of well-defined terms for use in rights expressions for DIs, but it is also designed to represent as many different definitions of terms as its users require and to show their relationships in a structured way.

REL and RDD together give meaning to the IPMP management. REL defines a set of XML Schema complex types called Multimedia Rights. Each activity associated with one Multimedia Right has a context that can be related to particular Act Types (activity types) within the RDD ontology.

> *Example: REL defines the render-right Copy, meaning the process of making a reproduction of a resource. This right, Copy, relates to the RDD Copy term and a set of activities. An activity that is defined with the RDD Copy is the process of determining how much the replica and source may differ to be considered close enough to represent a copy.*

3.3.3 DRM Use Case Scenario Using MPEG-21 REL

This simple use case scenario defines an MPEG-21 REL license containing the specification of the play rights for a DI referencing a piece of music. It is based on the example authorization process depicted in Exhibit 3.4. Two persons are involved in this use case scenario. The sample user, Harald, possesses a DI with the id (identification) urn:harald-1. This DI references to a resource starmania.mp3. The second sample user, Edith, likes to consume this DI, and she likes to hear starmania.mp3. The DI requested is the following:

```
<DIDL xmlns="urn:mpeg:mpeg21:2002:01-DIDL-NS"

xmlns:dii="urn:mpeg:mpeg21:2002:01-DII NS"

xmlns:xsi="http://www.w3.org/2001/XMLSchema-instance"
xsi:schemaLocation="urn:mpeg:mpeg21:2002:01-DIDL-NS
Mpeg21DIDL-2002.xsd">

  <Item>

    <! — Unique identifier of this digital item — >

    <Descriptor>

    <Statement mimeType="text/xml">

      <dii:Identifier>urn:harald-1</dii:Identifier>

    </Statement>

      </Descriptor>
```

113

```
<Component>

    <Resource ref="starmania.mp3" mimeType=
        "audio/mp3"/>

</Component>

</Item>

</DIDL>
```

Harald provides the following MPEG-21 REL license to Edith. The license allows Edith to consume the DI during 2003 (from 2003-01-01T00:00:00 to 2003-12-31T12:59:59).

```
<license
xmlns="http://www.xrml.org/schema/2002/05/xrml2core"
xmlns:mx="urn:mpeg:mpeg21:2002:01-REL-NS"
xmlns:dsig="http://www.w3.org/2000/09/xmldsig#"
xmlns:xsi="http://www.w3.org/2001/XMLSchema-instance"
xsi:schemaLocation="urn:mpeg:mpeg21:2002:01-REL-NS
mpeg-rel.xsd">

<! — The license is granted to Edith — >

    <grant>

        <keyHolder licensePartId="Edith">

            <info>

                <! — Digital Signature of Edith — >

                <dsig:KeyValue>

                    . . .

                </dsig:KeyValue>

            </info>

        </keyHolder>

        <mx:play/>

        <mx:diReference>

            <mx:identifier>urn:harald-1</mx:identifier>

        </mx:diReference>

        <validityInterval>

            <notBefore>2003-01-01T00:00:00</notBefore>

            <notAfter>2003-12-31T12:59:59</notAfter>

        </validityInterval>

    </grant>
```

```
<! — The license is issued by Harald — >
<issuer>
    <keyHolder>
      <info>
      <! — Digital Signature of Harald — >
        <dsig:KeyValue>

        . . .

        </dsig:KeyValue>
      </info>
    </keyHolder>
  </issuer>
</license>
```

The license above contains two parts: the declaration of the grant and the specification of the issuer.

The grant declaration contains four parts:

- keyHolder: identifies that Edith is being granted the rights. The keyHolder element may contain different info on the key holder like its digital signature. It is defined in the schema from XrML with the namespace xmlns = http://www.xrml.org/schema/2002/05/ xrml2core. To specify the signature, elements introduced in the XML signature syntax and processing from W3C with the namespace xmlns:dsig = "http://www.w3.org/2000/09/xmldsig# may be used.
- mx:play: identifies the right that Edith is being granted. The mx: prefix refers to the MPEG-21 REL namespace: xmlns:mx = "urn:mpeg:mpeg21:2002:01-REL-NS."
- mx:diReference: identifies the DI that contains the resource and that is identified by urn:harald-1.
- validityInterval: identifies the time interval, from 2003-01-01T00:00:00 to 2003-12-31T12:59:59, during which Edith is allowed to play the DI. It belongs to XrML.

The issue part contains principally the keyHolder, identifying that Harald issues the grant.

Note that many of the licensing elements stem from the Extensible rights Markup Language (XrML)* and some from the XML signature syntax and processing (xmldsig).** XrML provides a universal method for specifying rights and issuing conditions (licenses) associated with the use of all kinds

*http://www.xrml.org/.
**http://www.w3.org/TR/xmldsig-core/.

of resources, including digital content as well as services. xmldsig specifies XML syntax and processing rules for creating and representing digital signatures. xmldsig can be applied to any digital content, including XML.

The authorization process follows: Edith's MPEG-21-enabled terminal receives the license from Harald. The terminal relies on the REL authorization algorithm to decide whether Edith can play the requested piece of music. The authorization algorithms parse the REL license received, retrieve the current time from a trusted server, and process Edith's authorization query. If the right claimed by Edith matches the rights provided by the REL license, the resource is provided; otherwise, the access is denied.

3.4 Digital Item Adaptation

The DIA (ISO/IEC 21000-7) comprises descriptions of DIA architecture and descriptions specifying all factors that may influence and that may support the adaptation process. Specifying the adaptation of a digital item (DIA) is of importance, as the access to any multimedia resource from any type of terminal or network (often referred to as universal multimedia access) in an interoperable way is desired these days.[3,4]

There are many environmental factors that may influence the transparent access to the multimedia resource, including terminal, network, delivery, user, and natural environment factors. MPEG-21 regroups these factors and proposes a huge set of descriptors, the so-called usage environment descriptions, to specify these factors and their behavior.

In addition, MPEG-21 DIA introduces an adaptation architecture that is illustrated in Exhibit 3.5. As shown in this architecture, an input DI is adapted in the DI Adaptation Engine, containing a resource adaptation engine and a description adaptation engine. This separation is necessary, as the nature of the resource and the description associated are different and, therefore, require different adaptation processes. These engines together produce the modified DI. To achieve the goal of adaptation, it is essential to use a description of how the media resource adaptation may be performed. Therefore, DIA tools, which support the adaptation process, are the second input to the DI Adaptation Engine. A detailed overview of the DIA architecture is given in Section 3.4.1.

The descriptors and tools proposed in MPEG-21 DIA are specified in the DIA Schema, which is detailed in Section 3.4.2. Finally, Section 3.4.3 describes the relationship between DIA and the other parts of MPEG-21.

3.4.1 Overview of the DIA Architecture

The DIA architecture is broken into three main areas:

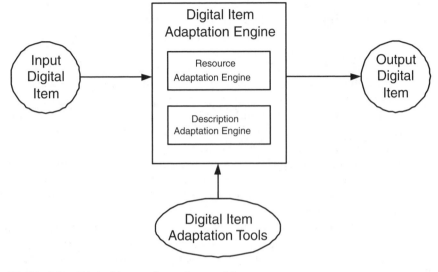

Exhibit 3.5.   Digital item adaptation architecture.

1. Usage environment descriptions
2. DI resource adaptation tools
3. DI declaration adaptation tools

The usage environment descriptions include descriptions for user, terminal capabilities, network characteristics, user preferences, and natural environment characteristics.

- Terminal capabilities include hardware properties, such as processor speed and memory capacity, and display properties, such as screen resolution and device profiles.
- Network characteristics specify delay characteristics, such as end-to-end delay, one-way delay, or delay variation, and bandwidth characteristics, such as amount of available bandwidth or bandwidth variation.
- User preferences include filtering and search preferences, quality of service preferences, and demographic information, such as gender and age.
- Natural environment characteristics include location information, such as Global Positioning System coordinates, the type of location (e.g., indoor and outdoor), and the illumination properties affecting a user or a terminal.

The DI resource adaptation tools comprise descriptions and algorithms that target the adaptation of resources in a DI.

- Bitstream syntax description (BSD) is the main descriptive element in this group. A BSD describes the syntax (called bistream) of a binary media resource. It does not, in general, detail each bit of the bitstream, but rather relies on logical units (so called syntactical units) of a bitstream. For a video, this is typically the frame level. A digital item resource adaptation engine can then transform the bit-stream and the corresponding BSD using editing-style operations such as data truncation and simple modifications. This transforma-tion can, for instance, be performed under control of an Extensible Stylesheet Language: Transformations style sheet. It is desirable that BSDs be independent of specific media resource formats. This enables adaptation of a binary resource to take place at adaptation nodes, for instance, network gateways, that are not aware of the specific resource representation format.
- Terminal and network quality of service descriptors and algorithms are the second category of descriptive elements within the DI resource adaptation tools. They describe the relationship between constraints (e.g., maintaining a certain bit rate), feasible adaptation operations satisfying these constraints (e.g., dropping of video B-frames), and associated qualities (e.g., peak signal-to-noise ratio [PSNR]). The descriptors proposed provide means to make trade-offs among these parameters so that an adaptation strategy can be formulated.
- Metadata adaptability descriptors are the third category of descrip-tors. They enable the filtering and scaling of XML instances with reduced complexity.

DID adaptation tools contain descriptions to specify session mobility, DID configuration preferences, and DIA description messages:

- Session mobility descriptions specify the configuration state infor-mation that pertains to the consumption of a DI on one device when it is transferred to a second device. This enables the DI to be con-sumed on the second device in an adapted way.
- DID configuration preferences provide mechanisms to configure the choices within a DID according to a user's intention and preference. This enables operations to be performed on elements within the DID, such as sorting and deleting.

3.4.2 DIA Schema

The DIA Schema assumes that a schema wrapper is provided that identifies the XML Schema namespace: urn:mpeg:mpeg21:dia:schema:2003. Two root elements for DIA descriptions are defined:

- DIA, if a complete description is used. A complete description is self-contained (see also the definition of a complete description in MPEG-7, Chapter 2, Section 2.5.3).
- DIADescriptionUnit, if a single DIA descriptor is used. A DIADescriptionUnit can be used to represent partial information from a complete description; for example, the description of only the display preferences of the user.

Exhibit 3.6 shows the top-level types that may be used in DIA descriptions (only the DIA root for complete descriptions is shown in Exhibit 3.6). Information and examples of use for the top-level types follow.

UsageEnvironmentType is the top-level type for describing a usage environment description. Elements of this type describe the user preferences, terminal, network, and natural environment characteristics.

Example: The static and dynamic capabilities of a sample network are described below. The static capabilities of the network are specified by using the capability element and the attributes maxCapacity and minGuaranteed (bandwidth in bps). The dynamics of the network are described by a condition and its subelement, utilization. Utilization contains means for specifying the current delay and error characteristics of the network.

```
<DIA xmlns="urn:mpeg:mpeg21:dia:schema:2003"

xmlns:xsi="http://www.w3.org/2001/XMLSchema-instance">

    <Description xsi:type="UsageEnvironmentType">

        <Network>

            <Capability maxCapacity="384000" minGuaranteed
                ="32000"/>

            <Condition>

                <Utilization instantaneous="78" maximum="90"
                    average="84"

                avgInterval="12"/>

                <Delay packetTwoWay="330"
                    delayVariation="66"/>

                <Error packetLossRate="0.05"/>

            </Condition>

        </Network>

    </Description>

</DIA>
```

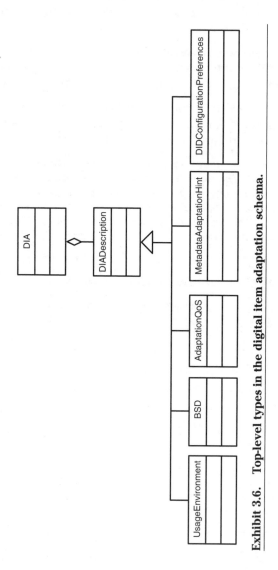

Exhibit 3.6. Top-level types in the digital item adaptation schema.

BSDType is the top-level type for the BSDs. These descriptions are not meant to replace the original binary format, but to act as an additional descriptive layer. Thus, they may be embedded as descriptors of a component in a DI. BSDs are employed for a more efficient adaptation process. This is because of the more compact representation of the BSD compared with the described bitstream (up to 98 percent of the bitstream size).[3]

Example: Exhibit 3.7 shows an extract of the BSD for the Coast Guard video from the MPEG-4 reference streams. We use for this example our standardized gBSD (generic BSD) schema,[2] which is independent of specific media resource formats. The example shows the use of the basic gBSD elements. The header defines the classification alias with its Uniform Resource Name. It is required to identify the meaning of the syntactical labels. The header also contains the default addressing values, which include the location of the bitstream and the mode used for addressing (absolute vs. relative). Subsequently, the description of the bitstream syntax follows. gBSDUnits are used to represent the frames in the bitstream. We have to distinguish between I-, P-, and B-frames; thus, the gBSDUnits are labeled with syntacticalLabel ":MV4:I_VOP" (for I-Frames), ":MV4:P_VOP" (for P-Frames), and ":MV4:B_VOP" (for B-Frames).

In addition (not shown in Exhibit 3.7), gBSDunits may be marked to support the adaptation process with hints. For instance, a B-VOP may be labeled with "important," so that it is saved from removal in adaptation. Further (also not shown in the simple example), gBSDUnits may be grouped to form other gBSDUnits; for instance, frames to form a group of Video Object Plans (VOPs).

AdaptationQoSType is the top-level type that specifies the relationship between constraints, feasible adaptation operations satisfying these constraints, and associated utilities (qualities). Therefore, AdaptationQoS descriptions let an adaptation engine know what adaptation operations are feasible for satisfying the given constraints and the quality resulting from each adaptation.

Example: The following fragment gives a simple AdaptationQoS example for the constraint "bandwidth." Two constraint points are specified, one for 1359 kbps (kilobits per second) and one for 1071 kbps. For a better readability, these constraint points are highlighted in the XML fragment below. For each of these points, an adaptation operator is declared to meet the constraints. In the first case, we have to perform a Coefficient Dropping (specified by the use of the element FrameCoeffDropping with the attributes as given below), and the second operator is B-Frame Dropping (here the attribute coeffDroppingRatio is set to 0.0 and the attribute numberOfBFrame to 1). The UtilityValue element specifies the quality of the adapted video in the metric given in attribute "name" of the element utility. The metric used in the example is the PSNR in decibels.

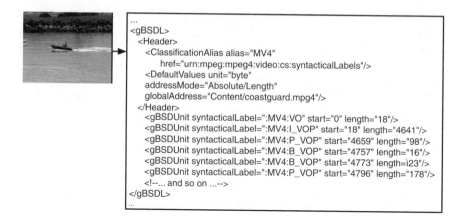

```
...
<gBSDL>
  <Header>
    <ClassificationAlias alias="MV4"
         href="urn:mpeg:mpeg4:video:cs:syntacticalLabels"/>
    <DefaultValues unit="byte"
         addressMode="Absolute/Length"
         globalAddress="Content/coastguard.mpg4"/>
  </Header>
  <gBSDUnit syntacticalLabel=":MV4:VO" start="0" length="18"/>
  <gBSDUnit syntacticalLabel=":MV4:I_VOP" start="18" length="4641"/>
  <gBSDUnit syntacticalLabel=":MV4:P_VOP" start="4659" length="98"/>
  <gBSDUnit syntacticalLabel=":MV4:B_VOP" start="4757" length="16"/>
  <gBSDUnit syntacticalLabel=":MV4:B_VOP" start="4773" length=i23"/>
  <gBSDUnit syntacticalLabel=":MV4:P_VOP" start="4796" length="178"/>
  <!--... and so on ...-->
</gBSDL>
...
```

Exhibit 3.7. Example of bitstream syntax description.

```
<DIA xmlns="urn:mpeg:mpeg21:dia:schema:2003"
xmlns:xsi="http://www.w3.org/2001/XMLSchema-instance">

  <Description xsi:type="AdaptationQoSType">

    <Adaptation adaptationMethod=
        "frameDroppingAndOrCoefficientDropping">

      <Constraint name="bandwidthInkbps"/>

      <Utility name="PSNRIndB"/>

      <AdaptationQoSData>

        <UtilityFunction>

          <ConstraintPoint>

            <ConstraintValues>1359</ConstraintValues>

            <AdaptationOperator>

              <FrameCoeffDropping numberOfBFrame="0"
                  numberOfPFrame="0"
                  coeffDroppingRatio="0.10"/>

              <UtilityValue>33.56</UtilityValue>

            </AdaptationOperator>

          </ConstraintPoint>

          <ConstraintPoint>

            <ConstraintValues>1071</ConstraintValues>

            <AdaptationOperator>
```

```
<FrameCoeffDropping numberOfBFrame="1"
    numberOfPFrame="0"
    coeffDroppingRatio="0.0"/>

<UtilityValue>31.58</UtilityValue>

</AdaptationOperator>

</ConstraintPoint>

</UtilityFunction>

</AdaptationQoSData>

</Adaptation>

</Description>

</DIA>
```

MetadataAdaptationHintType is the top-level type for describing adaptation hint information pertaining to metadata within a DI. This hint information is a set of syntactical elements with prior knowledge about the metadata that is useful for reducing the complexity of the description adaptation process.

> *Example: The following example shows the use of the MetadataAdaptationHint, including information about the metadata of a video resource. InstanceFileSize expresses the actual file size of metadata for a video resource, and TotalNumOfElements expresses the number of elements that are included in the metadata. The following hint informs the adaptation engine that there are 10 video segments in the metadata and that each of the video segments does not contain any temporal or spatial subsegments (elements MaxTemporalDepth and MaxSpatialDepth have the value 1). A description adaptation engine, which has to react to a resource constraint, may compute from this information the number of video segments to be removed from the description.*

```
<DIA xmlns="urn:mpeg:mpeg21:dia:schema:2003"
    xmlns:xsi=http://www.w3.org/2001/XMLSchema-
    instance>

  <Description xsi:type="MetadataAdaptationHintType">

    <InstanceFileSize>120000</InstanceFileSize>

    <TotalNumOfElements>100</TotalNumOfElements>

    <Component name="VideoSegmentDS" number="10">

      <MaxTemporalDepth>1</MaxTemporalDepth>

      <MaxSpatialDepth>1</MaxSpatialDepth>

    </Component>
```

```
</Description>

</DIA>
```

The remaining top-level types belong to the group of DI declaration adaptation tools, and they address the complete adaptation chain:

- SessionMobilityType is the top-level type that specifies a mechanism to preserve a user's current state (which is defined by the state of selection elements) of interaction with a DI. Examples of use include providing a mechanism to transfer a user's session between different terminals.
- DIDConfigurationPreferencesType is the top-level type that defines descriptions to express the user's intention of a DID choice configuration preferences.

3.4.3 Relation between DIA and Other Parts of MPEG-21

The fundamental unit of distribution and transaction in the MPEG-21 multimedia framework is the DI. Although the existing parts of ISO/IEC 21000 deal with different aspects of the DI, together they facilitate the complete multimedia framework. It is therefore crucial to understand the relationships between MPEG-21 DIA and the other parts to be able to achieve an interoperable framework. Exhibit 3.8 gives an overview of the DIA with respect to concepts defined in related MPEG-21 parts.

The input to the DIA Engine is a Content DI (CDI). The prefix Content is added to this DI to indicate that a resource is referenced and that descriptions for this resource are available and subject to adaptation. DIA tools may be embedded into the CDI using Part 2 of ISO/IEC 21000, the DID. For instance, the CDI may incorporate a BSD for the resource bitstream. The resource adaptation engine relies on the BSD to perform the adaptation. It transforms the BSD, for example, with an Extensible Stylesheet Language: Transformations style sheet, and then generates back an adapted bitstream. Another example of a DIA description that is useful for embedding into the CDI is an AdaptationQoS description offering a set of adaptation operations for different resource constraint points.

The type of the DI is indicated using descriptions provided by ISO/IEC 21000-3 and 5, the DII, and the REL. For instance, a particular user owing the rights of the CDI might define, in an adaptation specific license, the permissible types of adaptations that are allowed; for example, the bit rate should not be <1500 kbps.

DIA descriptions can also be carried in a Context DI (XDI). A XDI carries only descriptions to support the adaptation process and contains no resources. As shown in Exhibit 3.8, the XDI is used as input to the DIA Engine. The DIA descriptions in an XDI drive the adaptation and can provide parameters for both adaptation engines (resource and description).

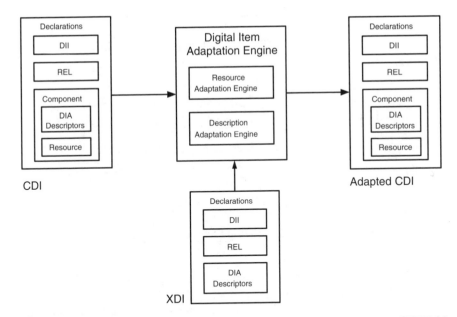

Exhibit 3.8. Digital item adaptation detailed with respect to the other MPEG-21 parts.

These descriptions are responsible for steering the adaptation process. For instance, a new network capacity may be specified by using the capability element of the network. This new situation is incorporated into an XDI and put into the DIA Engine. The DIA Engine analyzes the content of the XDI and decides to parse an available AdaptationQoS description (e.g., from the CDI) to obtain an appropriate adaptation operator, which is then applied to the resource.

The REL expressions of the XDI can be used for protection of user-sensitive information that may be conveyed by the DIA descriptions.

The DIA engine operates on the input CDI according to the DIA descriptions carried in the XDI, as well as the DIA descriptions that are carried in the CDI itself. The DID Identifiers, REL elements, DIA elements, as well as the resources themselves are all subject to change after being processed by the DIA engine and will be contained in the adapted CDI, which is the output of the DIA Engine.

3.5 Interoperable MPEG: From MPEG-1 to MPEG-21

The MPEG group introduced ISs within MPEG-1, MPEG-2, MPEG-4, MPEG-7 and MPEG-21 (parts of MPEG-21 are still under development). These standards address different issues (see Exhibit 3.9).

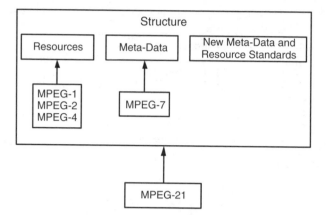

Exhibit 3.9.   Relationship of the Moving Picture Experts Group standards.

MPEG-1 and MPEG-2 provide interoperable ways of representing AV content. MPEG-4 extends this to many more application areas through features like extended bit-rate range, scalability, error resilience, integration of different types of objects in the same scene, interfaces to digital-rights management systems, and the integration of interactivity into content (see Chapter 1). In contrast to this, MPEG-7 defines an interoperable framework for content description. MPEG-7 has descriptive elements that range from very low level signal features like color, shape, and sound characteristics to high-level structural information about content collections (see Chapter 2).

MPEG-7 is not only a standard for the description of the content of MPEG-1, MPEG-2, and MPEG-4 encoded multimedia material but is also a coding standard for XML-based descriptions and a file format (by the use of the MPEG-7 systems tools). In particular, it employs the same time-dependent unit (AU, access units) used in the formats of MPEG-2 and MPEG-4. Thus, it is possible to reference metadata from media data or vice versa. This transferability enhances interactivity with the user to a great extent. A user may find the metadata for a media scene, similar scene descriptions may be searched (metadata search), and the appropriate media scenes may then be displayed. This requires means for synchronization of meta- and media data. Technical solutions have been found for MPEG-2 and MPEG-7, and solutions for MPEG-4 are under consideration.

The MPEG-21 multimedia framework gives the "big picture" and achieves end-to-end interoperability; that is, it offers a framework to build an infrastructure for the delivery and consumption of multimedia content. The components proposed are users that interact with DIs. A DI can be anything from an elemental piece of content, for example, a single picture or a sound track, to a complete collection of audiovisual material. Moreover, the content is not limited to existing formats. As the DI is only a container, it requires that its description be filled with existing metadata standards, for example, MPEG-7 for the description of the multimedia semantics, the media formats, and much more, to facilitate their integration in the whole distributed multimedia system.

In Chapters 4 and 5, we will detail the influence of the newest MPEG standards on distributed multimedia database technologies.

3.6 Ongoing MPEG-21 Research Projects

Several running research projects make use of the open MPEG-21 multimedia framework. They mainly focus on DI Processing and DI Adaptation. Examples are:

- The Multimedia Lab research group of the Department of Electronics and Information systems at Ghent University, Belgium, proposes several tools for MPEG-21 (http://multimedialab.elis.rug.ac.be/demo.asp).[5-7] First, a scalable MPEG-21 Video-on-Demand (VoD) application is introduced. The application contains a VoD Client that is able to consume a DI with constraints specifications of its current processing capabilities. Another tool is introduced that is able to resolve selection/choice elements of a DID. The user may specify its preferences toward the presentation, and a DI processor then selects the appropriate resource from the requested DI. Finally, an MPEG-21 DIA in a wireless network is proposed. It shows how Wireless Application Protocol and Wireless Markup Language technology can be used in combination with MPEG-21. The purpose is to create a device-specific interface to Wireless Application Protocol applications depending on the terminal characteristics of the mobile phone.
- The PAMLink (Personal Access over Mobile Link) project is to develop an end-to-end connectivity solution for Internet applications and Internet services.[8,9] PAMLink services are characterized by a personalized experience for the individual user to meet individual needs at any given moment. More information on PAMLink may be found at http://www.merl.com/projects/PAMLink21/.
- The CONTESSA project (http://contessa.intranet.gr/) describes a modular platform based on the MPEG-21 framework aiming at enabling users to transparently access and consume multimedia content through distinct access devices, including digital television set top boxes, personal digital assistants, mobile phones and personal computers, using distinct network connections.[10]
- The Universal Multimedia Access from wired or wireless systems project addresses issues regarding access to multimedia content

through a variety of possible systems having different terminal capabilities and network conditions (e.g., digital television networks, high-speed Internet protocol networks, etc.).[11,12] More information may be obtained from http://www.midgardmedia.net/.

References

1. Pereira, F., The MPEG-21 standard: why an open multimedia framework?, in *Proceedings of the 8th International Workshop on Interactive Distributed Multimedia Systems (IDMS 2001), LNCS 2158*, Lancaster, September 2001, Springer-Verlag, Heidelberg, pp. 219–220.
2. Hill, K. and Bormans, J., Overview of the MPEG-21 standard. ISO/IECJTC1/SC29/WG11 N4041 (Shanghai Meeting), October 2002, http://www.chiariglione.org/mpeg/.
3. Panis, G., Hutter, A., Heuer, J., Hellwagner, H., Kosch, H., Timmerer, C., Devillers, S., and Amielh, M., Binary multimedia resource adaptation using XML bitstream syntax description, *Image Communication*, 18(8), 721–747, 2003.
4. Vetro, A. and Devillers, S., Position Paper: Delivery Context in MPEG-21, W3C Delivery Context Workshop, March 2002, http://www.w3.org/2002/02/DIWS/agenda.html.
5. De Sutter, R., Lerouge, S., Bekaert, J., Rogge, B., Van De Ville, D., and Van de Walle, R., Dynamic adaptation of multimedia data for mobile applications, in *Proceedings of the International Conference on IT and Communications (ITCom 2002)*, Vol. 4862, Boston, MA, July–August 2002, pp. 240–248.
6. Lerouge, S., Rogge, B., De Sutter, R., Bekaert, J., Van De Ville, D., and Van de Walle, R., A generic mapping mechanism between content description metadata and user environments, in *Proceedings of the International Conference on IT and Communications (ITCom 2002)*, Vol. 4862, Boston, July–August 2002, pp. 12–21.
7. Rogge, B., Van De Ville, D., Lemahieu, I., and Van de Walle, R., Validating MPEG-21 encapsulated functional metadata, in *Proceedings of the IEEE International Conference on Multimedia and Expo,* Lausanne, Switzerland, IEEE CS Press, August 2002.
8. Vetro, A., Hata, T., Kuwahara, N., and Kalva, H., Complexity-quality analysis of MPEG-2 to MPEG-4 transcoding architectures, in *Proceedings of the IEEE International Conference on Consumer Electronics (ICCE 2002)*, Los Angeles, CA, June 2002, pp. 130–131.
9. Vetro, A., Divakaran, A., and Sun, H., Providing multimedia services to a diverse set of consumer devices, in *Proceedings of IEEE International Conference on Consumer Electronics (ICCE 2001)*, Los Angeles, CA, June 2001, pp. 32–33.
10. Tsakali, M. and Kaptsis, I., Cross-media content production and delivery: trends and challenges, in *Proceedings of the Euro-China 2002 Co-operation Forum on the Information Society*, April 2002.
11. Perkis, A., Zhang, J., Halvorsen, T., Kjøde, J., and Rivas, F., A streaming media engine using Digital Item Adaptation, in *Proceedings of the 2002 IEEE Workshop on Multimedia Signal Processing*, December 2002, St. Thomas.
12. Zhang, J. and Perkis, A., Multimedia adaptation for delivery and presentation, in *Proceedings of the Third COST #276 WORKSHOP on Information and Knowledge Management for Integrated Media Communication*, October 2002, Budapest, Hungary.

Chapter 4
Multimedia Database Management Systems

A multimedia database management system (MMDBMS) must provide a suitable environment for using and managing multimedia data. Therefore, it must support the various multimedia data types in addition to providing facilities for traditional DBMS functions like database creation, data modeling, data retrieval, data access and organization, and data independence.

The special nature of multimedia data also makes it important to support new and special functions. These include management of huge volumes of multimedia data and effective storage and delivery management in a multimedia storage server. The storage server may be part of the DBMS, but it may also be an individual physical component. In this case, to guarantee efficiency, the DBMS must be closely connected to the storage server.

In addition, a MMDBMS must provide the means for efficient information indexing and retrieval, support conceptual multimedia data models, and manage the query optimization and processing issues. MMDBMSs must also address problems specific to distributed databases, such as distributed query processing.

Network issues such as limited bandwidth and network delays are important considerations, as they would have adverse effects on the quality of service. Unlike in traditional DBMSs, data replication is often not encouraged in a distributed MMDBMS because of the large data volume exchanged. In this context, for simple pull applications (i.e., the client requests data from the server), the Client–Server (C–S) computing model is considered suitable for distributed MMDBMSs.[1] More complex multimedia applications might require a video server and MMDBMS architecture, which is more dynamic (Chapter 5 deals with this issue in detail).

Exhibit 4.1 shows the components that a general-purpose MMDBMS and video server (as an example of a multimedia storage server) may provide.

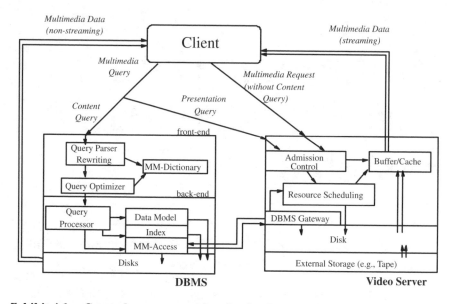

Exhibit 4.1.   General-purpose multimedia database management system and video server architecture.

The scenario chosen is a simple retrieval one. A client issues a multimedia query to the server system. The query is first analyzed, and the content-based query part is separated from the presentation part. The content-query goes to the MMDBS, as the presentation-related parts, that is, results that may be played or shown in specified composition, are submitted to the video server.

Let us concentrate on the content-query first. The query is parsed first, possible redundancy in the formulation is detected, and the query is rewritten. Then, the query optimizer prepares an execution plan for the query processor. The query processor searches for the content that corresponds to the query specification. This search process may involve complex operator processing mechanisms (like execution of multimedia joins, group by, etc.). Then, the MMDBMS informs the video server about the multimedia data to be delivered. If the MMDBMS and the video server are tightly coupled, for example, through a DBMS gateway available on the video server, no further query submission to the video server is necessary, and the data is then delivered, possibly by being streamed from the video server to the client. If this close connection is not available, the database results are returned to the client and may be submitted to the video server later.

Thus, the client may contact the video server directly, without involving the MMDBMS, or after having obtained the metadata on the videos from the MMDBMS. These queries may impose certain presentation constraints on the video server; for example, if two videos are demanded, the second video will be streamed 5 seconds after the end of the first one. The query is first analyzed by the admission control. The task of the admission control is to find an optimal schedule of the videos requested such that neither the presentation constraints nor the network and server constraints are violated. The latter assumes that the server has enough available resources (size of the buffer, disk bandwidth, etc.) to sustain the requirements of all actually supported video streams. Thus, for each newly submitted query, the admission control checks whether it can be admitted or not. On admission, the required resources for the video delivery have been reserved in advance. The resource-scheduling module is now responsible for managing the resources for all concurrently served video streams. Buffering is an important issue in video server resource management and is used to amortize different resource bandwidths; for instance, between disk, memory, and network.

Throughout this chapter the effect of MPEG-7 and MPEG-21 on the design and implementation process of a MMDBMS is discussed. Selected use cases are presented, as well as links to current projects. This chapter is organized as follows. Section 4.1 describes the indexing process and its effect on multimedia data modeling and highlights some of the important projects currently in progress. This is followed by a discussion in Section 4.2 of broadly used index structures to accelerate access to features extracted during the indexing process. Then, in Section 4.3, we sketch how a conceptual multimedia data model can be implemented in a MMDBMS and how it can be communicated in a distributed system. We also introduce SQL (Structured Query Language)/MM here and compare MPEG-7 with the object type hierarchy introduced in SQL/MM. Section 4.4 gives an overview of content-based retrieval systems. Section 4.5 introduces multimedia query languages (e.g., those used in Oracle interMedia and SQL/MM), query optimization, and processing and links them to content-based retrieval. Section 4.6 gives an overview of MMDBMS product (an historical sketch and an overview of actual developments) and details some selected products.

4.1 Multimedia Indexing

Keywords are by far the predominant features used to index multimedia data;[1-3] that is, an indexer using keywords or a textual abstract describes the content of the media. This is state of the art as far as most conventional DBMSs are concerned.

Another method, content-based indexing, refers to the actual contents of the multimedia data. Intensive research[4-13] has focused on content-based indexing in recent years, with the goal of indexing the multimedia data using certain features derived directly from the data.

These features are also referred to as low-level features. Examples of low-level visual features are color, shape, texture, motion, spatial information, and symbolic strings. Extracting such features may be done by an automatic analysis of the multimedia data. Section 2.5.3 explained extraction and representation methods for color in MPEG-7. Low-level features for audio are waveform and power (basic ones), spectral content, and timbre.

Indexing high-level features of audiovisual content is an active research area. Different detection mechanisms have been proposed for segmenting the multimedia material into regions of interest (moving regions for videos, parts of audio segments) and for attributing semantic meaningful annotation to each region and their relationships. In addition to this, and related to the previous issues, ongoing research concentrates on multimedia classification; for example, is this video a sport video? and more specifically, is this sport video a basketball video? The recognition of a video as basketball video facilitates the semantic annotation process, as we know what kind of objects and persons might appear.

Exhibit 4.2 gives an overview of different detection methods applied and points out their relationships. Multimedia classification is used for both

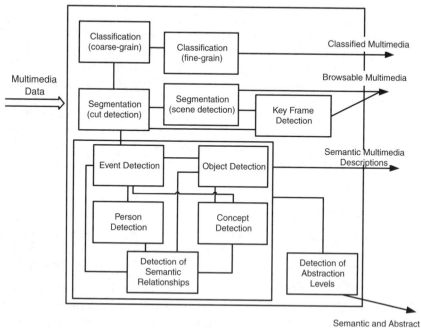

Exhibit 4.2. Overview of high-level multimedia indexing.

visual and audio material. For videos, first the genre of interest is detected, for example, news, commercial, cartoon, tennis, and car racing (coarse grain), and then, in a fine-grain classification, one may divide sports videos into basketball, football, and so forth.[14] For audio, classification by genre, such as pop, rock, and so on, is of interest.

Effective multimedia classification needs the help of a knowledge base that details the possible meaning of the low-level and high-level features extracted. Multimedia classification is used for browsing and prefiltering in searching applications and may also serve as an input to multimedia segmentation, which tries to identify meaningful segments. This can be done by detecting abrupt changes in time or space (called cut detection for continuous streams) or by detecting scenes (segment boundaries are separated by different semantic content). The core of the high-level indexing process is the detection of events, objects, persons, concepts, and their relationships. The detection tools depicted in Exhibit 4.2 are in strong relationship to the entities defined in the MPEG-7 semantic description scheme (DS), as described in section 2.5.3. Finally, abstraction layers may classify the semantic content. For instance, one describes in the lowest abstraction that a person is present in an image, in the higher abstraction one says that she is a woman, and finally in the highest abstraction one gives her a name.

It is clear that the process of high-level indexing is not an automatic process but has, in general, to be supported by manual annotation. The following paragraphs review current work in high-level multimedia indexing. We will see that for special applications, the automatic extraction methods give quite accurate indexing results.

Video classification[15] is based on different low-level characteristics performed conjointly on the audio and visual tracks of a video. Color is a good discriminator for both fine- and coarse-grain classification (e.g., football will reveal many green areas). These low-level results have to be interpreted by using a knowledge database and have to be usefully combined with results of more elaborated analysis tools; for example, caption detection with text recognition. Audio classification[16] focuses mainly on speech and music discrimination. Typical features for audio classification include cepstral coefficients, timbre, characteristics of the melody, and so on.

Multimedia segmentation is a well-known research area, and many good tools are available for both video and audio material. For video data, the video sequence is first divided into its constituent shots, using shot cut and change detection methods.[17,18] Then, representative abstractions, mainly key frames[19,20] are selected to represent each shot. Shot boundary detection deals with the detection of physical shot boundaries indicated by shot transitions. Most shot boundary detection techniques[18,21–25] define a measure of dissimilarity between successive frames that is then compared with a given threshold. Some other techniques transform the video before applying boundary detection. For instance, in the SMOOTH implementation,[26] we applied a shape analysis before comparing successive frames. Dissimilarity values exceeding the threshold value identify shot transitions, which are characterized by camera transitions. Recently, some important contributions concentrated on shot cut and change detection on compressed videos.[27,28] Such indexing methods are of great interest if resource availability for the indexing process is low. Once a video has been segmented, further indexing can be done on a key frame selection; for example, to generate a table of contents,[29] a video abstract,[30] or a hierarchical three-dimensional representation relying on ranked key frames.[31] Recently, in addition to key frame extraction, mosaicking of video clips has been used;[32] that is, the combination of subsequent frames to show a complete scene. In this case, frames that do not contribute to the motion of objects in the scene are discarded. For instance, Exhibit 2.7 shows the mosaic image for a 10-second short video on Pisa using an affine motion model. The mosaic has been created with the help of the MPEG-7 reference software (see Section 2.8).

For audio data, basic algorithms detect the segment boundaries by looking for abrupt changes in the trajectory of features. For instance, Tzanetakis and Cook[33] segment audio sources using spectral centroid, spectral skewness, audio flux, zero-crossing, and energy and do a peak detection on the derivative of the features with an absolute threshold. Rossignol et al.[34] use a measure of the in-harmonicity of the audio to segment transients and vibrato. Labeling the segment (as key frames in video) is done usually by attributing a note, a timbre, and a phrase to a segment.

Interesting to mention in this context is the yearly TREC (Text REtrieval Conferences) video evaluation series organized by the retrieval group of the NIST (U.S. National Institute of Standards and Technology). They call for novel video segmentation tools, which have to prove their efficiency and effectiveness on more than 120 hours of news videos. The homepage of TREC video is http://www-nlpir.nist.gov/projects/trecvid/. TREC also includes an audio segmentation track.

More precise image and video content retrieval is performed if regions of interest are extracted and indexed. The extraction process is called object segmentation and means (for images) identifying a group of pixels that have common low-level features (e.g., color and texture), and (for videos) identifying a group of pixels that move together into an object and track the object's motion.[27,35–37] For instance, Carson et al.[38] developed an image indexing and retrieval system that relies on the notion of "blobs." Each image is segmented into blobs by fitting a mixture of Gaussians to the pixel distribution in a joint color-texture-position feature space. Each blob is then associated with color and texture descriptors. Querying is based on the user specifying attributes of one or two regions of interest. Retrieval precision is improved, compared with methods relying on the description of the entire image.

In general, object segmentation is hard to perform. Exhibit 4.3 shows a typical example using the Blobworld algorithms for object segmentation. In the first line of Exhibit 4.3, the segmentation results for a simple image, offering clear discrimination between the foreground person and the background, are shown. In the second line, the result is shown for an image in which the regions of interest overlap and no clear discrimination of the persons and the background can be detected without human interaction.

Audiovisual indexing can efficiently be supported by common analysis of the visual and audio content. For instance, Chang et al.[39] have developed a demonstration video database that recognizes key sporting events from the accompanying commentary. Their work is based on spotting predetermined keywords. The recognition of captions in a video might enhance the video indexing efficiency as well. The difficulty here is to detect the place of the captions within the video frames and to transform the caption information into semantically meaningful information; for example, names, location, and so on. For instance, Assfalg et al.[40] propose for sport videos a method for detecting captions with a shape analysis followed by noise removal. The position of the captions is detected by a knowledge-based system for the sport domain.

The effectiveness of an automatic extraction process is determined to a great extent by the amount of a priori information available in the application domain. For some specific applications, it is possible to find a set of

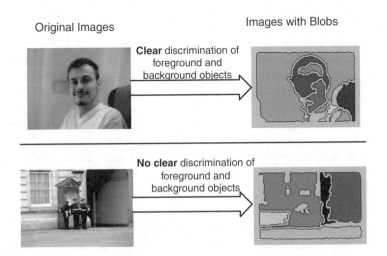

Exhibit 4.3. Examples of automatic object segmentation using the Blobworld algorithms.[38]

analysis tools that perform segmentation and feature extraction automatically as described in Okada and von der Malsburg[41] and Ide et al.[42] For instance, Correia and Pereira[43] discussed an analysis system for surveillance application in which the precise contours may be detected automatically by combining the partial results from tools based on the homogeneity of both motion and texture. However, there are many cases where fully automatic segmentation and feature extraction tools do not provide acceptable results. For example, a video classification in indoor or outdoor clips is, in general, not as good for pure automatic processing. Thus, guidance from the user must be incorporated into the indexing process to achieve valuable results.

Extracting high-level semantic content is influenced by at least two issues:[44] first, semantic content of multimedia data could mean different things to different users, and second, users typically have diverse information needs. Thus, it is evident that a single feature may not be sufficient to completely index a given multimedia data. To relate low-level features (or groups of them) to high-level content types, more research on additional domain-specific knowledge has to be done. In this sense, the process of semantic indexing must be in most cases a semiautomatic one; that is, a combined use of automatic analysis tools and of user interaction and domain knowledge.[43] For instance, in the domain of Web mining, WebSEEK[45] introduces a semiautomatic system for retrieving, analyzing, categorizing, and indexing visual images from the World Wide Web.

In this context, Jorgensen et al.[46] proposed a very compact model—the indexing pyramid for classifying levels of indexing. The pyramid, as shown in Exhibit 4.4, distinguishes between syntactic (first four levels) and semantic levels (next six levels). The syntactic levels hold attributes that describe the way in which the content is organized, but not their meanings. In images, for example, type could be "color image." Global distribution holds attributes that are global to the image (e.g., color histogram), whereas local structure deals with local components (e.g., lines and circles), and global composition relates to the way in which those local components are arranged in the image (e.g., symmetry). The semantic levels, however, deal with the meaning of the elements. Objects can be described at three levels: generic, representing everyday objects (e.g., person); specific, representing individually named objects (e.g., Roger Moore); and abstract, representing emotions (e.g., power). In a similar way, a scene can be described at these three levels.

Elements within each level are related according to two types of relations: syntactic and semantic. For example: two circles (local structure) can be related spatially (e.g., next to), temporally (e.g., before), or visually (e.g., darker than). Elements at the semantic levels (e.g., objects) can have syntactic and semantic relations (e.g., two people are next to each other,

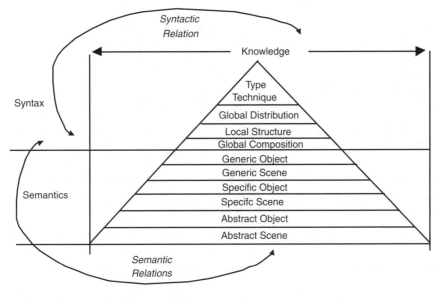

Exhibit 4.4.   Indexing pyramid.[47]

and they are friends). In addition, each relation can be described at different levels (generic, specific, and abstract).

The authors of the indexing pyramid also propose a retrieval system[47] that allows a search specific to the levels of the pyramid. For instance, if a user enters "soccer" for image search at the syntactical level, one retrieves images with a description containing the keyword soccer (which does not yet mean we have really a soccer game shown in the image). If a user enters soccer at the semantic level, only those images are retained in which the event, "soccer," took place. An online demo is available at http://www.ctr.columbia.edu/~ana/MPEG7/PyramidCE/search.html/.

Recently, several projects have aimed at coping better with multimedia indexing. Many of these projects rely on MPEG-7 as a description standard. A first project was MODEST, or multimedia object descriptors extraction from surveillance tapes, which belonged to the ACTS* program in the domain of Interactive Digital Multimedia Services. MODEST** was supported by a consortium of different universities and Philips Company. They defined and developed a framework for the analysis of video sequences from surveillance tapes to extract high-level semantic scene interpretation. Exhibit 4.5 shows an application case of a road-monitoring scene. Detailed information about the composition of the scene is obtained

*ACTS is an acronym for Advanced Communications Technology and Services Project supported by the EU 4th Framework.
**http://www.cordis.lu/infowin/acts/ienm/bulletin/01-1998/domain1/modest.html.

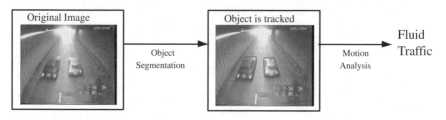

Exhibit 4.5. Indexing process in the ACTS project MODEST (multimedia object descriptors extraction from surveillance tapes) for road monitoring.

from object segmentation and tracking mechanisms. For instance, in the scenario shown in Exhibit 4.5, fluid traffic is concluded from the composition information.

A second interesting project is the IST* project ASSAVID,** supported by Sony and several European universities. This project aims to develop techniques for automatic segmentation and semantic annotation of sports videos. It is a straightforward continuation of the projects concentrating on simple surveillance scenarios, like MODEST, to complex "live" scenarios. In this project, algorithms to segment sport videos into shots, and to group and classify the shots into semantic categories, for example, type of sport, are being developed.[40] To do this, the system extracts information from each shot, based on speech and text recognition, and uses MPEG-7 descriptors where relevant; that is, where more complex (than keyword) indexing is required.

To continue on projects supported by the EU (European Union) Framework, one has to announce the initiatives in the 6th EU Framework in the field of multimedia systems, issued in 2003. Among others, the EU calls for projects in the thematic: full multimedia everywhere. Points of interest are networked audiovisual systems and home platforms with a strong emphasis on technologies for interoperability. This is obviously related to MPEG-21 (see Chapters 3 and 5). More information on the call for proposals in the 6th EU Framework may be found at http://www.cordis.lu/ist/.

Other industry-supported research consortia focus on meaningful multimedia indexing. For instance, the Digital Video Multimedia Group at Columbia University*** developed several techniques for identifying semantic content in sport videos. The applied strategy is to find a systematic methodology combining effective generic computational approaches with domain knowledge available in sport domains. Structures in sports video are characterized by repetitive transition patterns and unique views.

*Information Society Technologies Program of the EU 5th Framework.
**ASSAVID is an acronym for Automatic Segmentation and Semantic Annotation of Sports Videos. More information on ASSAVID may be found at http://www.viplab.dsi.unifi.it/ASSAVID/.
***http://www.ctr.columbia.edu/dvmm/.

For example, baseball videos normally consist of recurrent structures at different levels, such as innings, players, or pitches. A finite number of unique views are used because of the actual setup of cameras in the field. Therefore, the events at different levels can be characterized by their canonical visual views or the unique transition patterns between views. In this project,[48] a multistage detection system including adaptive model matching at the global level and detailed verification at the object level is introduced. The system demonstrates a high accuracy (>90 percent) for video segmentation with a real-time processing speed.

In addition, a personalized sports video streaming system based on the above results has been developed.[14] The system detects and filters the important events in live broadcast video programs and adapts the incoming streams to variable rate according to the content importance and user preference. Such application scenarios are powerful for streaming and filtering broadcast video to match the interest of users using pervasive computing devices. The techniques are also helpful for building personalized summarization or navigation systems, in which users can navigate efficiently through the video program at multiple levels of abstraction.

Singingfish.com uses MPEG-7 description schemes to describe the metadata characteristics of Internet streaming media. In particular, Rehm[49] demonstrated on Synchronized Multimedia Integration Language—Active Streaming Extensible Markup Language Format, or MPEG Audio Layer-3 URL (M3U)—specified presentations that the MPEG-7 Segment DS and Segment Decomposition DS allow one to model any currently available hierarchical playlist format. In addition to this observation, the author[49] also discusses MPEG-7 Multimedia Description Scheme (MDS) deficiencies. He mainly suggested an extension to the MediaInformation DSs to cope with scalable multimedia material. Detailed information on the MDS descriptors may be found in Chapter 2. These three projects are only a small portion of what is actually going on in the domain of semantic multimedia indexing and in MPEG-7 applications in general.

4.1.1 Use Case Study: Semantic Indexing of Images Supported by Object Recognition

Object recognition is a well-recognized technique for recognizing and classifying objects and thus attributing a semantic to them. The best-known work is probably that of Forsyth and Fleck.[50] Forsyth attracted much attention for his work on detecting naked human beings within images. His approach has been extended to a wider range of objects, including animals. Let us concentrate on their method for identifying a horse in an image (see also http://www.cs.berkeley.edu/~daf/horsedetails.html).

Exhibit 4.6 describes the indexing process. Images are first checked for pixels that have the right color and little texture. Second, a boundary

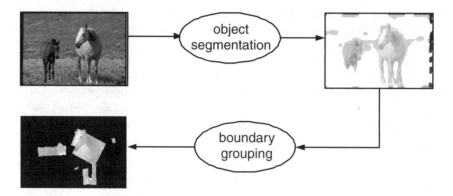

Exhibit 4.6.   Identifying horses in image collection: sample detection.

detection is applied that splits the regions of interest into curves. Groups of boundaries that could be views of cylindrical segments are then assembled (boundaries should be roughly parallel). These groups are then checked to see whether they are acceptably large and contain sufficient pixels, leading to a set of segments. They are then tested to see whether they could come from a view of a horse. The criteria are learned from images of horses and consist of a sequence of classification steps whose structure follows from the topology of the horse assembly. This process leads to a set of segments that could have come from a horse. The recognition technique works not as well if significant overlapping of fore- and background objects occurs in the image. Thus, the precision of the horse detection on real test data showing not exclusively horses did not exceed 66 percent.[50]

A promising technique to support the recognition process is to allow the system to learn associations between semantic concepts and the recognized objects through user feedback. These systems invite the user to annotate further regions of interest previously detected by object-recognition methods and then proceed to apply similar semantic labels to areas with similar characteristics. The pioneering system was FourEyes,[52] a learning system to assist users with the processes of segmentation, retrieval, and annotation. FourEyes extrapolates the semantic label of a selected region to other regions on the image and in the database by a selected model; for instance, by a Gaussian model of the label in that feature space. Moreover, FourEyes has a "society of models," from among which it selects and combines models to produce a labeling. This selection process is guided by the examples given by the user. More information on FourEyes may be obtained at http://web.media.mit.edu/~tpminka/photobook/foureyes/.

More recently, Wang et al.[51] proposed A-LIP, an automatic linguistic indexing system for images. This system learns automatically from already categorized images based on statistical modeling. To measure the association between an image and the textual description of a category of images, the likelihood of the occurrence of the image based on the stochastic process (a two-dimensional multiresolution hidden Markov model [2-D MHMM] is used) derived from the category is computed. An online demonstration of the system may be found at http://wang.ist.psu.edu/IMAGE/alip.html.

4.2 Multimedia Index Structures

The term indexing usually refers (as applied in the previous section) to the process of assigning terms or phrases that represent the information content of multimedia data. In contrast, the notion of an index from the point of view of a MMDBMS refers to the access structures built on the extracted low- and high-level feature vectors to accelerate data access. Most index access structures make use of multidimensional data structures. A multimedia object is represented, as a result of the indexing process, by an n-dimensional feature vector and, thus, constitutes a point in a multidimensional space.[53-55] Finding images similar to a query image involves retrieving those images whose corresponding locations in the n-dimensional space are within some measure of proximity to the point corresponding to the query object. This process is commonly referred to as similarity search.

Many works[56-63] are dedicated to the proposal of efficient methods for implementing the similarity search. The increasing need in applications to be able to store complex feature vectors, that is, high-dimensional vectors with more than 100 elements, and to index them based on their content has triggered a lot of research on multidimensional index structures, such as, for instance, those structures proposed in Chakrabarti and Mehrotra,[61] Cha and Chung,[62] White and Jain,[64] Kurniawati et al.,[65] and Cha et al.[66] The solutions proposed focusing on two main issues. The first solution class intends to reduce the dimension of the feature vectors, using transformation techniques like the Karhunen–Loeve Transform, Discrete Cosine Transform-based reduction methods or clustering techniques and then applying well-known indexing techniques. The second solution is the use of special indexing structures, such as the GC (Grid Cell)-trees, which may store and search efficiently long feature vectors as data points and that allow an effective partitioning of the large data space.

Existing multidimensional data structures for feature spaces can be classified into Data Partitioning (DP)-based and Space Partitioning (SP)-based structures.[61] A DP-based index structure consists of bounding regions (BRs) arranged in a spatial containment hierarchy. At the data level, the nearby points are clustered within BRs. At higher levels, nearby BRs are recursively clustered within bigger BRs, thus forming a hierarchical directory structure. The BRs can be bounding boxes, for example, R-trees[67] and

X-trees;[68] or bounding spheres or diamonds, for example, SS-trees[64,65] M-trees,[60] and TV-trees.[69] In contrast, an SP-based index structure consists of space recursively partitioned into mutually disjoint subspaces. The hierarchy of partitions forms a tree structure (e.g., KDB-trees[70] and hB-trees[59]) and the GC-tree for high-dimensional feature vector spaces.[62] The data partitioning is, in most cases, based on the values of the feature vectors along each dimension in the feature space.[61] This data partitioning is independent of the distance function used to compute the distance among objects in the database or between the query object and the database objects. Examples are R-trees and X-trees, as well as hB-trees. However, for SS-trees, the partitioning is based on the distance from one or more pivot points of the BRs.

Multidimensional data structures are also used to represent spatial and temporal relationships.[71,72] For instance, there are two major approaches to describing the spatial content of images: first, spatial content that is directional, and second, topological relationships between the domain objects. In the first approach, a single content element or structure captures the spatial content. In the second approach, several content elements collectively capture pair-wise spatial relationships between the domain objects. In both approaches, an algorithm is used to compute spatial similarity between two images. Some algorithms, based on the second approach, perform logical deduction or reduction before applying a similarity algorithm.

The assumption of most related works is that all elements of the feature vector are numeric. However, many vector elements are nonnumeric, and the domains are unordered. This introduces an additional problem of mapping the existing vector elements into a numeric domain. However, it may not be possible to find numerical substitutes for all contents. Furthermore, in perspective of the evolving number of extraction tools, more and more feature vectors will be extracted and have to be queried together. This query type is commonly referred to as a multifeature query.[73,74] Developing effective query processing techniques for high-dimensional multifeature queries is an open research issue. Finally, continuous nearest-neighbor (NN) search became of interest in the context of mobile spatial databases. Queries like, "give me all nearest hotels when I travel from Vienna to Hamburg" cannot be efficiently answered by subsequent k-NN search queries. Toa et al.[63] recently tackled this problem.

4.2.1 Use Case Study: The GC-Tree and the Curse of Dimensionality

With the proliferation of multimedia data and more accurate indexing methods, the feature vectors of low- and high-level multimedia describing features tend to have high dimensionalities, say, over 100. For instance, the Scalable Color Descriptor in MPEG-7, as described in Section 2.5.3, may scale to 256 values. So the main issue is to overcome the curse of dimensionality—a phenomenon in which the performance of indexing methods degrades drastically as the dimensionality increases.[66]

One promising solution to the dimensionality problem is the use of a vector approximation-based indexing method, namely, the LPC (Local Polar Coordinate) file[66] and the VA (vector approximation) file.[75] The vector-based search on a VA file is based on a simple filtering process. It eliminates those vectors that are considered worse than the first n vectors encountered during the sequential scan of the entire data file. This is accomplished by comparing the "lower bound" of a query vector with all the vectors in the file and storing potential records in a memory store; these records are considered to be within the acceptable region of the query vector. If a record satisfies the lower bound requirement, it will then be compared with the query item by computing the actual distance between them.

Although the LPC and VA file provided significant improvements compared with previous partitioning techniques, it suffers from performance degradation if the dataset is highly clustered because it employs a simple space partitioning strategy and a uniform bit allocation strategy for representing the partitioned region.[62] In this context, Cha and Chung[62] proposed the GC-tree indexing structure. The GC-tree is a SP-method that partitions the data space based on the analysis of the data distribution density; that is, it focuses the partitioning on the dense subspaces and dynamically constructs an index that reflects the partition hierarchy.

Exhibit 4.7 shows the difference between a typical SP method and a DP method based on the GC-tree. The DP method partitions the space by identifying BRs around the data points, and the SP method partitions the space recursively according to the density function.

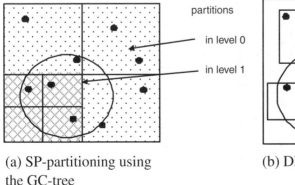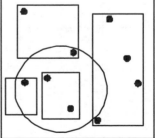

(a) SP-partitioning using the GC-tree

(b) DP-partitioning

Exhibit 4.7.   Data partitioning and space partitioning strategies.

The GC-tree consists of two components: directory nodes and data nodes. Directory nodes are employed for indexing the space partitioning, and data nodes are used for storing real objects. Each directory node corresponds to a region (cell) in the data space. Two types of regions are distinguished: those corresponding to clusters and those corresponding to outlier regions. The region corresponding to the cluster is a hyperrectangle with sides of equal length. The outlier region is the region remaining after removing the regions for clusters from the original region.

The GC-tree employs a density-based approach to partition the data space and to determine the number of bits to represent a cell vector for a partition. To approximate the density of the data points, the GC-tree partitions the data space into nonoverlapping hypersquare cells and counts the points that lie inside each cell of the partition—partitioning every dimension into the same number of equal length intervals at one time accomplishes this. This means that every cell generated from the partition of a space has the same volume, and therefore, the number of points inside a cell can be used to approximate the density of the cell.

Example: As an example, consider the two-dimensional GC-tree with a four-level index in Exhibit 4.8. At left, the two-dimensional data space is partitioned into 4×4 cells by using 2 bits per dimension as representation. At right, the directory nodes of the corresponding GC-tree are shown. The root directory contains two entries: the first from the left points to nodes that represents clusters, the second directory points to an outline region containing the singular points 1, 2, and 3. The directory entry with the cell vector (01, 01) in root points to the node C1 and represents the cell C1, which in turn forms a finer partition into an outlier region that contains the points 4 and 5 and another cluster, C2.

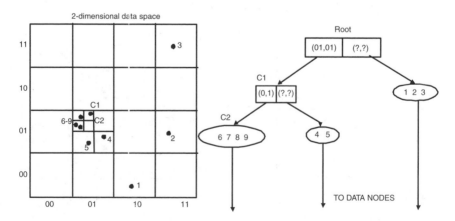

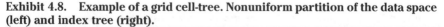

Exhibit 4.8.   Example of a grid cell-tree. Nonuniform partition of the data space (left) and index tree (right).

*The k-NN search is implemented as a branch and bound search approach
(similar to that employed in the R- and X-tree), and the search in the data
points is based on the vector-filtering technique from the VA files. The
combination of these two techniques shows the advantage for high-dimensional vector spaces, and Cha and Chung[62] could demonstrate a performance increase for real image datasets taken from the IBM QBIC (Query
by Image Content) stamp image database (see Section 4.4).*

4.3 Multimedia Data Models: Implementation and Communication

The multimedia data model deals with the issue of representing the content of all multimedia objects in a database; that is, designing the high- and
low-level abstraction model of the raw media objects and their correlations
to facilitate various operations. These operations may include media
object selection, insertion, editing, indexing, browsing, querying, and
retrieval. The data model relies, therefore, on the feature extraction vectors and their respective representations obtained during the indexing process. This section is divided into four main parts. In the first part, we concentrate on the conceptual design of multimedia data models. In the
second part, we introduce the object type hierarchy of SQL/MM and compare it with MPEG-7. In the third part, we focus on the implementation of
MPEG-7 in a DBMS and on the realization of descriptive multimedia information exchange in general. Finally, in the fourth part, we are showing how
the MPEG-21 DID may support legacy and semantic data integration in
multimedia databases.

4.3.1 Conceptual Multimedia Data Models

Continuous time-based multimedia such as video and audio involve
notions of data flow, timing, temporal composition, and synchronization.
These notions are quite different from the conventional data models, and
as a result, conventional data models are not well suited for multimedia
database systems. Hence, a key problem confronting a MMDBMS is the
description of the structure of time-constraint media in a form appropriate
for querying, updating, retrieval, and presentation.

One of the first pertinent approaches is introduced in Kim and Um.[76] In
this approach, a data model called timed stream is developed that
addresses the representation of time-based media. The model includes the
notions of media objects, media elements, and timed streams. Three general structure mechanisms are used: interpretation, derivation, and composition. This kind of data model is specialized in continuous media like
audio and video.

A more sophisticated approach is the VideoSTAR model.[77] The proposed
database system is closely aligned to the multimedia information system
architecture designed by Gross et al.[78] It constitutes a video database
framework and is designed to support video applications in sharing and

reusing video data and metadata. The metadata are implemented as a complex database schema. This schema realizes a kernel-indexing model valid for many application domains with a few precategorized entities like persons, events, and so on. Specific applications are able to enhance the descriptive power of the kernel model with specific types of content indexes.

The idea of the precategorization of content has been employed in many further models. Weiss et al.[79] have proposed a data model called algebraic video, which is used for composing, searching, and playing back digital video presentations. It is an important model in the sense that many of its features have been adopted in subsequent works. The authors use algebraic combinations of video segments (nodes) to create new video presentations. Their data model consists of hierarchical compositions of video expressions created and related to one another by four algebra operations: creation, composition, output, and description. Once a collection of algebraic video nodes is defined and made persistent, users can query, navigate, and browse the stored video presentations. Note that each algebraic video expression denotes a video presentation. An interesting feature of the proposed model, concerning the so-called interface operations like search, playback, and so forth, is that the hierarchical relations between the algebraic video nodes allow nested stratification. Stratification is a mechanism in which textual descriptions called strata are related to possibly overlapping parts of a linear video stream.[80] In the proposed model, a stratum is just an algebraic video node, which refers to a raw video file and a sequence of relevant frames. All nodes referring to the same video stream are used to provide multiple coexisting views and annotations and allow users to assign multiple meanings to one logical video segment. Moreover, the algebraic video model provides nested relationships between strata and thereby allows the user to explore the context in which a stratum appears.[81]

The algebraic video model has some shortcomings: first, the difficulty in adding automatic methods for segmenting video streams, and second, the need for an information retrieval engine for content-query execution because of the exclusive use of textual descriptions.

Zhong et al.[82] present a general scheme for video objects modeling, which incorporates low-level visual features and hierarchical grouping. It provides a general framework for video object extraction, indexing, and classification and presents new video segmentation and object tracking algorithms based on salient color and motion features. By video objects, the authors refer to objects of interest, including salient low-level image regions, moving foreground objects, and groups of objects satisfying spatio-temporal constraints. These video objects can be automatically extracted at different levels through object segmentation and object tracking mechanisms. Then, they are stored in a digital library for further access. Video objects can be grouped together, and high-level semantic annotations can be associated with the defined groups. The problem of this process is that visual features tend to provide only few direct links to high-level semantic concepts. Therefore, a hierarchical object representation model is proposed in which objects in different levels can be indexed, searched, and grouped to high-level concepts. However, content-based queries based on the proposed model can only retrieve whole video segments and set the video entry points according to some spatio-temporal features of the queried video objects rather than retrieving dedicated video units out of the whole video stream.

Jiang et al.[83–85] present a video data model, called Logical Hypervideo Data Model (LHVDM), which is capable of multilevel video abstractions. Multilevel abstractions are representations of video objects users are interested in, called hot objects. They may have semantic associations with other logical video abstractions, including other hot objects. The authors noted that very little work so far has been done on the problem of modeling and accessing video objects based on their spatio-temporal characteristics, semantic content descriptions, and associations with other video clips among the objects themselves. Users may want to navigate video databases in a nonlinear or nonsequential way, similar to what they can do with hypertext documents. Therefore, the proposed model supports semantic associations called video hyperlinks and video data dealing with such properties, called hypervideo. The authors provide a framework for defining, evaluating, and processing video queries using temporal, spatial, and semantic constraints, based on the hypervideo data model. A video query can contain spatio-temporal constraints and information retrieval subqueries. The granularity of a video query can be logical videos, logical video segments, or hot objects, whereas concerning hot objects, the results are always returned as logical video segments in which the hot objects occur.

LHVDM is one of the first models to integrate the concepts of hypervideo and multimedia data models and, therefore, attracted much attention. It has some shortcomings concerning the video abstraction levels and the free text annotations: first, the video abstraction hierarchy is not designed in full detail, meaning that the model does not distinguish between different video granularities, and second, there are no means for structured querying of the data model, only an information retrieval (IR) engine for querying is provided.

It has to be noted that in addition to LHVDM, many other related models also use exclusively, or as well as an MMDBMS, an IR engine to retrieve text documents containing multimedia elements. The domain of MultiMedia IR (MM-IR) has attracted interest in the last few years.[86] However, most of the annotations were keyword based.

Recently, researchers concentrated on an integrated approach for MM information systems, where MMDBMSs handle multimedia data in a structured way, whereas MM-IRs are used for retrieval of keywords.[1]

In this perspective, we proposed a generic indexing model, VIDEX,[87] which describes a narrative world as a set of semantic classes and semantic relations, including spatial and temporal relationships among these classes and media segments. The core of the indexing model defines base classes for an indexing system, whereas application-specific classes are added by declaring subclasses—so-called content classes—of the base classes. Furthermore, VIDEX introduces concepts for detailed structuring of video streams and for relating the instances of the semantic classes to the media segments. This approach tries to combine the advantages of the above-described methods, for instance, those in Weiss et al.,[81] Zhong and Chang,[82] Jiang et al.,[83] Little et al.,[88] and Hjelsvold et al.,[89] and extends them by the introduction of both means for structuring video steams and genericity in the indexing process. The SMOOTH multimedia information system realizes the high-level indexing part of the VIDEX video indexing model[26,90,91] and is detailed in Section 4.6 (Use Case 1).

Exhibit 4.9 shows the generic low- and high-level indexing parts of VIDEX in Unified Modeling Language notation.[87] It contains the basic set of high-level

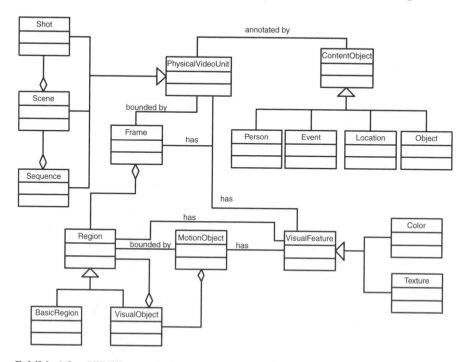

Exhibit 4.9. VIDEX generic low- and high-level indexing parts.[87]

content classes, which are events, objects, persons, and locations. These classes are subclasses of ContentObject, which builds the interface between the low- and high-level indexing parts with MotionObject. VIDEX provides a means for segmenting video streams in different granularities, such as shot, scene, and sequence. The class Frame denotes the entry point for low-level video access. It consists of one or more regions, realized through the abstract class Region, that can be either BaseRegions or VisualObjects. A region is a spatial object, whereas a Motion Object is a temporal and spatial object. This allows us to express temporal, spatial, and spatio-temporal relations between different low- and high-level objects.

4.3.2 Use Case Study: MPEG-7 versus SQL/MM

The International Standards Organization (ISO) subcommittee SC29, WG11, MPEG published in Spring 2002 their standard MPEG-7, the so-called Multimedia Content Description Interface.[92] MPEG-7 specifies a standard way of describing the content of different types of multimedia data. Chapter 2 provided a detailed description of the principles introduced in MPEG-7. It is important to remember here that the elements of MPEG-7 are coded as Extensible Markup Language (XML) documents following the rules of a data definition language (DDL), based on XML Schema. The DDL provides the means for defining the structure, content, and semantics of XML documents.

In this context, another International Organization for Standardization and International Electrotechnical Commission (ISO-IEC) Working Group, SQL, developed the SQL/MM–Multimedia extensions to SQL for creating multimedia extensions. In 2002, ISO-IEC also released the International Standard ISO-IEC 13249-5:2002 for image storage, manipulation and query.[93] A first version appeared in 2001; a second and improved version will appear in autumn 2003.[94] In the second version of the standard, a SI_StillImage type together with format descriptions and types for representing low-level features, such as SI_AverageColor, SI_ColorHistogram, and SI_Positional_Color, are proposed.

Both MPEG-7 and SQL/MM introduce a conceptual multimedia data model for use in multimedia database systems. MPEG-7 uses an extension to XML Schema, as SQL/MM extends the concept of the object-relational SQL-99.[95] To illustrate differences and commonness of the two models, consider the definition of the SI_StillImageType and related feature vector types in SQL/MM and of the StillRegionType in MPEG-7.

The SI_StillImageType in SQL/MM is defined as follows (main components):

```
CREATE TYPE SI_StillImage

AS (

    SI_content BINARY LARGE OBJECT(SI_MaxContentLength),

    SI_contentLength INTEGER,

    . . .

    SI_format CHARACTER VARYING(SI_MaxFormatLength),

    SI_height INTEGER,

    SI_width INTEGER

    )

INSTANTIABLE

NOT FINAL
```

SI_MaxContentLength is the implementation-defined maximum length for the binary representation of the SI_StillImage in the attribute SI_content. SI_MaxFormatLength is the implementation-defined maximum length for the character representation of an image format. The image format contains all information about format, compression, and so on. Height and width are self-explanatory.

In addition to the definition of an image, types for defining features for image comparison are proposed. The type SI_FeatureList provides the list of all available low-level features, and its definition is given below. The feature list principally contains means for color and texture indexing. It can be seen that for color, one histogram value is proposed (SI_ColorHistogram) and two nonhistogram color features are proposed: an average color (SI_AverageColor) and an array of dominant colors (SI_PositionalColor). The texture feature (SI_Texture) contains values represent the image texture characteristics.

The average color of an image is similar, but not identical, to the predominant color of an image. The average color is defined as the sum of the color values for all pixels in the image divided by the number of pixels in the image. For example, if 50 percent of the pixels in an image are blue and the other 50 percent are red, the average color for that image is purple. The histogram color of an image is specified as a distribution of colors in the image measured against a spectrum of N colors (typically 64 to 256). Positional color values indicate the average color values for pixels in a specific area of the image. The texture of an image is measured by three factors: coarseness, contrast, and directionality of the image. Coarseness indicates the size of repeating items in the image (e.g., pebbles versus boulders). Contrast is the variation of light versus dark. Directionality indicates whether the image has a predominant direction or not. An image of a picket fence, for example, has a predominant vertical direction, whereas an image of sand has no directionality. Texture is used to search for images that have a particular pattern.

SI_FeatureList is defined as:

```
CREATE TYPE SI_FeatureList
AS (
   SI_AvgClrFtr SI_AverageColor,
   SI_AvgClrFtrWght DOUBLE PRECISION DEFAULT 0.0,
   SI_ClrHstgrFtr SI_ColorHistogram,
   SI_ClrHstgrFtrWght DOUBLE PRECISION DEFAULT 0.0,
   SI_PstnlClrFtr SI_PositionalColor,
   SI_PstnlClrFtrWght DOUBLE PRECISION DEFAULT 0.0,
   SI_TextureFtr SI_Texture,
   SI_TextureFtrWght DOUBLE PRECISION DEFAULT 0.0
   )
INSTANTIABLE
NOT FINAL
```

The SI_ColorHistogramm is defined as follows:

```
CREATE TYPE SI_ColorHistogram
AS (
   SI_ColorsList SI_Color ARRAY[SI_MaxHistogramLength],
   SI_FrequenciesList
   DOUBLE PRECISION ARRAY[SI_MaxHistogramLength]
   )
INSTANTIABLE
NOT FINAL
```

SI_MaxHistogramLength is the implementation-defined maximum number of color/frequency pairs that are admissible in a SI_ColorHistogram feature value.

SQL/MM also defines elements for internal DBMS system behavior, such as SI_DLRead/WritePermission and the SI_DLRecoveryOption that fit well with the other system functionality.

Compared with SQL/MM, the MPEG-7 conceptual data model is richer; the following part of the DDL points out elements that are not covered by SQL/MM, such as:

```
. . .
<element name="TextAnnotation" minOccurs="0"
 maxOccurs="unbounded">
. . .
</element>
<choice minOccurs="0" maxOccurs="unbounded">
<element name="Semantic"
    type="mpeg7:SemanticType"/>
<element name="SemanticRef"
    type="mpeg7:ReferenceType"/>
</choice>
. . .
<element name="SpatialDecomposition"
type="mpeg7:StillRegionSpatialDecompositionType"
    minOccurs="0" maxOccurs="unbounded"/>
. . .
```

As a conclusion, the data model of SQL/MM covers the syntactical part of multimedia descriptions but allows no means for decomposition of an image, nor means for semantic description is given. Reconsidering the indexing pyramid, as shown in Exhibit 4.3, only features until level 3 may be presented (Local Structure). Means for a Global Structure are not given.

Note that almost all multimedia data models available in object-relational DBMS follow this conceptual modeling principle; for instance, Oracle 9i proposes in its interMedia Data Cartridge the type ORDImage that has similar elements as SI_StillImage enriched with more detailed format and compression information. More information on the retrieval capabilities of Oracle 9i is given in Section 4.5.

SQL/MM integrates well into the DBMS, as it proposes means for specifying access permissions, recovery options, and so on, and it is operational in the sense that the methods for retrieval and image processing are associated with the type hierarchy. MPEG-7 must rely on a DBMS implementation for storing and indexing MPEG-7 documents and must be associated with proprietary retrieval and processing mechanisms to be as functional as SQL/MM is. However, SQL/MM does not provide means for exchange of multimedia data and metadata.

The next section discusses implementation issues of MPEG-7 in DBMS and for information exchange in a distributed multimedia system.

4.3.3 Multimedia Data Model Implementation and Information Exchange in a Distributed Multimedia System

Most of the above-mentioned conceptual multimedia data models are implemented as database schemas or as object-relational types, benefiting from standard DBMS services like type extensions, data independence (data abstraction), application neutrality (openness), controlled multiuser access (concurrency control), fault tolerance (transactions, recovery), and access control. In our opinion, this will remain the predominant way of implementing a multimedia data model.

In addition to the above-mentioned criteria, a DBMS can provide a uniform query interface that is based on the structure of descriptive information implemented and the relationships between descriptive data. Finally, multimedia applications are generally distributed, requiring multiple servers to satisfy their storage and processing requirements. A well-developed distributed DBMS technology can be used to manage data distribution of the raw multimedia data efficiently, for instance, as BLOBs, and to manage remote access with the support of broadly used connection protocols, like JDBC (Java Database Connectivity).

However, none of the related works attributed significance to the question of how to communicate metadata effectively, in terms of interoperability of the information exchange in a distributed multimedia system. Designing models for information exchange, that is, descriptive information together with the described raw material, or as a standalone stream is a very important issue in a distributed multimedia system. Descriptive multimedia information can provide, for instance, active network components such as network routers and proxy caches, with valuable information to govern or enhance their media scaling, buffering, and caching policies on the delivery path to the client. Descriptive information can assist the client in the selection of multimedia data; for example, immediate or later viewing. It personalizes the data offered; for example, a user filters from broadcast streams according to the location encoded in the metadata.

In this context, MPEG-7 provides a coding schema, the BiM (binary) representation, for document transport. This choice has been made by taking into consideration the general development that XML documents are becoming a standard for a shared vocabulary in distributed systems.[96] Furthermore, it is based on the fact that compression is also important for MPEG-7 documents, as these documents may include, among others, large feature vectors for describing various low-level characteristics of the media data. The descriptive information contained in the DSs and Descriptors values (Ds) can be considered, to some extent, a summary of the contents and principles introduced by the models mentioned above.

However, the structural definition of the content differs, based on whether it is made for the storage in a database and further content querying, as considered in most related works, or whether it is designed for information exchange. This fundamental difference is revealed at several levels. The first one is in the overall organization of the content types. MPEG-7 tries to keep the hierarchy of content descriptions as flat as possible to minimize the number of dereferencing before reaching the desired information. This stems from the simple requirement that some network components and the client may not have enough computing power or storage space to process complicated unfolding of descriptive information. In contrast to this, multimedia database schema modeling semantically rich content, like VIDEX[87] and VideoSTAR,[77] for instance, have complicated hierarchies, in order to be as extensible as possible. Second, the difference is revealed in how both approaches attribute importance to single descriptive elements. For example, MPEG-7 proposes a variety of tools (MediaLocator DS) to specify the "location" of a particular image or audio or video segment by referencing the media data. This is important for cross-referencing of metadata and media data. However, such an effort is not of so much interest for a multimedia data model in a DBMS, as in most cases a simple reference to the video data, for example, as BFILE in Oracle 9i or other DBMSs, is sufficient for location (see also Kosch[97] for a discussion of commonness and differences). Obviously, a combination of data models for storage and querying on the one hand, and for information exchange on the other, must make a compromise between the requirements of both issues.

To store and communicate the XML-based MPEG-7 descriptions in and from a database, a first approach is the use of an extensible DBMS; for instance, an object-relational DBMS. Such an approach can be realized, for example, with the XML SQL Utility (XSU), a utility from Oracle (for more information on XSU, please visit http://technet.oracle.com). The MDC developed by us is an Oracle 9i system extension to store XML-based MPEG-7 documents and provide an interface for their exchange. The MDC is described in detail in Section 4.6, Use Case 2.

Alternatively, one can use a so-called XML-DBMS, which no longer relies on traditional database schemes and that stores XML documents directly. Such an approach is supported by recently developed multimedia data models, which rely on semistructured documents such as that proposed by Hacid et al.[98]

An XML-DBMS provides query interfaces and languages[99] with respect to the nature of XML documents. The broadly used query language is

XPATH. XPATH 1.0 provides the so-called path-query expression, and its specification can be found at http://www.w3.org/TR/xpath. XPATH 2.0 is under development and will simplify the manipulation of XML Schema–typed content. This is of obvious advantage for MPEG-7. The newest developments for XPATH 2.0 can be found at http://www.w3.org/TR/ xpath20req.

At present, several XML-DBMS products are in use. Examples are IPSIS from the GMD Darmstadt (http://xml.darmstadt.gmd.de/xql/) and Tamino from SoftwareAG (http://www.softwareag.com/tamino). These products are supported by the XML:DB initiative (http://www.xmldb.org), which intends to make XML-DBMS client–server capable by defining an XDBC standard similar to JDBC/ODBC. Whether an XML-DBMS or an extensible DBMS should be used depends mainly on the application area. An application requiring transaction management and recovery services will rely more on an extensible ORDBMS than on an XML-DBMS. However, in other applications, extensible DBMS technology might be too expensive in terms of storage space and processing costs. For instance, the M3box[100] project developed by Siemens Corporate Technology (IC 2) aims at the realization of an adaptive multimedia message box. One of its main components is a multimedia database for retrieving multimedia mails based on their structured content. The inputs to the database are MPEG-7 documents generated in the input devices (e.g., videophone, PDAs) and the outputs are again MPEG-7 documents to be browsed at the output devices. The system is performance critical and, therefore, relies on an XML-DBMS—actually dbXML—to avoid scheme translations of both the input and the output.[101]

4.3.4 MPEG-21 Digital Item: Legacy and Semantic Data Integration in MMDBMS

The importance of MPEG-7 serving as the conceptual data model in a MMDBMS has been intensively discussed. However, the fact that there exist many related multimedia metadata standards, which are in industrial use, should not be ignored. As described in Section 1.2, the Dublin Core metadata set,* based on RDF (Resource Description Framework), describes semantic Web documents. Dublin Core elements include creator, title, subject keywords, resource type, and format. The standards lack, however, elaborated means for describing the content of multimedia data. For instance, the only image-related aspects of the element set are the ability to define the existence of an image in a document ("DC.Type = image") and to describe an image's subject content by the use of keywords.

The issue of legacy in multimedia database is an important one, as many content providers and archives rely on metadata standards like Dublin Core and SMPTE (Society of Motion Picture and Television Engineers) and

*http://dublincore.org.

started to use MPEG-7 for content descriptions. A MMDBMS system must be able to deal with these different standards at the same time without bothering about complex transformation processes from one standard into the others, which is in general not supported by the providers.

In this context, the MPEG-21 Digital Item Declaration (DID) model may effectively be employed. As discussed in Chapter 2, the MPEG-21 DID provides means for integrating different description schema into one descriptive framework.

The following example shows how different descriptor formats can be used to express complementary metadata sets. The example shows an MPEG-7 description for the content and a RDF-based Dublin Core descriptor for title and rights of my passport image.

```
<?xml version="1.0" encoding="UTF-8?">

<DIDL xmlns="urn:mpeg:mpeg21:2002:01-DIDL-NS"

   xmlns:mpeg7="urn:mpeg:mpeg7:schema:2001"

   xmlns:RDF="http://www.w3.org/1999/02/22-rdf-syntax-
       ns#"

   xmlns:dc="http://purl.org/dc/elements/1.1/">

   <Item>

      <Descriptor>

         <Statement mimeType="text/xml">

            <mpeg7:Mpeg7>

               <mpeg7:DescriptionUnit
                   xsi:type="mpeg7:AgentObjectType">

               <mpeg7:Label>

                  <mpeg7:Name> Harald

                  Kosch</mpeg7:Name>

               </mpeg7:Label>

                  <mpeg7:Agent xsi:type="
                      mpeg7:PersonType">

                  <mpeg7:Name>

                     <mpeg7:GivenName>  Harald
                         </mpeg7:GivenName>

                     <mpeg7:FamilyName> Kosch
                         </mpeg7:FamilyName>

                  </mpeg7:Name>
```

```
        </mpeg7:Agent>
      </mpeg7:DescriptionUnit>
    </mpeg7:Mpeg7>
  </Statement>
</Descriptor>
<Descriptor>
  <Statement mimeType="text/xml">
    <RDF:Description>
      <dc:creator>Nowhere Photoshop</dc:creator>
      <dc:description>Passport Photo<
          /dc:description>
      <dc:date>2002-12-18</dc:date>
      <dc:rights>
        No reproduction allowed.
      </dc:rights>
    </RDF:Description>
  </Statement>
</Descriptor>
<Component>
  <Resource ref="myself.jpeg" mimeType=
      "image/jpeg"/>
</Component>
    </Item>
  </DIDL>
```

In addition to the legacy, the semantic integration aspect of the MPEG-21 DID is important. The syntactic properties of the MPEG-21 DID model facilitates interoperability among the semantic description formats, such as RDF(S)* or DAML+OIL.** This increases reusability of description, for example, MPEG-7 with metadata descriptions from other domains where multimedia data plays an important role, such as the Multimedia Home Platform (MHP) (as part of the Digital Video Broadcasting [DVB] Project) (http://www.dvb.org/), the TV Anytime Forum (http://www.tv-any-time.org/), the (NewsML,http://www.newsml.org/), the Gateway to Educational Materials project (http://www.thegateway.org/), or the Art and

*http://www.w3.org/RDF/.
**http://www.ontoknowledge.org/oil/.

Architecture Thesaurus browser (http://www.getty.edu/ research/tools/ vocabulary/aat).

4.4   Content-Based Retrieval

The key functionality in a multimedia database is how to retrieve continuous and noncontinuous multimedia information effectively. One broadly used method, the content-based retrieval (CBR) of multimedia objects, relies on simple extraction properties of multimedia objects.[102–104] In contrast, in concept-based content retrieval,[105] semantic interpretation of the objects is added; for example, objects are identified as a named person, and so forth. This semantic interpretation can be added by the indexer or obtained through a semiautomatic indexing process. We discussed this issue in Section 4.1.

To account for the broad use of CBR and the need for semantically rich indexing and querying, an MMDBMS must provide means for CBR as well as optimizer and processor engines for complex structured queries. This implies that the next-generation MMDBMSs must provide generic and reusable engines for different processing purposes, which must be built, preferably, on top of existing database engines. Two main description classes for CBR are actually distinguished and can be used in combination:

- A straightforward first approach is to use a "tag" to each object and to retrieve objects on the basis of their tags.[2] The tags could even be structured into multiple attributes. Traditional relational algebra is then applicable on all the attributes in the tag, and predicates on these can be used to retrieve the objects. Standard keyword-based indexing, as used in text retrieval, can then be used to retrieve the tags relevant to the query and the associated objects.
- The second approach to CBR is the similarity search between extracted multimedia features.[106] Here, the query is actually posed against the low-level feature vectors extracted from the multimedia object rather than against the tag.

4.4.1 Image CBR

There exist many Image CBR systems (CBIR), as discussed in Rui et al.,[103] Smith and Chang,[107] Flickner et al.,[108] Das et al.,[109] Shanbehazadeh et al.,[110] and Kelly and Cannon.[111] A broadly used system is the IBM QBIC (http://wwwqbic.almaden.ibm.com).[108]

4.4.2 Use Case: The QBIC System from IBM

The similarity search in QBIC relies principally on feature vectors generated from color, texture, and histograms. Exhibit 4.10 shows the graphical CBIR query mask of QBIC, in which, in addition to keywords, values for the

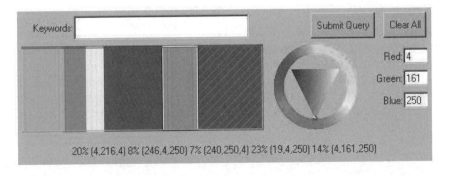

Exhibit 4.10. Image content-based retrieval query mask of Query by Image Content.[117]

RGB (red, green, and blue) color system can be entered. The computation of the features is the following:

- Color: QBIC computes the average Munsell[112] coordinates of each object and image, plus an *n*-dimensional color histogram (*n* is typically 64 or 256) that gives the percentage of the pixels in each image in each of the *n* colors.
- Texture: QBIC's texture features are based on modified versions of the coarseness, contrast, and directionality features. Coarseness measures the scale of the texture (pebbles versus boulders), contrast describes the vividness of the pattern, and directionality describes whether or not the image has a favored direction or is isotropic (grass versus smooth objects).
- Shape: QBIC uses several different sets of shape features. One is based on a combination of area, circularity, eccentricity, major axis orientation, and a set of algebraic moment invariants. A second is the turning angles or tangent vectors around the perimeter of an object, computed from smooth splines fit to the perimeter. The result is a list of 64 values of turning angle.

QBIC is integrated in the current Image Extender of IBM's commercial database system DB2. The QBIC functionality in the Image Extender is detailed in the product's Section 4.6. QBIC is also used in CBR Web-Application; for instance, it is integrated in a Web-based system for finding artwork in the digital collection of the Hermitage Museum; the Web site is http://hermitagemuseum.org/.

4.4.3 Video CBR

Video CBR is supported by fewer systems than CBIR.[113,114] For instance, VideoQ incorporates, in addition to traditional keyword search methods, the possibility to search video based on a rich set of visual features; that is, color, texture, shape, motion, and spatio-temporal relationships.

The VideoQ* system extracts regions and objects from the video shots using color and edge information and tracks their motion. Queries are entered in a graphical user interface by specifying the color, texture, the motion of the objects as well as their spatio-temporal relationship to other objects. Exhibit 4.11 shows a snapshot of the VideoQ query interface during the specification of a spatio-temporal query.

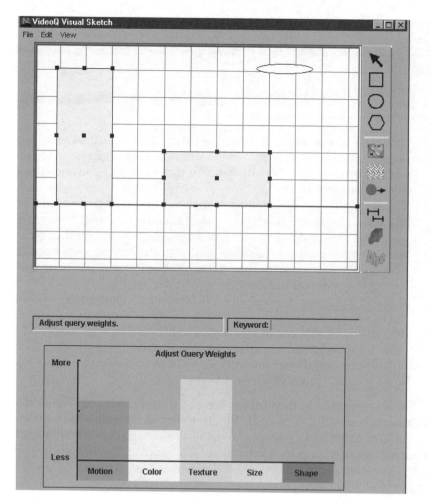

Exhibit 4.11. Query mask of VideoQ.[113]

---

*VideoQ has been developed within the ADVENT Project of the Image and Advanced TV Lab at Columbia University. A Web demonstration may be found at http://www.ctr.columbia.edu/VideoQ/.

Virage[114] is a broadly used commercial Video CBR (http://www.virage.com) that includes facilities for video analyzing, annotation, and retrieval. It also provides a speech recognition tool, based on a large set of speaker profiles, to encode content of audio in ASCII (American Standard Code for Information Interchange) text. This encoded data can then be used as the query content. However, Virage does not currently support any spatio-temporal querying.

There are similar CBR technologies currently in use in different applications.[109–111,113,114] An interesting approach is given by MetaSEEk (http://www.ctr.columbia.edu/MetaSEEk/). It is a meta-search engine for images based on the content of CBIRs that are located at IBM, Virage, and Columbia University servers. Furthermore, MetaSEEk[115] allows the search in categories, similar to WebSEEk[45] (http://www.ctr.columbia.edu/webseek/).

In this context, Colin C. Venters and Matthew Cooper provided a very comprehensive overview of currently used CBIR systems,[116] which can be found online at http://www.jisc.ac.uk/uploaded_documents/jtap-039.doc. In 2000, R.C. Veltkamp and M.Tanase[117] compared 43 available products. Their report may be found at http://give-lab.cs.uu.nl/cbirsurvey/. Finally, A.W.M. Smeulders et al.[118] overviewed CBIR in their overview paper and discussed open problems, such as the "semantic gap," which exists between low-level and high-level indexing and retrieval (as already discussed in Section 4.1). The focus of these overview articles is on algorithmic details and metadata models for retrieval in not detailed.

4.4.4 Audio CBR

One of the first systems available was QBH (Query by Humming), described at the ACM Multimedia Conference in 1995.[119] The system allows the user to query an audio database by humming the desired tune into a microphone. QBH tracks pitches with a modified form of autocorrelation method and converts them into a melody pattern encoded in a stream of U (up), D (down), and S (same) characters. Then, the system uses an approximate string match algorithm to match the patterns against the audio database.

The Melody Tools of MPEG-7 (see Section 2.8) can be used for query by humming. In a simple scenario, the audio input of a humming person is analyzed for the contour and beat (use of the MelodyContour DS) and is then compared with the melodies stored in the database. The song with the most similar contour and beat is retained. Additional MPEG-7 information on the author, the genre, and so forth, are equally returned. In some cases, however, it is useful to employ the MelodySequence DS for audio similarity matching; for instance, to identify melodies similar to humming by imperfect musicians. The MelodySequence DS can also be used to reconstruct a melodic line and lyrics from its MPEG-7 description. A working Query by Humming system can be found at www.musicline.de/de/melodiesuche.

In general, Audio CBR is the task used to find occurrences of a musical query pattern in a music database. A natural way to give such a query pattern is by humming (as described before), but recently, other forms have attracted interest. In the sample scenario from Chapter 1, the query pattern was recorded with the mobile phone. In such a case, the AudioSignature DS is a good representative for the content in the database and for the query pattern, as it provides an unique fingerprint. It has been shown that only 10 seconds of recorded pattern is sufficient to achieve a 90 percent recognition rate.[120] Another Audio CBR form is introduced in the Parfait Olé Melody Search Engine (http://www.parfaitole.com/). This engine allows one to identify an unknown melody from its first few notes, provided that one can describe the melody in terms of standard musical pitches. The pitches are allowed to be relative pitches, that is, the exact key need not be known, and the rhythm is ignored.

Jonathan Foote[121] gives a good overview of Audio CBR systems. He also realized several Audio CBR systems; in 1997,[122] he proposed a system for content-based retrieval of music and audio that can retrieve audio documents by acoustic similarity. In his approach, a template is generated using cepstral coefficients for each audio in the database and for the user's acoustic input. The query template is then matched against templates in the database to determine the query results. Later, he extended his methodology to retrieval by rhythmic similarity.[123]

4.4.5 Influence of MPEG-7 on CBR

MPEG-7 has a major influence on CBR implementations. It offers the unique possibility to have a standardized way of describing the low-level content and thus enables the realization of interoperable querying mechanisms. MPEG-7 applications for CBR may be found at http://mpeg-industry.com. Most of them focus on similarity search. Some of them try to integrate semantic meaningful annotation and advanced query mask for this purpose. For instance, Caliph and Emir from the I-Know Center in Austria propose an MPEG-7 based photo annotation and retrieval tool. The basic semantic entities, such as AgentObjectType and EventType, may be entered and reused. SemanticRelations may be graphically specified by connected respective semantic entities. The search mask follows the annotation mask and allows the same graphical concept. Caliph and Emir is available on 90-day license from http://www.know-center.at/en/divisions/div3demos.htm. Another interesting approach is used in the VAnnotator, developed in the IST VIZARD (Video Wizard) project. This MPEG-7-based annotation tool employs the concept of "video lenses" for providing different views on the materials being annotated. There are lenses for viewing and adding textual annotations and lenses that allow viewing the result of image processing algorithms such as cut detection. VAnnotator may be downloaded from http://www.video-wizard.com/index-n.htm on a 30-day trial license.

4.4.6 CBR Online Demos

Finally, the reader is advised to make his or her own judgment by looking at the following list (not complete) of available demos:

Online advanced CBIR systems include:

- Amore (Advanced Multimedia Oriented Retrieval Engine), http://www.ccrl.com/amore/: developed by C & C Research Laboratories NEC USA, this is a retrieval engine that adds category and a notion of the importance of a feature to a similarity search supported by a keyword search. The set of images to be searched stem principally from sport, art, and vehicles.
- Blobworld, http://elib.cs.berkeley.edu/photos/blobworld/: developed by the Computer Science Division, University of California–Berkeley, this engine performs an automatic segmentation of the query image into regions of interest and lets the user declare the importance of them for the query.
- The Department of Computer Science and Engineering, University of Washington, http://www.cs.washington.edu/research/imagedatabase/demo/: this department developed a handful of useful automatic annotation methodologies for CBR. The main focus is on semiautomated recognition of generic object and concept classes in digital images. In addition, a hierarchical multiple classifier methodology provides a learning mechanism for automating the development of recognizers for additional objects and concepts. Online demos are available for the object recognition techniques and the retrieval engine.
- LCPD (Leiden 19th-Century Portrait Database), http://ind156b.wi.leidenuniv.nl:2000/: LCPD is interesting from the application point of view. It is developed by the Department of Computer Science, Leiden University, The Netherlands. It offers a variety of search tools, one for studio applications (making carte de visite portraits), one for making family albums, one query by example, a relevance feedback based search, and finally a browsing interface.
- MuscleFish.com: this site provides several audio retrieval tools that can analyze audio files, cluster them according to categories, and search for audios that are similar or dissimilar to others. An online demo may be found at http://www.musclefish.com/cbrdemo.html.

- Themefinder, http://www.themefinder.org: Themedfinder is a Web-based melodic search tool. The database content consists of hand-picked monophonic incipit from classical and folksong repertoires. Queries are based on pitch information and can be given in many forms; for example, as intervals, scale degrees, pitch classes, or contour patterns. In addition, the search may be limited by entering the name of the composer and a time signature. Only exact matching is available.

Online MPEG-7-based retrieval and indexing systems include:

- MPEG-7 Retrieval Demo, http://vision.ece.ucsb.edu/demos.html: from the Department of Electrical and Computer Engineering, University of California, Santa Barbara, this demo exhibits the use of the MPEG-7 Homogeneous Texture Descriptor to a large collection of aerial images. The dataset consists of 54 large aerial images of the Santa Barbara, California, region. Each image is segmented into 1681 tiles using a rectangular grid. Each tile is a gray-scale image of 128×128 pixels.
- The MPEG-7-based SQUID (Shape Queries Using Image Databases), University of Surrey, http://www.ee.surrey.ac.uk/Research/VSSP/imagedb/demo.html: a tool for retrieving images by similar shape. It is based on the MPEG-7 Curvature Scale Space feature, which is a multiscale organization of the inflection points (or curvature zero-crossing points) of the object contour. The database contains about 1100 images of marine creatures. Each image shows one distinct species on a uniform background. Every image is preprocessed to recover the boundary contour, which is then represented by three global shape parameters and the maxima of the curvature zero-crossing contours in its Curvature Scale Space image.

4.5 Multimedia Query Languages, Optimization, and Processing

To retrieve multimedia data, described by a metadata model, a database system must provide a multimedia query language. This language must have capacities to handle queries specifying complex spatial and temporal relationships,[44,79,124] keywords, and objective and subjective contents of multimedia objects. In this context, Gudivada et al.[125] defined a set of generic query classes. These classes include:

1. Retrieval by browsing: employed by users who are not familiar with the structure and contents of MMDBMSs. Browsing is also often used for exploratory querying.
2. Querying objective and subjective attributes: An objective attribute query is a structured way of querying that is similar to queries on build-in datatypes used in contexts in which the syntactical form of

the query can be specified precisely. This is in contrast to situations where the user submits a fuzzy query formulation.

- A subjective attribute query is composed of attributes whose interpretation varies considerably from one user to another. For example, a query such as "give me all faces that have a beautiful nose" is subjective, and what "a beautiful nose" resembles is dependent on the taste of the user. Although subjective querying is of obvious interest, at present there is very little research work on this issue.

3. CBR queries: allow one to query the low-level characteristics of the media, for example, color, shape, and texture queries for visual media (see Section 4.4).
4. Correlation queries: used to retrieve media that are similar to the query object in terms of
   - Spatial relationship: directional and topological relationships between the corresponding pairs of objects in the query and the database
   - Temporal relationship: relations between the time instances at which the query object and objects in the database appear or disappear
   - Spatio-temporal relationship: a domain phenomenon that varies in space and time

There are recent works[126,127] that propose a framework for semantic integrated information indexing and retrieval by defining a semantic distance function between two conceptual entities in a linguistic ontology. However, these works focus on CBR exclusively. A next version of MPEG-7 will try to identify descriptors that are no longer representations of the fundamental qualities of audiovisual content, but represent subjective content. This obviously requires the notion of a common sense.[128] Somewhat in this direction, the current version of MPEG-7[92] (see also Chapter 2) introduces the principle of a ControlledTerm Datatype, by which one might control the value of a textual field using a classification scheme; for example, a sport expression can be controlled by the classification scheme provided by the Olympic movement (http://www.olympic.org). In the same manner, but considerably more complex, a commonsense principle might be set up for subjective descriptions.

Moreover, it is desirable to specify the presentation of the results within the query language. For this, several approaches[56,129–132] propose a combined multimedia query and presentation language; that is, a query expression consisting of two components: a query language to describe what information to retrieve and a presentation language to specify how to display query results. The advantage of an integrated presentation and query specification is that optimization issues for the presentation part can be addressed effectively with traditional query optimization methods. Adali et al.[133] apply such a principle.

Let us consider as an example the approach of Gonzalez et al.[130] They introduced SQL+D, a multimedia and presentation extension to an object-relational SQL that gives users the ability to specify, within an SQL query, a screen layout to be used to show the result of a query. For example, the following object-relational table MONUM contains video and audio information about the great world monuments: MONUM (name: string; country: string; a: audio; v: video). If a user wants now to see video clips showing monuments located in the U.S., together with its corresponding audio stream, the content query and presentation specifications can be formulated by the following SQL+D query:

```
SELECT a,v FROM MONUM

WHERE country='USA'

DISPLAY panel main

WITH a AS audio A, v AS video V ON main.Center(Overlay),

SHOW V,A
```

Exhibit 4.12 shows the principle steps of the SQL+D query processing and the result presentation of the sample query. The SQL+D interpreter receives the query and splits it into the SQL-based content query and the DISPLAY specification parts. Then, the SQL+D interpreter requests a connection to the database, which is obtained by the database interface. The database interface is responsible for starting the content query processing. The DISPLAY specifications and the result of the content query processing are sent as inputs to the display controller, which shows the multimedia display. The result window shows one monument video from the result set. The buttons in the interface allow the navigation through the query result set.

Note that the use of multimedia data and content required the introduction of new data types and associated methods in SQL+D. As a consequence, we have to employ an extensible DBMS for the processing of these enhanced features. Whether or not extensible DBMSs are the right technical platform for effective multimedia query processing and optimization is discussed in the next paragraph.

4.5.1 Multimedia Query Processing Platforms and Technologies

Object-Relational DBMSs (ORDBMSs), as broadly used extensible DBMS platforms, are actually the most promising technical platforms[134] to implement a multimedia data model and to realize query processing and optimization by providing the following facilities:

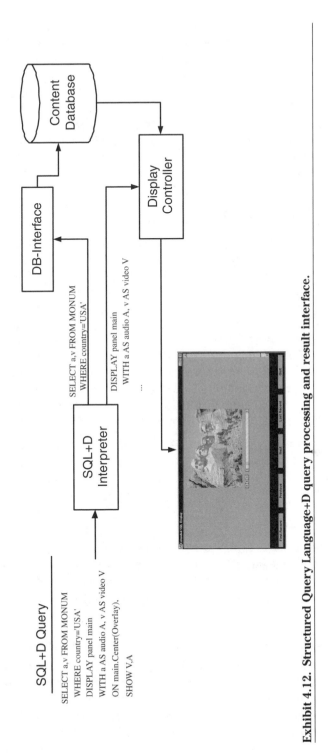

SQL+D Query

SELECT a,v FROM MONUM

WHERE country='USA'

DISPLAY panel main

WITH a AS audio A, v AS video V

ON main.Center(Overlay),

SHOW V,A

Exhibit 4.12. Structured Query Language+D query processing and result interface.

- Providing extensible data types with associated functions and operations and data access methods;
- Offering extensible indexing, processing, and optimization techniques (e.g., Oracle ORDBMS provides a facility called Data Cartridge Technology that includes the possibility to specify domain indexes and cost models for a newly introduced data type; the MDC proposed in Section 4.6. relies on this technology);
- Unifying declarative and navigable access on the same level for model and language; and
- Managing multimedia data externally and internally. Externally, data are stored as files, and the names of these files are stored in the database. With internal management, the fragments are stored as a series of separate objects in the database.

Object-Oriented DBMSs (OODBMSs) provide the above features as well. However, they do not rely on the relational table structure as a storage unit. This might sound like an advantage of OODBMSs at the first glance. It is, however, a disadvantage. Using tables in ORDBMSs allows these systems to use field-tested processing and storage strategies of relational databases, rendering these systems robust in an early introductive phase to the market. Second, tables provide regular access structures and thus enable the use of efficient and simple look-ahead optimization strategies. There are few OODBMSs with multimedia extensions that can compete with respective multimedia-enabled ORDBMSs in robustness and performance. One of them is the ObjectStore, which manages multimedia data; for more information, see http://www.exln.com/products/objectstore/.

Finally, the DISIMA (Distributed Multimedia DBMS) multimedia query processor[135,136] provides means for complex query processing and optimization of MOQL (Multimedia Object Query Language) queries and is built on top of ObjectStore. Chapter 6 describes the DISIMA system. Current market-leading ORDBMS products provide multimedia packages; that is, collection of data types to support multimedia processing.

IBM Informix packs different data types for images and videos in DataBlade modules; for example, image processing in the Excalibur Image DataBlade.[57] Oracle provides the Oracle Visual Information Retrieval system[137] for images, and IBM's DB2 Universal Database proposes multimedia extenders.[138]

4.5.2 Use Case Study: Oracle Visual Information Retrieval System

Let us consider as an example the Oracle Visual Information Retrieval system. This system is an extension of the Oracle 9i ORDBMS, providing image storage, CBIR functionality, and format conversion capabilities through a new object type ORDImage and associated methods and functions. CBIR functionality is provided by the ability to extract an image feature vector from four different visual attributes: global color, local color, texture, and shape. Moreover, Oracle provides a multidimensional index structure ORDImageIndex to accelerate access to the stored feature vectors.

In this system, simple CBR and attribute queries can be handled. However, complex join queries can only be partially treated. The following example shows the only possible formulation of a join between two image tables Pictures1 and Pictures2:

```
CREATE TABLE Picture1 (
    author VARCHAR2(30),
    description VARCHAR2(200),
    photo1 ORDSYS.ORDImage,
    photo1_sig ORDSYS.ORDImageSignature
);
CREATE TABLE Picture2 (
    mydescription VARCHAR2(200),
    photo2 ORDSYS.ORDImage,
    photo2_sig ORDSYS.ORDImageSignature
);
```

These tables are joined based on their feature vectors (called Signatures in Oracle), which are stored in the table element photo1_sig (photo2_sig) of type ORDSYS.ORDImageSignature. The Signatures have first to be generated for comparison with the member function photo1_sig.generateSignature(img). After this generation, the similarity function ORDSYS.IMGSimilar() is applied, which takes as inputs the two instances of the tables to be joined. The statement results in pairs of instances for which a user-defined threshold similarity value, which governs the difference of the respective feature vectors, has not been exceeded. This means that if the weighted sum of the distances for the visual attributes is less than or equal to the threshold, the images match. The join query expresses then as:

```
SELECT p1.description, p2.description
FROM Picture p1, Picture p2
WHERE
    ORDSYS.IMGSimilar(p1.photo1_sig, p2.photo2_sig,
    'color="0,6" texture="0,2" shape="0,1"
        location="0,1"', 20)=1;
```

The SQL/MM standard[93] (Section 4.3) introduces new OR-DB types to handle multimedia data. Notably, the SI_StillImage type is proposed for holding the image and, for example, SI_ColorHistogram and SI_AverageColor, for representing features. In addition to the type concept, several methods have been specified to allow CBR-functionality. For instance, the polymorph SI_Score Method compares two feature vectors. Assume that the object colorhist contains the color histogram of an image Picture1. Then, the method colorhist.SI_Score(Picture2) applied to another image, Picture2, returns a value greater than or equal to 0, with the meaning that the lower the returned value, the closer the color histogram values of Picture1 and Picture2 are.

Let us reconsider the ORDImage query from above and see how it looks in SQL/MM: Let us assume that the tables Pictures1 and Pictures2 contain an element of type SI_StillImage. Their definitions are given below. Note that each feature type used in the table definition must be explicit.

```
CREATE TABLE Picture1 (
    author VARCHAR2(30),
    description VARCHAR2(200),
    photo1 SI_StillImage,
    photo1_color SI_ColorHistogram,
    photo1_texture SI_Texture,
);
CREATE TABLE Picture2 (
    mydescription VARCHAR2(200),
    photo2 SI_StillImage,
    photo2_color SI_ColorHistogram,
    photo2_texture SI_Texture,
);
```

Furthermore, let us suppose that we like to join the two tables based on the ColorHistogram and the Texture features, where the difference of the ColorHistogram values should not exceed 0.5 and those of the Texture should not exceed 0.4. The SQL/MM query expresses then as

```
SELECT p1, p2
FROM Picture1 p1, Picture2 p2
WHERE
    p1.photo1_color.SI_Score(p2. photo2) > 0.5 AND
    p1.photo1_texture.SI_Score(p2.photo2) > 0.4
```

A similar join definition can be found in other systems, for example, the IBM Informix[57] Excalibur Image DataBlade module and prototype implementations and the DISIMA system.[135]

However, it is not possible in these systems to formulate in a single SQL statement a join through the method of the NN search; that is, retain for all tuples of the left-input relation the k-NN in the right-input table. Processing a multimedia join operation through the NN-search method is, however, an alternative and useful form of multimedia join.

In this context, a complete framework for the integration of NN-search supporting operators in an Image DBMS was proposed by us.[139–141] This framework includes an image data type and associated operators, image algebra, optimization strategies, and finally, appropriate processing strategies. The framework is designed and implemented for an image database relying on the efficient multidimensional index structure of X-trees.[68]

Another important point of concern is the formulation and processing of correlation queries. The above-mentioned multimedia database products, like the DataBlade modules, the Oracle Cartridge ORDImage, and the Multimedia Extenders, as well as the standardized proposition of SQL/MM, do not support correlation queries. For example, these systems are unable to handle image queries like "give me all images where a person stands in front of a car." Lack of such a support might increase the number of undesired matches for CBR queries. For example, if a user wants to find all images showing red automobiles and if each automobile has a person standing in front of it, the color, shape, and position of the person (skin and clothing) will cause color and shape similarities to be detected. This might reduce the importance of color and shape similarities between automobiles because part of the automobile is behind the person and thus not visible. Some MMDBMSs, such as the DISIMA[136] system, overcome this shortcoming. For instance, DISIMA accepts queries in MOQL[135] that extend OQL by adding new predicate expressions, which allow the specification of correlation queries.

4.5.3 Multimedia Query Optimization

In addition to the limited functionality of the proposed query-processing strategies discussed above, effective query optimization mechanisms for multimedia databases are rarely provided. There have been quite a number of proposals of object-oriented and object-relational query algebras, such as the AQUA algebra[142] and the KOLA algebra.[143,144] Most of them also handle the problem of query optimization in the presence of methods or foreign functions.[145–147] These later works mainly focus on the appropriate position of the method evaluation within a query execution plan. They are, however, less practical for managing multimedia data and multimedia index structures. This is because of the large data volume introduced by these kinds of media and also because of their complicated access functionality by feature vectors and the complex searching and matching algorithms involved in similarity searching.

There have been some systems introduced that focus on similarity-based query optimization. Adali et al.,[148] for example, propose a similarity algebra at a higher abstraction level that integrates heterogeneous similarity measures coming from different similarity implementations into one common framework. For instance, it allows the formulation and optimization of a query returning the union of the best 10 matches from a black-and-white and a color image database. The framework is implemented on top of an integrated search engine. However, it does not provide the implementation level required for processing a multimedia join through the NN search method, nor does it deal with combined multimedia and relational queries.

Ciaccia et al.[149] developed recently the algebra SAME[W]. This algebra introduces, in addition to the operators introduced in Adali et al.,[148] user preferences such as weights and also captures imprecision in feature representations. However, implementation issues of the complex operations introduced are not addressed.

Possibilities for optimizing complex multimedia expressions were introduced by Stonebraker[134] for simple multimedia join processing. Stonebraker gives some initial optimization ideas. For example, he observes that the traditional select-push rule, which is to push the select operator as close to the base table as possible, might no longer apply to MM query optimization.

Let us imagine a query to be composed of a highly selective, nonmultimedia join between an image table, "Picture," and a traditional table, "Example," and a select operator, "redness(pict)<0.1," on the instances pict of the table "Picture." Assume further that the redness has to be computed on the fly (i.e., no feature vector was stored in the database). Looking then at the processing complexity, one will observe that the computation of the redness of a picture is a computationally intensive operation, which will be better if applied to the result of the join. The reason is that the result of the join produces fewer images than the base table, "Picture," contains.

This example gives a flavor of the complexity of query optimization in multimedia databases. Actually, optimization strategies for complex multimedia processing, including the optimization of compound expressions of relational and multimedia operators, is an open research area.

Finally, it has to be noted that multimedia processing implemented on top of an ORDBMS can deal only with well-defined queries, including the NN-search, where users can specify exactly the nature of their query intentions. However, knowledge of the intentions is sometimes not available, at the level of exactness required by the query interface. Therefore, fuzzy querying is required where the properties of query objects are ambiguous or unclear.

In this context, the CHITRA system uses a fuzzy object query language (FOQL)[150,151] that is an extension of OQL. Another alternative to a well-defined query statement is the query formulation through query refinement. The Multimedia Analysis and Retrieval System (MARS)[152,153] system allows complex query formulation by an intelligent query refinement tool. The query processor of the MARS system uses a query expansion approach[154] in which relevant objects are added to a new query representation. However, this approach is user-interaction centric and does not allow the declarative definition of similarity-based joins.

4.6 Multimedia Database Management System Products

The first MMDBMSs rely mainly on the operating system for storing and querying files. These were ad hoc systems that served mostly as repositories.

The mid-1990s saw a first wave of commercial, implemented from scratch, and full-fledged MMDBMS. Some of them were MediaDB, now MediaWay,[155] JASMINE,[156] and ITASCA, which is the commercial successor of ORION.[157] They were all able to handle diverse kinds of data and provided mechanisms for querying, retrieving, inserting, and updating data. Most of these products disappeared from the market after some years of existence, and only a few of them continued and adapted themselves successfully to the hardware and software advances as well as to application changes. For instance, *MediaWay* provided early very specific support for a wide variety of different media types. Specifically, different media file formats varying from images, and video to PowerPoint documents,[155] can be managed segmented, linked, and searched. Information on the database management system available can be found at http://www.mediaway.com.

In a second wave, commercial systems were proposed that handle multimedia content by providing complex object types for various kinds of media. The object-oriented style provides the facility to define new data types and operators appropriate for the new kinds of media.[2] Therefore, broadly used commercial MMDBMSs are extensible ORDBMSs.

The most advanced solutions are marketed by Oracle 9i, IBM DB2, and IBM Informix. We already discussed the main characteristics of the Oracle interMedia and the related ORDImage, ORDAudio, and ORDVideo object types at several places in this book and we, therefore, refer the reader to Section 4.5 for further details.

The *IBM DB2 Universal Database Extenders* extend the ORDBMS management to images, video, audio, and spatial objects. All these data types are modeled, accessed, and manipulated in a common framework. Features of the multimedia extenders include importing and exporting multimedia objects and their attributes into and out of a database, controlling access to nontraditional types of data with the same level of protection as traditional data, and browsing or playing objects retrieved from the database.

For instance, the DB2 Image Extender defines the distinct data type DB2IMAGE with associated user-defined functions for storing and manipulating image files (http://www-3.ibm.com/software/data/db2/extenders/image.htm). The actual contents of the image file that DB2Image describes can be stored as binary large objects (BLOBs) or outside of the database in a file system. The following SQL-insert statement shows how an image is stored into a column named "image," in a table named "Picture." In this example, the content of the image comes from a server file and stored as a BLOB in the database:

```
INSERT INTO Picture (image) VALUES(

DB2IMAGE (

CURRENT SERVER, /* database server name located in a
    DB2 environment variable */

'pisa.jpg', /* source_file */

'JPG',                  /* source_format */

1,                      /* 1=BLOB, 2=file pointer */

'my Image File'    /* comment */

)

)
```

The DB2 Image Extender provides similarity search functionality based on the QBIC technology[108] (in detail in Section 4.4) for images stored in the DB2IMAGE type. The QBIC technology provides the ability to query, or search, for images based on their content. Using this query mechanism, one may specify image content features, such as color values, and another image file as input to a query. These features are matched against the contents of the images stored in the database, and a score is assigned to each image. A score is a double-precision floating-point value between 0 and 1 that indicates how closely an image's features match those specified in the QBIC query. The lower the score, the closer the match.

DB2IMAGE columns must be explicitly enabled for QBIC queries by specifying on which image features one wants to be able to query. For each column enabled, the DB2 Image Extender analyzes the images in that column and stores their features in a QBIC catalog. These features are stored as additional administrative files that are maintained by the DB2 Image Extender.

The image features that can be used in QBIC queries are average color, histogram color distribution, positional color values, and the texture of an image. This is in line with the SQL/MM standard, as described in Section 4.3; however, different query syntax has been defined by IBM. For instance, the following SQL statement shows an example of executing a QBIC query that ranks each image in the image column based on how closely its average color matches red:

```
SELECT CONTENTS(image),

QBScoreFROMStr('averageColor=<255,0,0>', image) AS
SCORE

FROM signs ORDER BY SCORE
```

The IBM Informix DataBlades provides similar multimedia search functionality as the IBM DB2 Multimedia Extenders, and details are not given here. Note that IBM Informix is the commercial development of the Postgres Database, which is the result of a research project at the University of California–Berkeley that was initiated by Stonebraker and Rowe.[158]

In addition to the commercial products, several research projects have implemented full-fledged multimedia database systems. Recently, successfully terminated projects include the following:

MIRROR,[159] an acronym for multimedia information retrieval reducing information overload, developed at the University of Twente, is a research MMDBMS that is developed to better understand the kind of data management that is required in the context of multimedia digital libraries. Its main features are an integrated approach to both content and traditional structured data management. MIRROR provides probabilistic inference mechanisms during the interaction with the user,[160] which has been adopted from cognitive theories. MIRROR is implemented on top of the ORDBMS Monet database system. More information on MIRROR may be obtained at http://wwwhome.cs.utwente.nl/~arjen/mmdb.html. On top of MIRROR runs the Acoi system (http://monetdb.cwi.nl/acoi/), which is a platform for the indexing and retrieval of video and image data. The system provides a plug-in architecture to subsequently index multimedia objects using various feature extraction algorithms.[161] Acoi relies on the COBRA (content-based retrieval) video data model (only low-level descriptors). COBRA introduces a feature grammar to describe the low-level persistent metadata and the dependencies between the extraction mechanisms.[162] Exhibit 4.13 shows the system architecture of the MMDBMS product.

In addition, the system distinguishes four distinct layers within video content: the raw data, the feature, the object, and the event layer. The object and event layers are concept layers consisting of entities characterized by spatial and temporal dimensions, respectively. This goes in line with the concepts of the MPEG-7 standards; however, no standardized

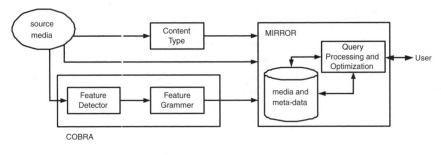

Exhibit 4.13. Architecture of the Acoi/MIRROR System.[161]

entities are employed, and interoperable exchange of metadata is therefore not enabled. A description of the whole system, including a Web demonstration, may be found at http://wwwhome.cs.utwente.nl/~blokh/ VLDB2001/.

DISIMA,[135,136] developed at the University of Alberta, is an image database system that enables content-based querying.

Exhibit 4.14 shows the system architecture of DISIMA.

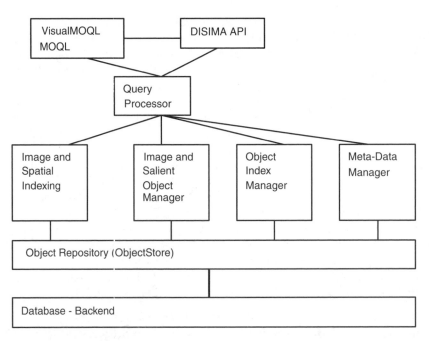

Exhibit 4.14. Architecture of the Distributed Multimedia Database Management System (DISIMA).[135,136]

The prototype was implemented on top of the OODBMS ObjectStore. Queries are specified in the query language MOQL (or Visual MOQL for images only), which relies on a new type of concept model for both image and spatial applications. The associated query languages (MOQL and Visual MOQL), extending OQL, allow spatio-temporal querying as well as the definition of a presentation specification. For instance, the following simple query allows us to find all images in which a person appears (assuming that an Image table m and Person table p is defined beforehand).

```
SELECT m

FROM Images m, Persons p

WHERE m contains p
```

The distributed architecture of DISIMA involves different image sources including servers and file systems. Please refer to http://db.uwaterloo.ca/ ~ddbms/projects/multimedia/ for more information on DISIMA, a Web demonstration, and related projects.

The third wave, that is, currently running projects, addresses the needs of applications for richer semantic content. Most of them rely, thereby, on the new MPEG standards, MPEG-4 and MPEG-7. Representative running projects include, among others, the European Project ASSAVID, described in Section 4.1; the MARS project carried out at the University of Illinois at Urbana-Champaign; and the SMOOTH multimedia database and the MPEG-7 MDC developed by us.

MARS[152–154] realizes an integrated multimedia information retrieval and database management system that supports multimedia information as first-class objects suited for storage and retrieval based on their semantic content. MARS proposes a set of tools for an MMDBMS back end, as shown in Exhibit 4.15.

The MARS project includes the conception of a multimedia data model for content indexing and retrieval and for database management. The presented multimedia data model influenced the development of the descriptors in the MDS of MPEG-7.[163] MARS is a from-scratch management system, based on a query refinement processing.[153] Furthermore, a table of contents (ToC) extraction mechanism for videos has been developed.[164] A hybrid tree data structure to support high-dimension feature indexing in multimedia databases[61,165] has also been realized. For the multimedia information retrieval, an adapted relevance feedback approach that is able to learn users' information needs in image databases is proposed.[152,154] More information on MARS may be obtained from http://www-mars.ics.uci.edu. A Web demo page is available at http://www-db.ics.uci.edu/pages/demos/ index.shtml.

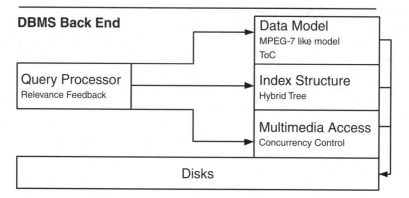

Exhibit 4.15. Set of tools proposed in the Multimedia Analysis and Retrieval System Projects (MARS).[152–154]

Here we will detail two research MMDBMS developed by us: first, the SMOOTH multimedia database that relies on a metadatabase implementation, and second, the MDC that extends Oracle 9i with multimedia extensions relying on the MPEG-7 standard.

4.6.1 Use Case Study 1: The SMOOTH Multimedia Database

The SMOOTH[26,87] prototype of a distributed multimedia database system integrates a query, navigation, and annotation framework for video media material driven by the content of a metadatabase. This metadatabase implements the semantic and structural part of our multimedia data model VIDEX, as presented in Section 4.3.

Exhibit 4.16 displays the general systems' architecture of SMOOTH. The video server provides selective access to the physical video streams (the Oracle Video Server with the supported protocol types UDP [User Datagram Protocol] and RTP [Real-Time Transport Protocol] was used).

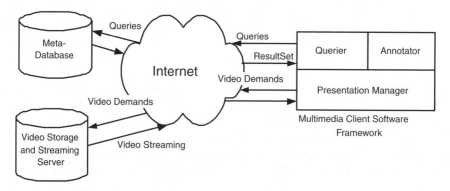

Exhibit 4.16. SMOOTH distributed multimedia system scenario.

As described in Section 4.3 and Exhibit 4.9, the core of the metadatabase are the base classes: events, objects, persons, and locations. These classes are subclasses of a general ContentObject, which may refer to low-level motion objects. Application-specific classes are added by declaring subclasses (content classes) of the base classes. Furthermore, the metadatabase contains classes for a detailed structuring of video streams and for relating the instances of the semantic classes to the media segments.

The interfaces provide means to annotate, query, and navigate through video material. The core components of the client include the annotator, querier, presentation manager, and navigator. The annotator allows the structuring of the video into segments and the annotation of high-level content objects. The querier follows a text-based, structured query specification technique. It enables the definition of video queries by specifying conditions on content objects and the specification of semantic and temporal relations to other content objects. The results of a query are presented in a compact form; that is, server address, length, video description, and so forth. In the presentation manager, the user can compose presentations, with temporal constraints, from the query results. The navigator allows the navigation through the contents of the metadatabase.

Querier: The user is able to submit query conditions through a combination of fill-in forms, menu selections, and text fields. Furthermore, query refinement, query storage, and a replay mechanism are provided. For instance, in our soccer application, queries such as, "Find all video shots, where the player Lothar Matthäus scores a goal" can be specified. Exhibit 4.17 shows an extract of the SMOOTH query interface that allows the specification of this query. We need to declare two conditions, one for the subclass "Player" of "Person" and one for the subclass of "Goal" of "Event." Results may be displayed directly, as shown in Exhibit 4.17 or through a presentation dialog, seen later. In many cases, it is useful to specify a temporal constraint between two events; for example, a goal should strictly occur after the pass. This temporal constraint between the two events "Goal" and "Pass" is entered in the "Event" dialog, shown in Exhibit 4.18.

Annotator: The underlying multimedia data model is generic and could lead to complex annotation processes. Therefore, SMOOTH provides an annotation tool to help the user annotate the videos and refer to already annotated units for reuse of information. For instance, Exhibit 4.19 shows a typical annotation situation. The already annotated segments are displayed in the upper panel, allowing the definition of larger segments in the bottom panel; for example, a "Scene" can be built from two "Shots." In addition, text fields and menu selections are provided to enter the content information for the events.

Presentation Manager: The query results can be composed into a presentation in the dialog presentation manager shown in Exhibit 4.20. In the

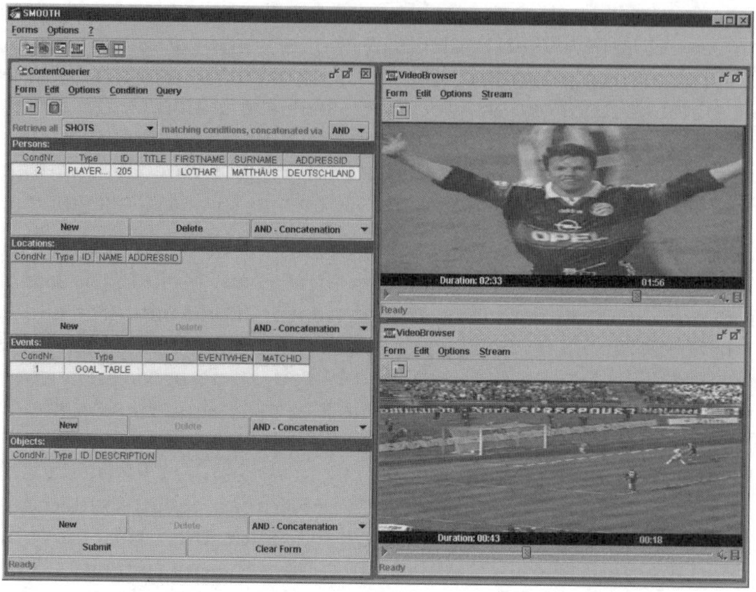

Exhibit 4.17. SMOOTH query dialog.

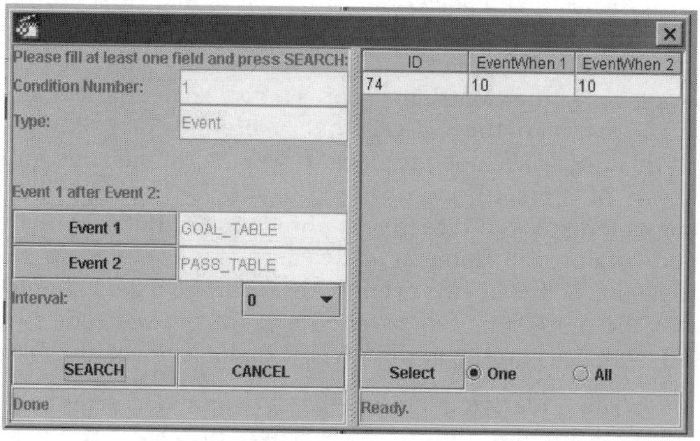

Exhibit 4.18. Specification of a temporal constraint between two events in SMOOTH.

upper-left corner, the query results are displayed as beams with respective length in a pool ready to be used for a presentation composition. These query results are then dragged and dropped from the pool to be arranged along a time chart. Users may specify complex presentation scenarios by imposing temporal constraints on the video delivery. Temporal constraints comprise precedence constraints related to the ordering of the videos and

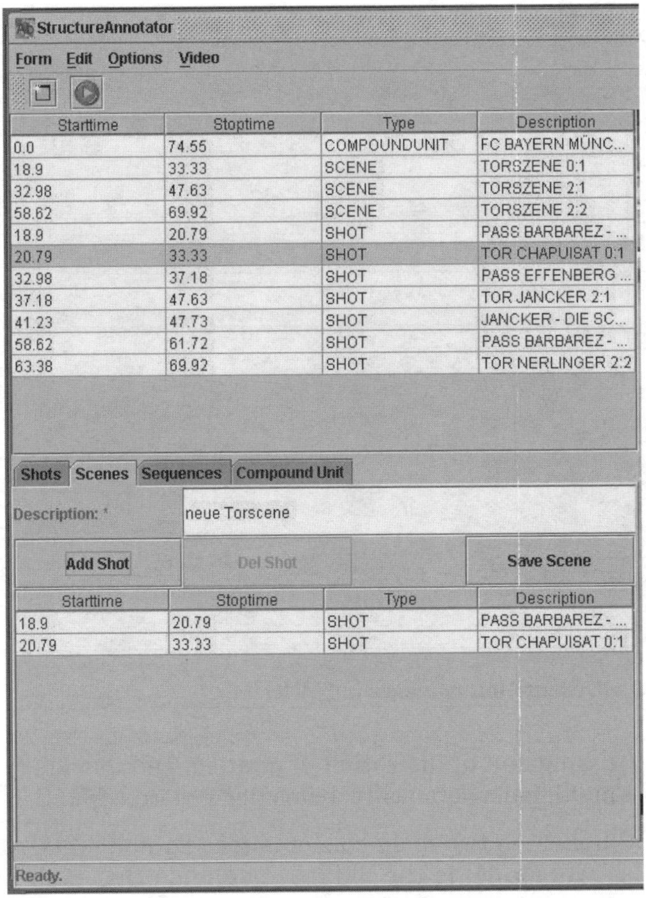

Exhibit 4.19. Extract of the annotator frame in SMOOTH.

delay constraints related to the waiting time between the videos. For instance, in Exhibit 4.20, we specify that the second video starts in Window 1 immediately after the completion of the first video. Then, upon the completion of the second video (after 28 seconds), two new videos are displayed in parallel in Windows 2 and 3. Exhibit 4.20 snapshots the situation after 32 seconds with two running videos in the bottom Windows 2 and 3, whereas the upper Widow 1 shows the last frame of the second video. The server addresses, ports, stream identifiers and time intervals of the requested video units are obtained from the result sets of the video queries.

4.6.2 Use Case Study 2: The MPEG-7 MDC

The MPEG-7 Multimedia Data Cartridge (MDC)[166,167] is a system extension of the Oracle 9i DBMS providing a multimedia query language, access to

Exhibit 4.20. Presentation manager in SMOOTH.

media, processing and optimization of queries, and indexing capacities relying on a multimedia database schema derived from MPEG-7.

The MDC builds on two main concepts (see Exhibit 4.21). At first, the Multimedia Data Model is the database schema that is derived from MPEG-7 descriptions. It is realized with the help of the extensible type system of the cartridge environment; that is, descriptors in the MPEG-7 schema are mapped to object types and tables. Second, the Multimedia Indexing Framework (MIF), which provides an extensible indexing environment for multimedia retrieval. The indexing framework is integrated into the query language and enables efficient multimedia retrieval.

The Multimedia Schema of MDC relies on the one hand on the structural and semantic parts of the MPEG-7 standard (high-level descriptions). On the other hand, object types for the MPEG-7 low-level descriptors, such as color, shape, and texture, are provided and linked to the high-level descriptions. This enables one to retrieve multimedia data not only by low-level features but also by semantics in combination with low-level characteristics.

Exhibit 4.22 displays an extract of the multimedia schema derived from MPEG-7. It shows the mapping of an MPEG-7 StillRegionType, which is a delegate for images in MPEG-7 (i.e., StillRegion denotes complete images and parts of them) to object-relational database types. In the database

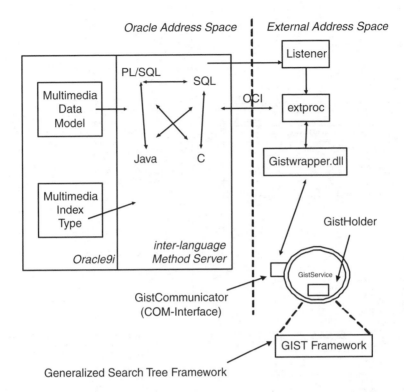

Exhibit 4.21. Architecture of the MPEG-7 multimedia data cartridge.[167]

schema, an object type of the same name (StillRegionType) is created. Some of its attributes are declared as separate object types, and some are defined by the specific SYS.XMLType.

The decision of which type to use was carried on importance of the description for a possible query. For instance, the attribute with type TextAnnotationType was chosen to be detailed further because it is of importance for free-text search in the database, whereas the UsageInformation was chosen to be declared as SYS.XMLType. The latter type is suspected to contain only a little information for a concrete image, because meta-information on the usage may already be declared at the MPEG-7 root level; furthermore, it spans a DS that might contain many different descriptions with similar content. This would lead to many database object and tables, probably containing little content. Therefore, it was decided to store the subtree of the MPEG-7 document containing UsageInformation directly in the database type or table using the XMLType. Note that all information not retained in object types is not lost for querying. The reason is that the XMLType provides XPATH query functionality that enables one to reach elements and attributes of this document by XPATH. In other

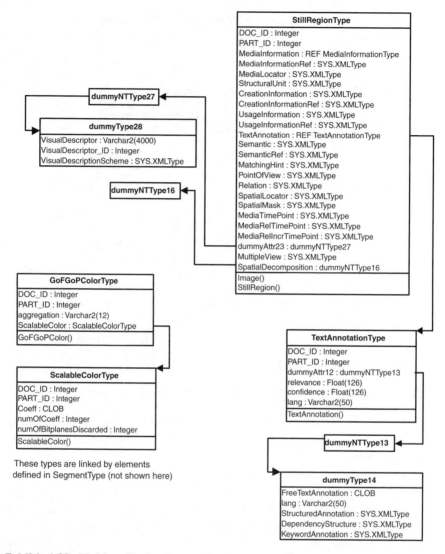

Exhibit 4.22. Multimedia database schema of the MPEG-7 multimedia data cartridge.[167]

words, with a combined SELECT and XPATH query, any information may be reached.

However, as pointed out earlier, important information can be reached directly through object navigation, as, for instance, from StillRegion to TextAnnotation.

Other explicitly used object types include MediaInformation (MediaInformationType, MediaProfile, MediaFormat, etc.). These types describe information on the coding, media attributes, locations, and physical structure of the data.

Semantic content of an image may be obtained through the semantic reference linking to a SemanticBagType, which is an abstract root object type for concrete semantic indexing classes, such as events, places, and time.

Finally, the decomposition of the image (structural aspect) is specified by following the reference of the SpatialDecomposition attribute in the StillRegionType. Further important object types are ScalableColorType and ColorStrucutureType. They are used to store the feature vectors of the color histograms extracted from the images described by the StillRegionType and are indexed with the help of our MIF extension.

The MIF offers advanced indexing services to the MMDBMS. It is generic in a way that new index types may be added without changing the interface definitions. The MIF is divided into three modules (as seen in Exhibit 4.21). Each module, especially the GistService and the Oracle Enhancement, may be used on its own and may be distributed over the network.

The GistService is the main part and is realized in the external address space. It offers services for index management based on the Generalized Search Trees (GiST)[52,168] (e.g., X-tree and SR-tree; see Section 4.2) and on access methods not relying on balanced trees (VA files). This service is split into two components: GistCommunicator and GistHolder. The GistCommunicator is a COM-object (component object model) used for interprocess communication between the database (by passing through the GistWrapper shared library) and the implemented access methods. Thus, the GistCommunicator supplies the necessary functionality (e.g., creating, inserting, deleting) for accessing the index structures. The GistHolder manages all currently running index trees and the accesses to them. Each index tree is identified through a global and unique identifier, which is forwarded to the accessing process.

The integration of MIF into the MDS is done via the index extension mechanisms of Oracle 9i. For each new index, a new Oracle indextype has to be defined, but the interface to the Gist remains unchanged.

4.7 Summary

Since the first multimedia database system was developed in 1987 (ORION),[157] the area and applications have experienced tremendous growth. As described in the previous section, all popular commercial database systems propose multimedia extenders to store, access, and query multimedia material and its metadata. Especially with the rapid development of network technology, multimedia database systems get more tremendous development, and multimedia information exchange becomes very important. Here, the reliance on standard technology is crucial to guarantee the interoperability of a multimedia database system and, thus, its commercial success. Hence, from the multimedia database viewpoint, the following issues have to be considered.

4.7.1 Issues on Multimedia Data Modeling

A multimedia data model must deal with the issue of representing the multimedia objects; that is, designing the high and low-level abstractions of the media data to facilitate various operations. These operations may include media object selection, insertion, editing, indexing, browsing, querying, retrieval, and communication. A good data model should fulfill the following issues:

- It is necessary to model and store media components in the database. Its storage mechanism will play an important factor affecting the performance of a multimedia system.
- A representation should be provided for the logical media structure. It is essential to represent this structure explicitly both for querying and for representation.
- Semantic meaning should be modeled and linked to low-level characteristics and the structure of the media.
- The metadata necessary for the operation of the system components needs to be determined and stored in the database.
- It is necessary to rely on international standards, for example, MPEG-7, to guarantee interoperability for data sharing and data exchange.

4.7.2 Issues on Multimedia Indexing, Querying, and Presentation

The key functionality in a multimedia database is how to access and how to exchange multimedia information effectively. No matter what data model is used or data store mechanisms are employed, the most important thing is how to retrieve and communicate continuous and noncontinuous media with a short real-time constraint. The key to the retrieval process is similarity between two objects. The content of the object is analyzed and used to evaluate specified selection predicates, a process called content-based retrieval. For instance, features described for visual retrieval include measures expressing the color distribution of the image or video. Other features express the texture and the composition of the image. An image query is translated into a point query in some multidimensional feature space. The similarity between a query and a database object is estimated using a distance function. The efficiency of the similarity search can be significantly improved by the use of multidimensional indexing structures.

To retrieve multimedia data from a database system, a query language must be provided. A multimedia query language must have the ability to handle complex spatial and temporal relationships. A powerful query language should have to deal with keywords, an index of keywords, and the semantic contents of multimedia objects.

The key to efficient communication is to rely on standards for communicating metadata and associated media data. An important contribution is the development of the system parts of MPEG-7 and the file format of MPEG-21.

Finally, the issues considered above on data model, storage retrieval and query should not be limited to atomic multimedia data such as image, audio, or video. It is also interesting to retrieve composite objects, such as when we read news text and, at the same time, open a window to see video documentaries. Hence, we need the ability to deal with several atomic multimedia data and media data presentations at the same time. MPEG-21 goes in this direction with the provision of the notion of a Digital Item, which surely will influence the multimedia database world in the future. In addition, and related again to MPEG-21, it is important for a multimedia database system to use multiple representations of data for different users and profiles, for intellectual property management and for adaptation purposes. In this context, the next chapter will detail technologies used in a distributed multimedia database environment.

References

1. Lu, G., *Multimedia Database Management Systems*, Artech House, 1999.
2. Subrahmanian, V.S., *Principles of Multimedia Database Systems*, Morgan Kaufman Press, 1998.
3. Ono, A., Amano, M., and Hakaridani, M., A flexible content-based image retrieval system with combined scene description keywords, in *Proceedings of the IEEE Conference on Multimedia Computing and Systems*, Hiroshima, Japan, June 1996, pp. 201–208.
4. Sebe, N. and Lew, M.S., Color-based retrieval, *Pattern Recog. Lett.*, 22, 223–230, 2001.
5. Deng, Y., Manjunath, B.S., Kenney, C., Moore, M.S., and Shin, H., An efficient color representation for image retrieval, *IEEE Trans. Image Process.*, 10, 140–147, 2001.
6. Adjeroh, D.A. and Lee, M.C., On ratio-based color indexing, *IEEE Trans. Image Process.*, 10, 36–48, 2001.
7. Berens, J., Finlayson, G.D., and Qiu, G., Image indexing using compressed colour histograms, *IEEE Vision Image Signal Process.*, 147, 349–355, 2000.
8. Chahir, Y. and Chen, L., Searching images on the basis of color homogeneous objects and their spatial relationship, *J. Visual Comm. Image Representation*, 11, 302–326, 2000.
9. Syeda-Mahmood, T. and Petkovic, D., On describing color and shape information in images, *Signal Process. Image Comm.*, 16, 15–31, 2000.
10. Berretti, S., del Bimbo, A., and Pala, P., Indexed retrieval by shape appearance, *IEEE Vision Image Signal Process.*, 147, 356–362, 2000.
11. Huet, B. and Hancock, E.R., Shape recognition from large image libraries by inexact graph matching, *Pattern Recogn. Lett.*, 20, 1259–1269, 1999.
12. Wu, P., Manjunath, B.S., Newsam, S.D., and Shin, H.D., A texture descriptor for browsing and similarity retrieval, *Signal Process. Image Comm.*, 16, 33–43, 2000.
13. Tao, B. and Dickinson, B.W., Texture recognition and image retrieval using gradient indexing, *J. Visual Comm. Image Representation*, 11, 327–342, 2000.

14. Zhong, D., Kumar, R., and Chang, S.-F., Personalized video: real-time personalized sports video filtering and summarization, in *Proc. of ACM Multimedia 2001*, AMC Press, Ottowa, 2001, pp. 623–625.

15. Snoek, C.G.M. and Worring, M., Multimodal Video Indexing: A Review of the State-of-the-Art. Multimedia Tools and Applications, to appear; also available as ISIS TR, Vol. 2001-20, December 2001.

16. Zhang, T. and Kuo, C.C. Jay, *Content-Based Audio Classification and Retrieval for Audiovisual Data Parsing*, Kluwer, Dordrecht.

17. Hampapur, A., Semantic video indexing: approach and issues, *ACM Sigmod Rec.*, 28, 32–39, 1999.

18. Lee, M.S., Yang, Y.M., and Lee, S.W., Automatic video parsing using shot boundary detection and camera operation analysis, *Pattern Recog.*, 34, 711–719, 2001.

19. Dimitrova, N., McGee, T., and Elenbaas, H., Video keyframe extraction and filtering: a keyframe is not a keyframe to everyone, in *Proceedings of the 6th International Conference on Information and Knowledge Management (CIKM-97)*, Las Vegas, NV, November 1997, ACM Press, pp. 113–120.

20. Dufaux, F., Key frame selection to represent a video, in *Proceedings of the IEEE International Conference on Image Processing*, Vancouver, Canada, September 2000.

21. Zhang, H.J., Kankanhalli, A., and Smoliar, S.W., Automatic partitioning of full-motion video, *ACM Multimedia Syst.*, 1, 10–28, 1993.

22. Boreczsky, J.S. and Rowe, L.A., A comparison of video shot boundary detection techniques, *J. Electron. Imaging*, 5, 122–128, 1996.

23. Ahanger, G. and Little, T.D.C., A survey of technologies for parsing and indexing digital video, *J. Visual Comm. Image Representation*, 7, 28–43, 1996.

24. Patel, N.V. and Sethi, I., Video segmentation for video data management, in *The Handbook of Multimedia Information Management*, Grosky, W.I., Jain, R., and Mehrotra, R., Eds., Prentice-Hall, Englewood Cliffs, NJ, 1997.

25. Yu, H.H. and Wolf, W., A hierarchical multiresolution video shot transition detection scheme, *Comp. Vision Image Understanding*, 75, 196–213, 1999.

26. Kosch, H., Tusch, R., Böszörményi, L., Bachlechner, A., Dörflinger, B., Hofbauer, C., Riedler, C., Lang, M., and Hanin, C., SMOOTH—a distributed multimedia database system, in *Proceedings of the International VLDB Conference*, Rome, Italy, September 2001, pp. 713–714.

27. Schonfeld, D. and Lelescu, D., Vortex: video retrieval and tracking from compressed multimedia databases—multiple object tracking from MPEG-2 bit stream, *J. Visual Comm. Image Representation*, 11, 154–182, 2000.

28. Milanese, R., Deguillaume, F., and Jacot-Descombes, A., Efficient segmentation and camera motion indexing of compressed video, *Real-Time Imaging*, 5, 231–241, 1999.

29. Rui, Y., Huang, T.S., and Mehrotra, S., Exploring video structure beyond the shots, in *Proceedings of the IEEE International Conference on Multimedia Computing and Systems*, Austin, Texas, June 1998, pp. 237–240.

30. Toklu, C., Liou, S.P., and Das, M., Video abstract: a hybrid approach to generate semantically meaningful video summaries, in *Proceedings of the IEEE International Conference on Multimedia and Exposition*, New York, July 2000, pp. 57–61.

31. Manske, K., Mühlhäuser, M., Vogel, S., and Goldberg, M., OBVI: hierarchical 3D video-browsing, in *Proceedings of the 6th ACM International Conference on Multimedia (Multimedia-98)*, New York, September 1998, ACM Press, pp. 369–374.

32. Sawhney, H., Ayer, A., and Gorkani, M., Model based 2D and 3D dominant motion estimation for mosaicing and video representation, in *Proceedings of the International Conference on Computer Vision*, Cambridge, MA, 1995, IEEE CS Press, pp. 583–590.

33. Tzanetakis, G. and Cook, P., Multifeature audio segmentation for browsing and annotation, *IEEE Workshop on Applications of Signal Processing to Audio and Acoustics*, New Paltz, New York, October 1999.

34. Rossignol, S., Rodet, X., Soumagne, J., Collette, J.-L., and Depalle, P., Feature extraction and temporal segmentation of acoustic signals, in *Proceedings of the International ICMC: International Computer Music Conference*, Ann Arbor, MI, October 1998.
35. Eren, P.E. and Tekal, A.M., Keyframe-based bi-directional 2-d mesh representation for video object tracking and manipulation, in *Proceedings of the IEEE International Conference on Image Processing*, Kobe, Japan, 1999, IEEE CS Press, pp. 968–972.
36. Eng, H.L. and Ma, K.K., Spatio-temporal segmentation of moving video objects over mpeg compressed domain, in *Proceedings of the IEEE International Conference on Multimedia and Exposition*, New York, July 2000, pp. 1531–1534.
37. Jang, D.S., Kim, G.Y., and Choi, H.I., Model-based tracking of moving object, *Pattern Recog.*, 30, 999–1008, 1997.
38. Carson, C. et al., Blobworld: image segmentation using expectation-maximization and its application to image querying, *IEEE Trans. Pattern Anal. Machine Intell.*, 24, 1026–1038, 2002.
39. Chang, Y.L., Kamel, W., and Alfonso, R., Integrated image and speech analysis for content-based video indexing, in *Proceedings of the 3rd IEEE International Conference on Multimedia Computing and Systems*, Hiroshima, Japan, 1996, pp. 306–313.
40. Assfalg, J., Bertini, M., Colombo, C., and Del Bimbo, A., Semantic characterization of visual content for sports videos annotation, in *Proc. of Multimedia Databases and Image Communication*, Amalfi, September 2001, Springer-Verlag, Heidelberg, LNCS 2184, pp. 179–191.
41. Okada, K. and von der Malsburg, C., Automatic video indexing with incremental gallery creation: integration of recognition and knowledge acquisition, in *Proceedings of the Third International Conference on Knowledge-Based Intelligent Information Engineering Systems*, Adelaide, August 31, 1999, pp. 431–434.
42. Ide, I., Yamamoto, K., and Tanaka, H., Automatic video indexing based on shot classification, in *Proceedings of the International Conference on Advanced Multimedia Content Processing*, Osaka, 1999, Springer-Verlag, Heidelberg, LNCS 1554, pp. 87–102.
43. Correia, P. and Pereira, F., The role of analysis in content based video coding and indexing, *Signal Process.*, 66, 125–142, 1998.
44. Chen, S.-C., Kashyap, R.L., and Ghafoor, A., *Semantic Models for Multimedia Database Searching and Browsing*, Kluwer, Dordrecht, 2000.
45. Smith, J. and Chang, S.F., Visually searching the web for content, *IEEE MultiMedia*, 4, 12–20, 1997.
46. Jorgensen, C., Jaimes, A., Benitez, A.B., and Chang, S.-F., A conceptual framework and research for classifying visual descriptors, *J. Am. Soc. Info. Sci.*, 52(11), 938–947, 2001.
47. Benitez, B., Chang, S.-F., and Smith, J.R., IMKA: a multimedia organization system combining perceptual and semantic knowledge, *Proceeding of the 9th ACM International Conference on Multimedia (ACM MM-2001)*, Ottawa, September 30–October 5, 2001, pp. 630–631.
48. Zhong, D. and Chang, S.-F., Structure analysis of sports video using domain models, *IEEE Conference on Multimedia and Exhibition*, Tokyo, August 22–25, 2001.
49. Rehm, E., Representing Internet streaming media with MPEG-7, in *Proceedings of the ACM Multimedia 2000 Workshop Standards, Interoperability and Practice: Who Needs Standards Anyway?*, New York, November 4, 2000, ACMPress, pp. 93–106.
50. Forsyth, D. and Fleck, M., Automatic detection of human nudes, *Int. J. Comput. Vision*, 32, 63–77, 1999.
51. Wang et al., Automatic linguistic indexing of pictures by a statistical modeling approach, *IEEE Trans. Pattern Anal. Machine Intelligence*, 25(10), 14–20, 2003.
52. Minka, T.P. and Picard, R.W., Interactive learning using a "Society of Models," *Pattern Recognition*, 30, 1997.
53. Roussopoulos, N., Kelley, S., and Vincent, F., Nearest neighbor queries, in *Proceedings of ACM-SIGMOD Conference on Management of Data*, San Jose, June 1995, pp. 71–79.

54. Berchtold, S., Bohm, C., Keim, D.A., and Kriegel, H.P., A cost model for nearest neighbor search in high-dimensional data space, in *Proceedings of the ACM PODS Conference*, Tucson, May 1997, pp. 78–86.
55. Pramanik, S., Alexander, S., and Li, J., An efficient searching algorithm for approximate nearest neighbor queries in high dimensions, in *IEEE International Conference on Multimedia Computing and Systems*, Vol. 1, Florence, Italy, June 1999, pp. 865–869.
56. Li, J.Z., Özsu, M.T., Szafron, D., and Oria, V., MOQL: a multimedia object query language, in *3rd International Workshop on Multimedia Information Systems*, Como, September 1997, Springer-Verlag, Heidelberg, LNCS Series, pp. 19–28.
57. Excalibur Image DataBlade Module User's Guide, Version 1.2, Informix Press, 1999.
58. Oracle9i interMedia Audio, Image, and Video User's Guide and Reference, http://technet.oracle.com.
59. Evangelidis, G., Lomet, D., and Salzberg, B., The hB tree: a multi-attribute index supporting concurrency, recovery and node consolidation. *VLDB J.*, 6, 1–25, 1997.
60. Ciaccia, P., Patella, M., and Zezula, P., M-Tree: an efficient access method for similarity search in metric spaces, in *Proceedings of the VLDB Conference*, Athens, August 1997, pp. 426–435.
61. Chakrabarti, K. and Mehrotra, S., The hybrid tree: an index structure for high dimensional feature spaces, in *Proceedings of the International Conference on Data Engineering (ICDE)*, Sydney, March 1999, pp. 440–447.
62. Cha, G.-H. and Chung, C.-W., The GC-Tree: a high-dimensional index structure for similarity search in image databases, *IEEE Trans. Multimedia*, 4, 235–247, 2002.
63. Tao, Y., Papadias, D., and Shen, Q., Continuous nearest neighbor search. *International Conference on VLDB 2002*, Hong Kong, August 2002, pp. 287–298.
64. White, D.A. and Jain, R., Similarity indexing with the SS-tree, in *Proceedings of the 12th IEEE Intl. Conference on Data Engineering*, New Orleans, February 1996, pp. 516–523.
65. Kurniawati, R., Jin, J.S., and Shepherd, J.A., The SS+-tree: an improved index structure for similarity searches in a high-dimensional feature space, in *Proceedings of the SPIE storage and Retrieval of Image and Video Databases*, San Jose, February 1997, pp. 110–120.
66. Cha, G.-H., Zhu, X., Petkovic, D., and Chung, C.-W., An efficient indexing method for nearest neighbor searches in high-dimensional image databases, *IEEE Trans. Multimedia*, 4, 76–87, 2002.
67. Guttman, A., R-trees: a dynamic index structure for spatial searching, in *Proceedings of ACM SIGMOD Conference of Management of Data*, Boston, June 1984, pp. 47–57.
68. Berchtold, S., Keim, D.A., and Kriegel, H.-P., The X-tree: an indexing structure for high-dimensional data, in *Proceedings of the VLDB Conference*, Bombay, September 1996, pp. 28–39.
69. Lin, E.T., Omiecinski, E.R., and Yalamanchili, S., Large join optimization on a hypercube multiprocessor. *IEEE Trans. Knowl. Data Eng.*, 6(2), 304–315, 1994.
70. Robinson, J.T., The K-D-B tree: a search structure for large multidimensional dynamic indexes, in *Proceedings of ACM-SIGMOD International Conference on Management of Data*, April 1981, pp. 10–18.
71. Wang, W., Yang, J., and Muntz, R.R., PK-tree: a spatial index structure for high dimensional point data. Technical Report 980032, Computer Science Department, University of California, Los Angeles, September 22, 1998.
72. Kim, B. and Um, K., 2d+ string: a spatial metadata to reason topological and directional relationships, in *Proceedings of the 11th International Conference on Scientific and Statistical Database Management*, Cleveland, July 1999, IEEE CS Press, pp. 112–121.
73. Goh, S.-T. and Tan, K.-L., MOSAIC: a fast multi-feature image retrieval system. *Data Knowl. Eng.*, 33, 219–239, 2000.
74. Guntzer, U., Balke, W.-T., and Kiesling, W., Optimizing multi-feature queries for image databases, in *Proceedings of the International Conference on Very Large Databases*, Cairo, September 2000, pp. 419–428.

75. Weber, R., Schek, H.-J., and Blott, S., A quantitative analysis and performance study for similarity-search methods in high-dimensional spaces, *International Conference on VLDB 1998*, New York, August 1998, pp. 194–205.

76. Gibbs, S. Breiteneder, C., and Tsichritzis, D., Data modeling of time-based media, in *Proceedings of the ACM SIGMOD International Conference on Management of Data*, Minneapolis, May 1994, Snodgrass, R.T., and Winslett, M., eds., Vol. 23, pp. 91–102.

77. Hjelsvold, R. and Midtstraum, R., Databases for video information sharing, in *IS&T/SPIE's Symposium on Electronic Imaging Science and Technology*, 1994, pp. 268–279.

78. Gross, M.H., Koch, R., Lippert, L., and Dreger, A., Multiscale image texture analysis in wavelet spaces, in *Proceedings of the IEEE International Conference on Image Processing*, 1994.

79. Weiss, R., Duda, A., and Gifford, D.K., Content-based access to algebraic video, in *Proceedings of the International Conference on Multimedia Computing and Systems*, Boston, May 1994, pp. 140–151.

80. Smith, T.G.A. and Davenport, G., The stratification system: a design environment for random access video, in *Proceedings of the 3rd International Workshop on Network and Operating System Support for Digital Audio and Video*, 1992.

81. Weiss, R., Duda, A., and Gifford, D.K., Composition and search with a video algebra, *IEEE MultiMedia*, 2, 12–25, 1995.

82. Zhong, D. and Chang, S.-F., Video object model and segmentation for content-based video indexing, in *IEEE International Symposium on Circuits and Systems (ISCAS'97)*, Hong-Kong, June 1997.

83. Jiang, H., Montesi, D., and Elmagarmid, A.K., Integrated video and text for content-based access to video databases, *Multimedia Tools Appl.*, 9, 227–249, 1999.

84. Jiang, H. and Elmagarmid, A.K., Spatial and temporal content-based access to hyper-video databases, *VLDB J.*, 7, 226–238, 1998.

85. Jiang, H. and Elmagarmid, A.K., WVTDB—a semantic content-based videotext database system on the World Wide Web, *IEEE Trans. Knowl. Data Eng.*, 10, 947–966, 1998.

86. Bertino, E., Catania, B., and Ferrari, E., Multimedia IR: models and languages, in *Modern Information Retrieval*, Baeza-Yates, R. and Ribeiro-Neto, B., Eds., Addison-Wesley, Reading, MA, 1999.

87. Tusch, R., Kosch, H., and Böszörményi, L., VideX: an integrated generic video indexing approach, in *Proceedings of the ACM Multimedia Conference*, Los Angeles, October–November 2000, pp. 448–451.

88. Little, T.D.C., Ahanger, G., Folz, R.J., Gibbon, J.F., Reeve, F.W., Schelleng, D.H., and Venkatesh, D., A digital on-demand video service supporting content-based queries, in *Proceedings of 1st ACM International Conference on Multimedia*, 1993, pp. 427–436.

89. Hjelsvold, R. Midtstraum, R., and Sandstå, O. *Multimedia Database Systems: Design and Implementation Strategies*, Kluwer, Dordrecht, 1996, pp. 89–122.

90. Kosch, H., Slota, R., Böszörményi, L., Kitowski, J., and Otfinowski, J., An information system for long-distance cooperation in medicine, in *Proceedings of the 5th International Workshop on Applied Parallel Computing, New Paradigms for HPC in Industry and Academia (PARA)*, Bergen, Norway, June 2000. Springer-Verlag, Heidelberg, LNCS 1947, pp. 233–241.

91. Kosch, H., Tusch, R., Böszörményi, L., Bachlechner, A., Dörflinger, B., Hofbauer, C., and Riedler, C., The SMOOTH Video DB—demonstration of an integrated generic indexing approach, in *Proceedings of the ACM Multimedia Conference*, Los Angeles, October–November 2000, pp. 495–496.

92. Martínez, J.M. Overview of the MPEG-7 Standard. ISO/IEC JTC1/SC29/WG11 N4980, (Klagenfurt Meeting), July 2002, http://www.chiariglione.org/mpeg/.

93. Melton, J. and Eisenberg, A., SQL multimedia and application packages (SQL/MM), *SIGMOD Rec.*, 30(4), 97–102, 2001.

94. Information technology—Database languages—SQL Multimedia and Application Packages—Part 5: Still Image, ISO/IEC FCD 13249-5, 2003(E), December 2002.
95. Melton, J. and Eisenberg, A., SQL: 1999, formerly known as SQL3, *SIGMOD Rec.*, 28(1), 131–138, 1999.
96. Harold, E.R. and Means, W.S., *XML in a Nutshell*, 2nd ed., O'Reilly and Associates, 2002.
97. Kosch, H., MPEG-7 and Multimedia Database Systems, *SIGMOD Rec.*, 31(2), 34–39, 2002.
98. Hacid, M.-S., Decleir, C., and Kouloumdjian, J., A database approach for modeling and querying video data, *IEEE Trans. Knowl. Data Eng.*, 12, 729–750, 2000.
99. Bonifati, A., Comparative analysis of five XML query languages, *SIGMOD Rec.*, 29(1), 68–79, 2000.
100. Heuer, J., Casas, J.L., and Kaup, A., Adaptive multimedia messaging based on MPEG-7—the M3 box, in *Proceedings of the Second International Symposium on Mobile Multimedia Systems & Applications*, Delft, November 2000.
101. Kofler, A., Evaluation of Storage Strategies for XML Based MPEG-7 Data. Master's thesis, Institute of Information Technology, University Klagenfurt, 2001.
102. Amato, G., Mainetto, G., and Savino, P., An approach to a content-based retrieval of multimedia data, *Multimedia Tools Appl.*, 7, 9–36, 1998.
103. Rui, Y., Huang, T.S., and Chang, S.-F., Image retrieval: past, present and future. *J. Visual Comm. Image Representation*, 10, 1–23, 1999.
104. Yoshitaka, A. and Ichikawa, T., A survey on content-based retrieval for multimedia databases, *IEEE Trans. Knowl. Data Eng.*, 11, 81–93, 1999.
105. Apers, P.M.G. and Kersten, M.L., Content-based retrieval in multimedia databases based on feature models, in *Proceedings of the International Conference on Advanced Multimedia Content Processing*, Osaka, Japan, November 1998, Springer-Verlag, Heidelberg, LNCS 1554, pp. 119–130.
106. Apers, P.M.G., Blanken, H.M., and Houtsma, M.A.W., *Multimedia Databases in Perspective*. Springer-Verlag, Heidelberg, 1997.
107. Smith, J. and Chang, S.-F., VisualSEEk: a fully automated content-based image query system, in *Proceedings of the Fourth ACM Multimedia Conference (MULTIMEDIA'96)*, New York, November 1996, ACM Press, pp. 87–98.
108. Flickner, M., Sawhney, H., Niblack, W., Ashley, J., Huang, Q., Dom, B., Gorkani, M., Hafner, J., Lee, D., Petkovic, D., Steele, D., and Yanker, P., Query by image and video content: the QBIC system. *IEEE Comput.*, 28, 23–32, 1995.
109. Das, M., Riseman, E.M., and Draper, B.A., FOCUS: searching for multi-colored objects in a diverse image database, in *IEEE Conference on Computer Vision and Pattern Recognition (CVPR)*, 1997, pp. 756–761.
110. Shanbehazadeh, J., Moghadam, A.M.E., and Mahmoudi, F., Image indexing and retrieval techniques: past, present, and next, in *Proceedings of SPIE: Storage and Retrieval for Media Databases 2000*, Yeung, M.M., Yeo, B.-L., and Bouman, C.A., eds., Vol. 3972, 2000, pp. 461–470.
111. Kelly, P.M. and Cannon, T.M., Query by image example: the CANDID approach, in *Proceedings of SPIE: Storage and Retrieval for Media Databases 1995*, 1995, pp. 238–248.
112. Ortega, M., Rui, Y., Chakrabarti, K., Porekaew, K., Mehrotra, S., and Huang, T.S., Supporting ranked Boolean similarity queries in MARS, *IEEE Trans. Knowl. Data Eng.*, 10, 905–925, 1998.
113. Chang, S.-F., Chen, W., Meng, H., Sundaram, H., and Zhong, D., VideoQ: an automated content-based video search system using visual cues, in *Proceedings of the 5th ACM International Multimedia Conference (MULTIMEDIA '97)*, New York/Reading, November 1998. ACM Press/Addison-Wesley, pp. 313–324.
114. Bach, J.R., The VIRAGE image search engine: an open framework for image management, in *Proceedings of SPIE-96, 4th Conference on Storage and Retrieval for Still Image and Video Databases*, San Jose, 1996, pp. 76–87.

115. Beigi, M., Benitez, A.B., and Chang, S.-F., Metaseek: a content-based metasearch engine for images, in *Proceedings of the International Conference of Storage and Retrieval for Image and Video Databases (SPIE)*, 1998, pp. 118–128.
116. Venters, C.C. and Cooper, M., A review of content-based image retrieval systems. Technical Report JTAP-054, JISC Technology Applications Programme (JTAP) at University Manchester, Manchester, 1999.
117. Veltkamp, R.C. and Tanase, M., Content-based image retrieval systems: a survey Technical Report UU-CS-2000-34, Utrecht University, Utrecht, March 2001.
118. Smeulders, A.W.M., Worring, M., Santini, S., Gupta, A., and Jain, R., Content based image retrieval at the end of the early years. *IEEE Trans. Pattern Anal. Machine Intell.*, 22, 1349–1380, 2000.
119. Ghias, A., Logan, J., Chamberlain, D., and Smith, B.C., Query by humming-musical information retrieval in an audio database, in *Proceedings of the ACM Multimedia*, San Francisco, 1995, pp. 231–236.
120. Crysandt, H. and Wellhausen, J., Music classification with MPEG-7, *Proceedings of the SPIE International Conference on Electronic Imaging—Storage and Retrieval for Media Databases*, Santa Clara, January 2003.
121. Foote, J., An overview of audio information retrieval, *ACM Multimedia Syst.*, 7, 2–10, 1999.
122. Foote, J.T., *Multimedia Storage and Archiving Systems II, Proceedings of SPIE*, Kuo C.-C.J., et al., eds., Vol. 3229, 1997, pp. 138–147.
123. Foote, J., Cooper, M., and Nam, U., Audio retrieval by rhythmic similarity, in *Proceedings of the Third International Symposium on Musical Information Retrieval*, Paris, September 2002.
124. Li, J.Z., Goralwalla, I.A., Özsu, M.T., and Szafron, D., Modeling video temporal relationships in an object database management system, *Multimedia Comput. Networking*, 80–91, 1997.
125. Gudivada, V.N., Raghavan, R., and Vanapipat, K., *A Unified Approach to Data Modelling and Retrieval for a Class of Image Database Applications*, Springer-Verlag, Heidelberg, 1996.
126. Park, Y., Kim, P., Golshani, F., and Panchanathan, S., Concept-based visual information management with large lexical corpus, in *Proceedings of the International Conference on Database and Expert Applications (DEXA)*, Munich, September 2001. Springer-Verlag, Heidelberg, LNCS 2113, pp. 350–359.
127. Li, W.-S., Selçuk Candan, K., Hirata, K., and Hara, Y., Supporting efficient multimedia database exploration, *VLDB J.*, 9, 312–326, 2001.
128. Brewer, E.A., When everything is searchable. *Comm. ACM*, 44, 53–54, 2001.
129. Aloia, N., Matera, M., and Paterno, F., Presentations for databases in multimedia environments. *Multimedia Syst.*, 6, 408–420, 1998.
130. Baral, C., Gonzalez, G., and Nandigam, A., SQL+D: extended display capabilities for multimedia database queries, in *ACM International Conference on Multimedia*, Bristol, England, September 1998, pp. 109–114.
131. Marcus, S., *Multimedia Database System: Issues and Research Direction*, Springer-Verlag, Heidelberg, 1996.
132. Adiba, M. and Zechinelli-Martin, J.L., Spatio-temporal multimedia presentations as database objects, in *International Conference on Database and Expert Systems Applications (DEXA)*, Florence, September 2000, Springer-Verlag, Heidelberg, LNCS Series 1677, pp. 974–985.
133. Adali, S., Sapino, M.L., and Subrahmanian, V.S., A multimedia presentation algebra, in *Proceedings of the ACM SIGMOD International Conference of Management of Data*, Philadelphia, June 1999, pp. 121–132.
134. Stonebraker, M., *Object-Relational DBMS: The Next Wave,* 2nd edition, Morgan Kaufmann, 1998.

135. Oria, V., Özsu, M.T., Xu, B., Cheng, L.I., and Iglinski, P., VisualMOQL: the DISIMA visual query language, in *IEEE International Conference on Multimedia Computing and Systems*, Florence, Italy, June 1999, Vol. 1, pp. 536-542.

136. Oria, V., Özsu, M.T., Iglinski, P., Lin, S., and Ya, B., DISIMA: a distributed and interoperable image database system, in *Proceedings of the ACM SIGMOD International Conference of Management of Data*, Dallas, May 2000, p. 600.

137. Freeman, R.G., *Oracle 9i New Features*, McGraw-Hill Osborne Media, 2002.

138. Chamberlain, D., A complete guide to DB2 Universal Database. Academic Press/Morgan Kaufmann, 1998.

139. Atnafu, S., Brunie, L., and Kosch, H., Similarity-based operators and query optimization for multimedia database systems, in *Proceedings of the International Database Engineering and Applications Symposium (IDEAS)*, Grenoble, July 2001, IEEE CS Press, pp. 346–355.

140. Atnafu, S., Brunie, L., and Kosch, H., Similarity-based operators in image database systems, in *Proceedings of the International Conference on Advances in Web-Age Information Management (WAIM)*, Xi'an, China, July 2001, Springer-Verlag, Heidelberg, LNCS 2118, pp. 14–25.

141. Kosch, H. and Atnafu, S., A multimedia join by the method of nearest neighbor search. *Info. Processing Lett.,* 82, 269–276, 2002.

142. Leung, T.W., Mitchell, G., Subramanian, B., Vance, B., Vandenberg, S.L., and Zdonik, S.B., The Aqua data model and algebra. Technical Report CS-93-09, Brown University, Providence, 1993.

143. Cherniack, M. and Zdonik, S.B., Rule languages and internal algebrs for rule-based optimizers, in *Proceedings of the ACM SIGMOD International Conference of Management of Data*, Montréal, June 1996, pp. 401–412.

144. Cherniack, M. and Zdonik, S.B., Changing the rules: transformations for rule-based optimizers, in *Proceedings of the ACM SIGMOD International Conference of Management of Data*, Seattle, June 1998, pp. 61–72.

145. Hellerstein, J.M. and Stonebraker, M., Predicate migration: optimizing queries with expensive predicates, in *Proceedings of the ACM SIGMOD International Conference of Managment of Data*, Washington, DC, May 1993, pp. 256–257.

146. Chaudhuri, S. and Shim, K., Query optimization in the presence of foreign functions, in *Proceedings of the International Conference on Very Large Databases*, Dublin, 1993, pp. 529–542.

147. Scheufele, W. and Moerkotte, G., Efficient dynamic programming algorithms for ordering expensive joins and selections, in *Proceedings of the International Conference on Extending Database Technology*, Valencia, March 1998, pp. 23–27.

148. Adali, S., Bonatti, P., Sapino, M.L., and Subrahmanian, A.S., A multi-similarity algebra, in *Proceedings of the ACM SIGMOD International Conference of Management of Data*, Seattle, June 1998, ACM Press, pp. 402–413.

149. Ciaccia, P., Montesi, D., Penzo, W., and Trombetta, A., Imprecision and user preferences in multimedia queries: a generic algebraic approach, in *Foundations of Information and Knowledge Systems, First International Symposium*, Burg Spreewald, February 2000. Springer-Verlag, Heidelberg, LNCS 1762, pp. 50–71.

150. Nepal, S., Ramakrishna, M.V., and Thom, J.A., A fuzzy object query language (FOQL) for image databases, in *International Conference on Database Systems for Advanced Applications*, Hsinchu, April 1999. IEEE CS Press, pp. 117–124.

151. Nepal, S., Ramakrishna, M.V., and Thom, J.A., A fuzzy system for content based image retrieval, in *Proceedings of the IEEE International Conference on Intelligent Processing Systems*, Gold Coast, August 4–7, 1998, pp. 335–339.

152. Porkaew, K., Ortega, M., and Mehrotra, S., Query reformulation for content based multimedia retrieval in MARS, in *IEEE International Conference on Multimedia Computing and Systems*, Florence, June 1999, Vol. 2.

153. Chakrabarti, S., Porkaew, K., and Mehrotra, S., Efficient query refinement in multi-media databases, in *Proceedings of the IEEE International Conference on Data Engineering (ICDE)*, San Diego, February–March 2000, p. 196.

154. Rui, Y., Huang, T., and Mehrotra, S., Relevance feedback: a powerful tool for content-based image retrieval. *IEEE Trans. Circuits Syst. Video Technol.*, 8, 25–36, 1998.

155. Phillips, B., Mediaway presses access to multimedia database. *PC Week*, 13, 39–40, 1996.

156. Khoshafian, S., Dasananda, S., and Minaasian, N., *The Jasmine Object Database: Multimedia Applications for the Web*, Morgan Kaufmann Publishers, 1998.

157. Woelk, D., Kim, W., and Luther, W., An object-oriented approach to multimedia databases, in *SIGMOD Conf.*, Washington, D.C., 1986, pp. 311–325.

158. Stonebraker, M.R. and Rowe, L.A., The Design of POSTGRES, in *Proceedings of the ACM SIGMOD International Conference on Management of Data*, Washington, DC, May 1986, pp. 340–355.

159. de Vries, A.P., van Doorn, M.G.L.M., Blanken, H.M., and Apers, P.M.G., The MIRROR MMDBMS architecture, in *Proceedings of the International Conference on Very Large Databases*, Edinburgh, 1999, pp. 758–761.

160. van Doorn, M.G.L.M. and de Vries, A.P., The psychology of multimedia databases, in *Proceedings of the Fifth ACM Conference on Digital Libraries*, San Antonio, June 2000, pp. 1–9.

161. de Vries, A.P., Windhouwer, M.A., Apers, P.M.G., and Kersten, M.L., Information access in multimedia databases based on feature model, *New Generation Comput.*, 18, 323–339, 2000.

162. Blok, H.E., Windhouwer, M.A., van Zwol, R., Petkovic, M., Apers, P.M.G., Kersten, M.L., and Jonker, W., Flexible and scalable digital library search, in *Proceedings of the International Conference on Very Large Data Bases (VLDB)*, Rome, September 2001, pp. 705–706.

163. Rui, Y., Huang, T.S., and Mehrotra, S., MARS and its applications to MPEG-7. Technical Report TR-DB-97-05, Department of Computer Science, University of Illinois, Chicago, 1998.

164. Rui, Y., Huang, T.S., and Mehrotra, S., Constructing table-of-content for videos. *ACM Multimedia Syst.*, 7, 359–368, 1999.

165. Chakrabarti, K. and Mehrotra, S. Efficient concurrency control in multidimensional access methods, in *Proceedings of the International ACM SIGMOD Conference on Management of Data*, Philadelphia, June 1999, pp. 25–36.

166. Döller, M., Kosch, H., Dörflinger, B., Bachlechner, A., and Blaschke, G., Demonstration of an MPEG-7 Multimedia Data Cartridge, ACM Multimedia 2002, Juan-Les-Pins, December 2002, pp. 429–430.

167. Döller, M. and Kosch, H., An MPEG-7 Multimedia Data Cartridge, *SPIE Conference on Multimedia Computing and Networking 2003 (MMCN 2003)*, Santa Clara, January 2003.

Chapter 5
Distributed Multi-media Database Systems

This chapter describes the architecture and components of distributed Multimedia Database Systems (MMDBMS) responsible for delivering, streaming, and receiving multimedia data, and the effect of MPEG-21 on the implementation of the components is described in particular.

We will start by illustrating different distributed MMDBMS architectures in use; namely, the client–server (C-S), peer-to-peer, and an MPEG-21-based architecture. The remaining parts of this chapter are mainly the descriptions of the different components: multimedia storage servers, network and client considerations, and finally, adaptation issues.

5.1 Architectural Considerations

5.1.1 C-S System

Many distributed MMDBMSs[1,2] for pull applications rely on C-S architectures. In this scenario, client applications request multimedia data from the server, which are then processed locally. Obviously, this architecture minimizes the degree of parallel processing that can occur because of the synchronous nature of the request function.[3]

Furthermore, it is a common experience that pure C-S systems do not scale well with respect to the number of users, the heterogeneity of the terminals employed, and the size of the data requested. Exhibits 5.1 and 5.2 give an example in which two media storage and streaming servers are available for media requests. The three terminals here support, because of their hardware characteristics, three different coding standards—MPEG-4 Simple, Core, and Complex—and different display capabilities. Moreover, the network between the server and the terminal differs, as the personal computer (PC) in the example has a direct and good connection via LAN

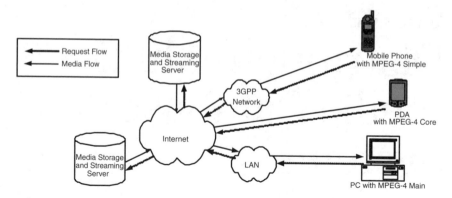

Exhibit 5.1. Client–server-based multimedia system.

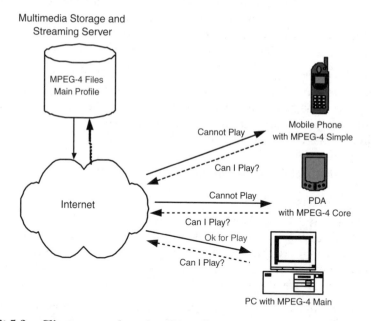

Exhibit 5.2. Client–server-based multimedia system with different profiles.

(local area network) to the Internet and the mobile phone must go over a mobile network.

All terminals in Exhibit 5.1 wish to be provided with rich multimedia access. A simple C-S system would scale poorly in this context, because the server proposes only a video encoded using the MPEG-4 main profile, and as a consequence, the mobile phone and the personal digital assistant (PDA) would not receive a stream at all. Thus, the mobile phone and the

PDA, when they request the content desired, will receive a "Cannot Play" answer, although the PC will receive fine. The situation is shown in Exhibit 5.2.

A more scalable architecture would feature interdependent servers of variable availability and reliability, owned by competing organizations (peer-to-peer architecture, see below). Moreover, it would manage content encoded in different formats to be consumed by heterogeneous terminals. Finally, for dynamic changes in the delivery situation (e.g., when the content is streamed through the Internet), the server will provide information to steer dynamic adaptation.

We introduced a scalable video server architecture[4,5] that allows the migration of modules to a proxy or client. In such an architecture, which relies on competition and on cooperation, mobile agents are also a possible paradigm for a more flexible usage.

5.1.2 Peer-to-Peer System

To allow greater flexibility, multimedia systems evolve from pure C-S system to peer-to-peer (P2P) systems with the notion of a "user," which is defined in MPEG-21 as an entity to consume and to produce digital multimedia items.[6–8] A P2P architecture is shown as in Exhibit 5.3, where portable devices with various capabilities send and transfer multimedia content from one device to another. Exhibit 5.3 shows a PDA user, a mobile phone

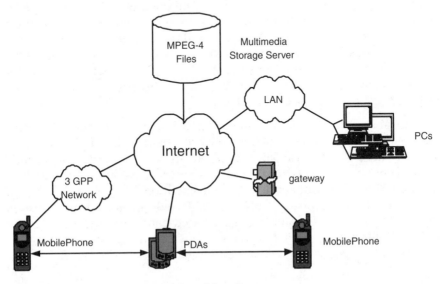

Exhibit 5.3.   Peer-to-peer-based multimedia system.

user, and PC users consuming content from the multimedia storage server but also communicating with each other, including making phone calls, sending e-mail, images, music, and videos to the other, although the terminal capability is quite different from PDAs to mobile phones or PCs. Such a system must provide peer-to-peer services in the form of, for instance, operators, which may have the following functions:

- To hold the content from the creation to the delivery
- To check the capability of the other peer party and see whether it can process the multimedia data before delivering
- To create metadata (e.g., in the form of a MPEG-21 Digital Item [DI]) to describe content received from the users

Many technical challenges arise from the architecture shown in Exhibit 5.3. They concern mainly the realization of generic information communication between peers. A set of open peer-to-peer protocols that allow any connected device on the network to communicate and collaborate in a peer-to-peer manner has to be defined. All the negotiation messages will sit on top of the generic peer-to-peer communication protocols that are up-layers of physical network protocols; for instance, the CC-PP exchange protocol based on HTTP Extension Framework by the W3C* or the JXTA v1.0 Protocols Specification, by Sun Microsystems.**

In addition, the protocol considerations communication paradigm has to be reconsidered. Mobile agents are an important paradigm in a peer-to-peer multimedia environment. Mobile agents are autonomous, that is, they have their own goals and can negotiate and compete with other agents. They are mobile, so that they can search for a better environment, and are local, so that they may "own" their own data. The great advantage of a mobile agent is that it is simultaneously a client and a server. This obviously fits well with the idea of peers. Moreover, mobile agents make better use of communication bandwidth and protect the privacy of the community, operating on a need-to-know basis.

Natural applications in distributed MMDBMSs are multiuser applications, such as video conferencing, network management, and distributed search. Therefore, several works recently attempted to integrate mobile agent technology into distributed MMDBMSs. The main issue is actually a more efficient quality of service (QoS) negotiation.[9,10] For instance, Manvi and Venkataram[10] propose a mobile agent–based QoS management system that provides means for efficient agent-based bandwidth negotiation. The idea of mobile agents in distributed multimedia systems can be extended to database functionality, such as content-based retrieval, as well.

*http://www.w3.org/Mobile/CCPP/.
**http://www.jxta.org/.

In this context, one attempt to be mentioned here is our mobile agent system, which was developed on top of the multimedia extension of Oracle 9i that allows the execution of personal multimedia-searching algorithms in the core of the Oracle database.[11] The system uses the JServer functionality of Oracle 9i, including its CORBA services, which are provided by a VisiBroker CORBA ORB. This distributed implementation allows an agent, during its visits to different DBMSs, to learn from the results of previous visits; for example, an agent trying to find the most similar face to a reference one in a distributed face database can revert in each visit to the previously best match, stored in the agent.

5.1.3 MPEG-21-Based Architecture

A possible architecture for a Web-based distributed MMDBMS relying on MPEG-21 is depicted in Exhibit 5.4. It consists of the following main components:

- The Multimedia Database holds a collection of MPEG-21 DIs. The DID may contain DI identification(s) for describing the item, DI adaptation(s) for describing its quality of service characteristics and Rights Expression Language (REL) descriptor(s) for describing its

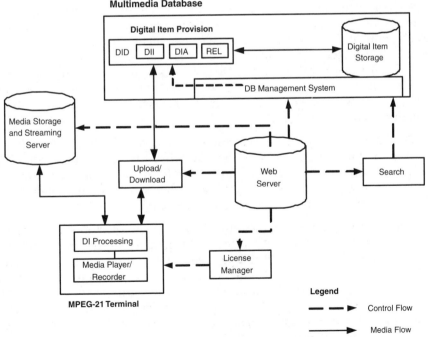

Exhibit 5.4.   Peer-to-peer-based multimedia system relying on MPEG-21.

usage rights. The provision module of the database is responsible for aggregating the different descriptors available. The resource described is either included in the DID or the DID contains a reference to the resource. Remember that this does not exclude MPEG-7, which may be one descriptor of a DI.

- The Web server is the front end for all users to the framework providers. It serves several needs, including the following:
  Searching for items in the database
  Uploading and downloading DIs
  Purchasing licenses to contents and trading with them
  Controlling the execution of the media streaming
- The MPEG-21 terminals are where users consume and create DIs for the use in the distributed system.

The system is Web based, which means that DIs may be searched, uploaded, and so forth by Web applications. To interface with the database, middle tiers to the database have to be employed[12] (not shown in Exhibit 5.4). This naturally leads to the specification of a multimedia middleware. The middleware implements complex services; for instance, looking up available services that match a user's service description. There are few works considering how to design a multimedia middleware; for more information, see Chapter 6.

A media streamer is a unit that streams content to a user for immediate consumption. It can stream on a one-to-one connection, as in on-demand (pull) applications, or it can broadcast (push). In both cases, resources will usually be protected, and only licensed users can play it. The REL descriptions are matched against the user descriptors, and if they match, the user may play the resource. In some cases, the DIs are available to the user before the resource is streamed. In other cases, the DIs are delivered together with the resource.

The MPEG-21 terminal enables the user to consume the content delivered in the form of a DI. It could be a Web browser application, a media player, or potentially a media recorder. The terminal contains software to upload or download content, buy or sell licenses, activate the on-demand media streamer, or tune into a broadcast session.

In a peer-to-peer manner, the terminal may create DIs, too. For instance, the user creates the resource with available media recorder and then generates descriptions for the resource. These descriptions include the identification in the form of the DI Identification, information for adaptation engines in the form of DI adaptation, and the rights associated to the resource in the form of a REL description. The resource and the descriptions are bundled in the DID and are uploaded to the Web server for further use in the system; for example, to be stored in the database or delivered directly to another user.

5.1.4 Roadmap of This Chapter

The following sections detail the different components of a distributed multimedia database system and how they are supposed to work together for an end-to-end multimedia delivery.

The first component described is the video server and streamer (Section 5.1). It may be coupled more or less strongly with the database. It is clear that a stronger connection to the database lets the server be more metadata aware, with the consequence of a considerable performance and functionality improvement in the admission control and the buffer management. Section 5.2 is dedicated to multimedia communication. It includes a discussion of communication protocols (e.g., reservation-based and QoS supporting protocols) and secure and reliable communication. Section 5.3 introduces client-design issues, mainly on hardware and software requirements and implementations. Section 5.4 discusses content adaptation* and presents a comprehensive adaptation architecture. Finally, Section 5.5 summarizes the main concepts introduced and points to future developments.

5.2 Video Servers and Streaming

Stored multimedia data can be classified into fundamentally two types: noncontinuous media such as text and image and continuous media such as audio and video. Continuous media data have the real-time property, whereas noncontinuous data do not. These two types of data will use different storage mechanisms. Videos are, therefore, stored using separate multimedia storage servers[13] to meet the real-time requirement. Noncontinuous media, however, may be stored in the database together with their descriptive information.[13]

For instance, Oracle provides infrastructures for a coexisting and interacting MMDBMS: the Oracle 9i interMedia system[14] and the Oracle Video Server/Client.[15] Exhibit 5.5 shows the architecture of the Oracle Video Server/Client. The Oracle Video Server stores video files, actually MPEG-1/2 but not yet MPEG-4, in a so-called Media Data Store (MDS) structure and controls the access to the videos. Moreover, it allows an application to browse the list of available videos in the MDS. The server handles video requests and informs the video pump which portion of the video file to deliver to meet a particular user request. The Oracle Video Client receives the delivered video data for display. Moreover, it provides libraries

---

*Throughout this chapter we will use the term content adaptation to describe the adaptation of the media content to an alternative form to meet current usage and resource constraints. MPEG-21 prefers the term resource instead of content to avoid the mismatch between content as semantic content and media content. However, most related papers use the term media content in this context, and to avoid confusion with respect to these papers, we adopted content.

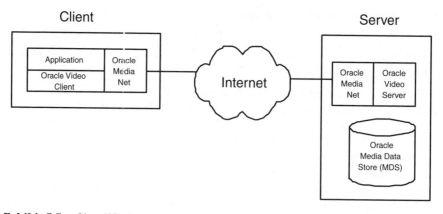

Client   Server

Exhibit 5.5. Simplified architecture of the Oracle video server.

for developing client applications, such as the Java Media Framework (JMF) libraries.[16] This means that a JMF player can access and play audio or video from Oracle 9i interMedia.

Oracle 9i interMedia objects have a common storage model for media data. Media data of the ORDImage, ORDAudio, or ORDVideo object types can be stored in the database using binary large objects (BLOBs). A BLOB can be as big as 4 Gb in size. Media data maintained outside the database can be stored, retrieved, and managed as a binary file (BFILE) or as a source on an Oracle Video Server or on a Real Network streaming server. Video data in the Oracle Video Server can be managed by inter-Media services, including methods for retrieval of the data and inserting new information. Manipulation is, however, limited to some simple filtering, based on the metadata stored; for example, format. The requirements of video servers are quite different from those of the existing network-based servers.[17,18]

The real-time nature of multimedia data needs guaranteed periodic retrieval and transmission of data. A video server that stores a large number of videos will usually rely on storage devices of various types.[19] Video servers, for instance, video-on-demand (VoD), may have to support hundreds or even thousands of concurrent clients.[20] In addition, the server architecture must have the ability to scale in terms of throughput and number of clients. Moreover, multimedia servers should meet the requirements of user interaction.[21] That means the server must be able to support various user interactions such as rewind, fast forward, pause, and so forth. Because of these requirements, research in video servers has been directed mainly toward[22]:

- Striping of data across storage devices for the purpose of efficient exploitation of resources (load balancing)

- Replication of videos, or parts of them, to improve availability and achieve better load balancing among servers
- Efficient retrieval of data from disks to amortize seek time and to avoid jitter
- Scheduling of system resources to guarantee the real-time requirements of the multimedia data requested
- Buffer and cache management to save resource utilization

It can be seen clearly that a video server places several demands on its computing, storage, and communication environments. The communication requirements concern the network services. The video data must arrive at the users with low jitter and perhaps low latency. In conventional, wired networks, real-time support may be given by network: Some protocols are able to allocate network resources to individual connections to provide bounds on throughput, delay, jitter, and congestion loss (see Section 5.2). However, mobile networks will in general not offer support for QoS, and they require that the connections used to deliver the video data be rerouted as the user terminal's location changes. In addition, they have to deal with loss of data and dynamically changing resource availability much more than wired networks. Therefore, adaptive multimedia streaming becomes important for mobile multimedia application. New scalable coding schemes, as well as the retrieval of composite elements and their QoS management, in the server support adaptation (see Section 5.3).

5.2.1 Striping Policy

Striping policies for multimedia data are crucial for overall performance. Although simple circular striping can be employed for long, sequential accesses, associative access to smaller units requires complex block-allocation policies that take into account bandwidth and storage capacities.[23] To decrease the complexity of the block-allocation policy, an alternative approach is to partition the storage devices into sets of homogeneous striping groups.[24] A higher-level policy assigns media objects to these devices, matching the storage and bandwidth requirements of the multimedia data.[25] We distinguish here between disk striping and network striping. Disk striping refers to the process of allocating the striping units to different devices of one server, whereas network striping allocates the units to different servers. Obviously, the usage of network striping requires multiple server resources and the application type dictates the usage of each technology. However, network striping is more resistant against failure.

5.2.2 Load Balancing

Another related problem is the dynamic load balancing across servers or striping groups[26] because of varying access patterns. For instance, Dan et al.[27] propose a policy of temporarily replicating hot data segments, that is, frequently accessed parts of the media objects, to dynamically balance the load across striping groups. Chou et al.[28] study methods for dynamic replication in a distributed VoD system to achieve load balancing among the servers. Furthermore, in a subsequent paper, Chou et al.[29] try to identify a good compromise between striping and replication for highly scalable systems. They argue for the use of a hybrid approach in which, instead of striping each object across all the nodes of the video server system, the striping is constrained to a single node and popular objects are replicated to other nodes. Finally, we would like to remark that striping and replication proposed in video server systems are similar to the data-placement policies proposed in parallel databases. For instance, in the system Bubba, dynamic replication and striping policies, based on the access frequency, have been defined.[30]

5.2.3 Admission Control

To guarantee QoS, that is, to meet the real-time requirements of the video data requested, video servers employ admission control. A new request is admitted only if enough server resources are available.[31,32] This implies that a multimedia server has to know, in advance, the number of streams it can serve while satisfying their real-time requirements. The capacity of a multimedia server can be expressed in statistical terms; for example, the number of streams it can serve with a certain level of jitter.

The admission control relies on finding a delivery path from the storage devices to the selected network interface and reserving appropriate capacities on all components on this path for the multimedia delivery. Therefore, one of the main tasks here is to maintain the continuity of continuous data. Furthermore, hard and soft admission controls are distinguished. In hard admission control, the video server must exclusively offer services that provide deterministically bounded delay guarantees; that is, all tasks to be scheduled must have hard deadlines.[33] In contrast, soft admission control may accept some task types that may finish after the deadline.[34] An example of a hard deadline may be the maximal delivery delay between two clips of a video edition application, and that of a soft deadline may be the start-up time of a video in a VoD application, where exceeding 10 percent, for instance, may be tolerable.

5.2.4 Disk Scheduling Strategy

Because disk operations are nondeterministic, because of random access time and sharing with other operations, special disk scheduling algorithms have to be developed to retrieve the multimedia data continuously. The overall goal of these scheduling algorithms is to meet the deadlines for all time-critical tasks and to minimize the buffer space requirement while dealing with both concurrent streams and aperiodic requests.

Techniques employed are, for instance, the Early Deadline First (EDF), SCAN-EDF, and Group Sweeping Scheduling (GSS) algorithms.[13] The EDF algorithm serves requests with earliest deadlines first. SCAN-EDF combines the seek optimization of SCAN, which serves requests in the order of disk head movements, and the real-time guarantees of EDF. When deadlines are equal, a SCAN prioritization is used. To provide different data rate requirements, all requests are served in a cycle and each request gets an amount of service time proportional to the required data rate. GSS organizes the set of requested streams into a number of groups. These groups are served in a fixed, round-robin order. Streams within a group are served according to SCAN. This method has the advantage of reducing the required buffer space for user interaction. The SCAN technique, without grouping, requires the playback of a stream to start after the end of the first cycle, that is, all streams are retrieved once, whereas with the GSS technique, playback can begin as soon as the group has been served. The SCAN scheduling requires buffers for all streams, whereas GSS can reuse the buffer for each group.

Many authors have proposed optimization techniques for the basic scheduling strategies.[22,35,36] First of all, optimization techniques are employed for near video-on-demand, where requests for the same video, arriving within a specified period of time, are grouped together.[35] Later, Lau et al.[36] have studied piggypacking of I/O streams to reduce I/O demands. They have found that small variations in the delivery rate of streams can enable enough merging, called piggypacking, of I/O streams to achieve significant reduction of I/O bandwidth. A well-accepted technique to reduce the buffer requirements and to improve the bandwidth use is the so-called double buffering technique.[22] One buffer is provided for the producer of a stream and another buffer for the consumer. The buffers are switched at each time cycle. Double buffering allows one to smooth different device access times; for example, between the disk and the network devices.

5.2.5 Server, Proxy, and Client Caching

Besides the necessary use of buffers to smooth the flow of data between various devices, caching must be a central issue in the server. The advantages of multimedia object caching are obvious; for one, previously cached videos can be immediately streamed to the client without triggering disk retrieval.[37–39] Even in the case of partial caching, that is, when only parts (frames, elementary streams) of a video are cached, resource consumption is reduced. Caching can be employed among different levels in the server and among servers and clients and the network.

In its abstract view, caching means the design of an object management mechanism that minimizes the migration of objects among different levels of the hierarchical storage system;[40] that is, tertiary storage and disk, disk and memory, and among servers, proxy, and client caches.

Efficient caching depends on the quality of the used cache replacement algorithm.[41,42] The replacement algorithm determines which objects are removed from the cache when storage space is needed for placing new objects into the cache. These algorithms must predict which currently cached objects will not be accessed in the near future, so that they can be removed.

However, these algorithms must also be fast; that is, they must not be computationally too complex. The reason is that these algorithms are run often on caches that contain a large number of objects requiring a real-time reaction to cache saturation. Current implementations of caches can be classified as[42]

- The traditional replacement policy, least recently used (LRU), and its direct extensions; for example, not frequently used (NFU) and least frequently used (LFU).
- Key-based replacement policies. The replacement policies in this category evict objects based on a primary key. For instance, the SIZE strategy evicts the largest object.
- Cost-based replacement policies. The replacement policies in this category employ a cost function derived from different factors such as time since last access, entry time of the object in the cache, and so forth. For instance, the least normalized cost replacement (LCN-R) strategy employs a cost function incorporating the access frequency, the transfer time cost and the object's size.

Prefetching can augment the efficiency of caching. For example, in Sen et al.,[43] a methodology to store prefixes of multimedia streams in proxy caches to improve startup latency in addition to perform smoothing is proposed.

In the context of client caching, a prefetching strategy for a news-on-demand video server was proposed, based not only on run-time information like objects access frequencies, for example, but also on knowledge about clips structures.[44] That means that by considering the degree of overlapping between contextually correlated streams, a simple prefetching algorithm can be designed, which anticipates the load of future accessed streams. The information on the clip's structure can simply be obtained during the annotation process of the video and may be encoded in the SegmentDecomposition DS of MPEG-7.[45] Simulation experiments show that, on average and compared with a nonprefetching strategy, an 18 percent higher buffer hit rate can be achieved without additional cost.

Let us finally note that there is a fundamental difference between realizing cache replacement algorithms for server caches and doing so for proxy caches. The available bandwidth between the various levels of a hierarchical storage system is fixed and known a priori. In contrast, available bandwidth between server and proxy or proxy and client may randomly change with time. As a result, applying resource management schemes from the server across the network becomes problematic, and alternative solutions have to be sought.

User interaction, that is, VCR-like (video cassette recorder) control operations, requires more complex techniques than those employed for simple request servicing.[21] Resources may be released and reacquired on resumption. However, it may not be possible to guarantee that resources are available on resumption. For example, a new playback stream must be created on resumption of a client stream that was originally served via batching. Therefore, in large-scale servers, a small amount of capacity may be set aside as contingency capacity for dealing with VCR-like control operations.[22]

5.2.6 Presentation Management

In addition to addressing the above resource optimization issues, video servers must address the challenges in the retrieval of composite multimedia documents,[46,47] also referred to as a presentation.

A presentation may consist of many different parts, for example, video and audio clips, image, and text, with very different storage and bandwidth requirements that are to be presented in a synchronized fashion. Therefore, the bandwidth requirement may vary over time. An example of a presentation is a multiclip query that requests multiple video clips from a video server and that can contain complex structural and temporal constraints defined by QoS,[48] application-specific (e.g., video editing),[49] or user-specific requirements (e.g., sequential presentation of the news highlights of the day).[47] Other examples of a multimedia presentation specification are multimedia query languages that integrate means for presentation languages.

Section 4.5 gives an example of a combined query and presentation language. The issue of managing presentations must be addressed at the clients as well as at the servers. The prefetch schedule for various media objects should also take into account the bandwidth fragmentation in a server, where different components may be located in different storage devices, as well as having to consider grouping of presentations for bandwidth sharing.[47,50,51]

In this context, we propose an efficient heuristic for the scheduling of the presentation's clips in a VoD server with respect to previously submitted presentations as proposed in Kosch et al.[52,53] The key idea is to use object sharing between presentations queued for schedule. This idea relies on the observation that in many multimedia applications,[46,48,49,54] a subset of clips is more frequently requested than the rest of the data. For instance, in Tele-Learning applications,[46,48] clips explaining core problems of a course are hot in the preparation period of exams and are, therefore, likely to be requested almost simultaneously. The developed heuristic aims at the maximization of clip sharing between submitted presentations and consequently reduces the workload of the video server; that is, increases the number of admitted clips in the admission control. In a simulation-based evaluation, using two video access patterns, hot-spot access and Zipf-like distribution, we have obtained a significant reduction in workload (an average reduction of 33 percent) over a broadly used baseline algorithm. The supplemental optimization costs were also very small.

5.2.7 *Adaptive Continuous Multimedia Streaming*

The currently used streaming techniques of continuous multimedia data are mostly proprietary solutions and do not provide a framework that is adaptive to changing network bandwidths, as well as handling of errors such as packet loss, over the Internet. However, the scalable object coding of MPEG-4[55] offers the possibility of building a flexible platform for developing Internet-capable streaming media applications. However, there are as yet very few works that focus on the development of an adaptive streaming framework.

For instance, Haghighi et al.[56,57] propose the implementation of a scalable QoS-aware server architecture compatible with the Delivery Multimedia Integration Framework (DMIF) of MPEG-4, which provides means for variable bit coding. Starting with a relatively high bit rate, to fill the client buffer, the stream is then adapted to the client capacities. To control the amount of data to be delivered, a flexible transmission rate is determined. Feamster et al.[58] propose a framework that is adaptive to variable bandwidth in the network. The authors focus on the effect of various congestion control algorithms and receiver buffering strategies on the performance of streaming continuous multimedia data. They extend, in this context, the results of a previous work from Rejaie et al.[59] and find that a strategy that provides a combination of low playout delay and congestion control may improve the adaptability of continuous media streaming. However, there is as yet no streaming framework available that supports the layered coding capabilities of MPEG-4.

5.2.8 *Architectures of Video Servers*

In the last few paragraphs, we described broadly used techniques for maintaining the real-time requirements of video servers. Orthogonal to this, fundamentally different architectures have to be considered.[60] They vary from single processor and central disk architectures, to distributed disk and single processor, and finally to entirely distributed architectures.[61]

The servers running on one single processor are bound to the limited resources of this particular processor, whereas a parallel video server is scalable to a certain extent.[62] This means that new resources can be added without a big effort. Furthermore, with this architecture, load balancing can be achieved when using an intelligent query-scheduling algorithm.[63,64]

Parallel servers are able to accept more requests in total than a video server located on one processor.[65] A currently available prototype is the parallel Tiger video file server,[66] a project running at Microsoft Research, which we will use as an example video server here. Tiger is now commercialized through the product name NetShow Theater Server. More information on this video server can be obtained from http://www.microsoft.com/catalog/display.asp?subid = 21&site = 734.

Research prototypes to mention here are, for instance, the ELVIRA (experimental video server for ATM) video server[67] and the parallel SESAME-KB server,[68] a parallel and multithreaded (using the PM^2-library)[69] video server.

In this architectural context, Shahabi and Alshayeji[70] propose an interesting distributed architecture: the SuperStreaming architecture. The main idea of the SuperStreaming technique is to use the client-side resources of modern multimedia-enabled PCs to improve the use of the multimedia servers. A distributed cooperative technique enables the media servers to start the delivery of continuous media at a rate higher than that required by the display bandwidth. Then, if necessary, alternative policies to downgrade superstreams in favor of regular streams when the resources are scarce can be employed.

5.2.9 Example Video Server

The Tiger Video Server, developed by Microsoft Research and intended to support VoD applications, is a parallel and fault-tolerant real-time fileserver.[66] It relies, to a great extent, on off-the-shelf components that are inexpensive and, therefore, allow the architecture to remain scalable. Tiger is designed to support a high number of clients and, therefore, a high-performance architecture was chosen as technical platform video. The basic architectural layout of Tiger is depicted in Exhibit 5.6.

The central component is the controller, whose task is to serve as query interface to the client and to perform the admission control. When the controller has accepted a new query, it contacts the cub, a node in the parallel architecture that holds the first block of the requested video, and then it withdraws from the current request. The cub returns the video directly to the client, bypassing the controller. The video files are striped in a circular fashion. Based on the striping mechanism, a scheduler is defined that efficiently makes use of the distributed I/O system. The

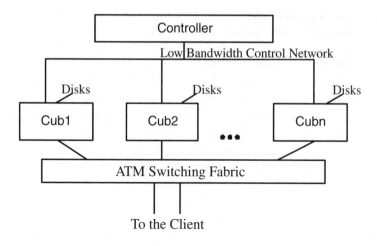

Exhibit 5.6. **Architecture of the parallel video server, Tiger.**

schedule is distributed over the cubs; that is, each cub has only a partial knowledge of the whole disk schedule. Tiger's schedule management is based on a so-called coherent hallucination strategy that is a distributed implementation of a shared object where no physical instantiation of the object is available.[71] None of the cubs are holding the whole schedule, but they behave as if they can see the global schedule.[71] Another important feature of the Tiger video server is its fault tolerance strategy. If the server is extended to a huge number of cubs, it becomes more and more likely that one of the cubs fails. To recognize the failure of a cub, a so-called deadman protocol is executed among them.[71]

In the architecture proposed, the cubs are logically organized in a ring. Every cub observes its left neighbor and sends ping messages to its right neighbor. The communication of the control information is done via a separate, low-bandwidth control network.

Tiger uses a replication strategy, that is, blocks are replicated on other disks as well, to prevent a complete server failure. The blocks are not necessarily replicated to successive cubs. It is also possible to specify a so-called declustering factor, which determines how many cubs, in addition to the cub holding the primary copy, should be involved for storing the secondary copies. A declustering factor of 2 means that the primary copy is spread over 2 other cubs. Bolosky et al.[66] state that a declustering factor between 4 and 8 combined with a block size of 500 kb was the most appropriate choice for the tested VoD applications. They argue that a too-small declustering factor, say 2, would mean that one-third of the system bandwidth would need to be reserved for failure recovery. A too-high declustering factor also would not be a good choice because of the higher probability of failure of cubs holding secondary copies.

5.3 Multimedia Communication

Multimedia communication knows two principle ways of delivery. The multimedia files are downloaded and played back, or the multimedia data is usually sent across the network in streams. Streaming breaks multimedia data into packets with sizes suitable for transmission between the servers and clients. The real-time data flows through the transmission, decompressing and playing, just like a water stream. A client can play the first packet and decompress the second while receiving the third, just as in a water pipeline. Thus, the user can start enjoying the multimedia without waiting to the end of transmission. Modern software frameworks, such as the Java Media Framework (JMF), comfortably support both principles (see Section 5.3).

This section discusses first the issues that relate mainly to multimedia communication in its streamed form. We will then discuss networks and network protocol issues. Finally, security aspects are assessed.

For a distributed multimedia system, several features should be of concern:

- Remote control: allowing long-distance execution, manipulation, and synchronization of multimedia objects
- Unreliable communication handling: taking care of possible data loss or data delays including insertion of frames, frame composition, and so forth
- Adaptation of the storage and streaming to different applications, to different network bandwidth and to different presentation devices
- Data compression and decoding for multiple platforms, which will concern different data representations
- Secure communication, authentication, and copyright protection

Heterogeneous network topologies create delivery paths through different network subsystems from the multimedia servers to the individual clients. As intercontinental network links provide, in time of low congestion, sufficient bandwidths for video streaming (several megabits per second), the network to the home scales for most cases only to the order of 1 megabit per second for Asymmetric Digital Subscriber Line (ADSL) and Very High Bit Rate DSL (VDSL) technologies.

However, despite these technological advances, raw bandwidth is not enough for effective delivery of multimedia services, especially when this bandwidth is shared among several systems or applications. It is necessary to provide guaranteed QoS for a flawless end-to-end service; that is, so that the end user receives a continuous flow of audio or video without interruption or noticeable degradation of quality.[72]

Communication protocols used for multimedia transmission play an important role in achieving the above goals; that is, to provide high bandwidth to the user with the appropriate QoS.

5.3.1 Reservation-Based versus Reservationless Protocols

Transmission over the Internet with the use of the currently broadly used communication IPv4 protocol family cannot guarantee on-time delivery of time-sensitive information. Hence, two main classes of QoS-aware protocols have been defined.

Reservation-based: In this model, resources are reserved explicitly. The network classifies incoming packets and uses the reservations made to provide a differentiated service. Typically, a dynamic resource reservation protocol is used in conjunction with admission control to make reservations. In the Resource Reservation Protocol, RSVP,[73] resources are reserved for unidirectional data going from sender to receiver. The new Internet protocol (IP) generation, IPv6,[74] proposes both reservation-based and reservationless QoS. The integrated services model, the int-serv model, in IPv6 reserves resources explicitly using a dynamic signaling protocol. It employs admission control, packet classification, and intelligent scheduling to achieve the desired QoS. Protocols of this type lack the implementation support, as broadly used router technology allows no reservation of a delivery path.

Reservationless: In this model, no resources are explicitly reserved. Instead, traffic is differentiated into a set of classes, and the network provides services to these classes based on their priority. It is necessary to control the amount of traffic in a given class that is allowed into the network so as to preserve the QoS being provided to other packets of the same class. For example, IPv6[74] uses for its diff-serv model the so-called Flow Label and Priority fields in the IP header. A host may use them to identify those packets for which it requests special handling by routers. This presupposes that network nodes have to use intelligent queuing mechanisms to differentiate traffic.[75] Several commercial router producers adapted this new protocol family (http://playground.sun.com/pub/ipng/html/ipng-implementations.html). However, old technologies that are not able to differentiate traffic are yet in worldwide use.

5.3.2 Real-Time Delivery Supporting Protocols

In addition to reservation-based protocols, there exits a class of protocols that support the transport of continuous media.[76] The most prominent member is the Realtime Transport Protocol (RTP). RTP is an IP-based protocol providing support for the transport of real-time data such as video and audio streams. The services provided by RTP include time reconstruction, loss detection, security, and content identification. RTP is designed to work in conjunction with the auxiliary control protocol RTCP to get feedback on quality of data transmission and information about participants in the ongoing session.

On top of RTP is the Real-Time Streaming Protocol (RTSP).* RTSP is a C–S multimedia presentation protocol to enable controlled delivery of streamed multimedia data over IP networks. It provides VCR-style remote control functionality for audio and video streams, such as pause, fast forward, reverse, and absolute positioning. RTSP is an application-level protocol designed to work with lower-level protocols such as RTP and RSVP to provide a complete streaming service over Internet. It provides a means for choosing delivery channels (such as UDP [User Datagram Protocol], multicast UDP, and TCP [Transmission Control Protocol]) and delivery mechanisms based on RTP.

5.3.3 *Multimedia Session Protocols*

In addition to real-time supporting and reserving protocols, mechanisms for setting up multimedia sessions are important. In principle, no formal session that sets up mechanisms is needed for multicast communication — senders send to a group address, receivers subscribe to the same address, and communication ensures. However, in practice, we normally need means for users that wish to communicate to discover which multicast address to use, to discover which protocols and codecs to transmit and receive with, and to discover that a session is going to take place at all. Note that session management may be described by MPEG-21 descriptors (see Chapter 3). The view is the following: MPEG-21 provides the open framework, that is, the application interface for the system, and a session protocol provides the implementation of this interface.

The Internet Engineering Task Force (IETF) Section Initiation Protocol (SIP)** protocol is currently the most promising protocol for session initiation and management available.

There are different entities defined in SIP. At first there are the SIP user agents (UAs), which could be separated into UA servers and UA clients. UA clients initiate a call, whereas UA servers only react to calls. Both are statefull devices. "State full" means that in the terminal the state of a call has to be known. The second important entity in SIP is the SIP network server, which could act as proxy or as redirect server. Because of scalability, the network server in the core net should be stateless, whereas the edge servers have to be statefull to provide all required functionality. Location server and register server complete this enumeration.

*http://www.rtsp.org/.
**http://www.ietf.org/ids.by.wg/simple/html.

The session concept of SIP offers a generic way to establish, control, and tear down multimedia sessions between communication end-points. At the time, SIPs mostly concentrate on the implementation of voice over IP (VoIP) services, but there is much ongoing research to show that SIP sessions can be used to establish multimedia streaming sessions as well as interactive multimedia communications.[77]

5.3.4 Secure Multimedia Communication

It is also imperative that the network infrastructure support security to appropriate levels to protect customers and ensure privacy.[78] The aim of security techniques in this field ranges from authentication and verification to classical encryption and, recently, to copyright protection. The proposal of copyright protection mechanisms is one of the main standardization aims in MPEG-21[79] (Intellectual Property Management; see Chapter 3).

Application-specific data structures are exploited to create more efficient encryption systems. Relevant work for MPEG encryption can be found in Shi and Bhargava[80] and Tang.[81] Digital watermarking is a recent technology[82–84] that covers more issues than related approaches; that is, it can be used for copyright protection of digital content, multimedia data authentication, and other purposes. Here, the problem is to embed an imperceptible mark in multimedia data in a secure and robust way so as to establish ownership claims or prove integrity. Watermarking does not depend on any specific data representation, for example, file format, and tolerates distortions resulting from common image processing operations, which is a major robustness requirement.

5.3.5 Reliable Multimedia Communication

Reliable multimedia communication introduces an error-control mechanism. This is mostly used with error-prone wireless links. Two basic approaches are employed, the forward error correction (FEC) and automatic repeat request (ARQ). FEC adds parity bits to the transmitted packets, and this redundancy is used by the receiver to detect and correct errors. FEC maintains constant throughput and has bounded time delay. ARQ only provides error detection capability by requesting retransmission when errors are detected by the receiver. ARQ is simple, but the delay is variable and unbounded. Many alternatives to FEC and ARQ have also been proposed.[85]

Supplemental and regularly updated information on multimedia communication techniques, including internet transmission protocols, networks, media packaging, encryption, and watermarking may be found at http://streamingmedialand.com/technology_frameset.html.

5.4   Client-Design Issues

The design of the client will, as always, be dominated by questions of cost, functionality, and convenience. The variety of available client devices is high, ranging from a full-fledged personal computer or workstation, an optimized personal computer, an upgraded television set with internal or external set-top capability, or a mobile phone with video/graphical capabilities. For instance, the IST SAMBITS* project, driven by Siemens Corporate Technology, Heinrich-Hertz Institute, Philips France, and Frauenhofer Gesellschaft, aimed to provide digital video broadcasting (DVB) with complementary Internet services to set-top boxes at home.

In contrast to a pull application, where users issue a request to a MMDBMS, it is a push application, where media and metadata are continuously streamed to the end-user. The aim of the SAMBITS and related projects is to develop real-time technology for interactive multimedia services in a push scenario.

Metadata play an important role in the future of interactive television. Interactive broadcasting will combine traditional television with additional services including Internet access, content-environment DVB-MHP (DVB–multimedia home platform), interactivity through the use of MPEG-4, and content navigation and search through the use of MPEG-7.[86] Television viewers will be able to watch background information related to the program. For an advertisement, one may receive additional information on the product features and prices and may display the homepage of the product. In a music contest, the viewer can look at the show and see, in addition, backstage, look at a video clip showing the actor at home, and retrieve metadata on the song and the actor, such as his or her birthday, favorite meal, and so on.

In view of the emerging scalable coding technologies, synchronization of different streams of an audiovisual document is of importance, as well as synchronization of the media documents with the exchanged descriptive information. As there is a solution proposed for MPEG-2 and metadata (e.g., MPEG-7), solutions for synchronization mechanisms of MPEG-7 and MPEG-4 access units and cross-referencing of MPEG-7 and MPEG-4 data are under development.

Apart from the above hardware considerations, decisions about the software interfaces are of importance. Most related works have proposed very proprietary solutions, reflected by the hardware prerequisites and the software tools employed.[87–89] Moreover, the possible limited client resource availability led not only to the question of which functions to be

*SAMBITS is an acronym for System for Advanced Multimedia Broadcast and Information Technology Services. More information on SAMBITS may be found at http://www.irt.de/sambits/.

executed locally or at the server but also to the question of how to adapt the content of the media to use the client resources effectively. This is accentuated by the growing need for personalized environments.

Several multimedia software frameworks have been defined to help the programmer to define and implement the multimedia applications; for instance, the JMF for Java (Java Media Framework* for Java) and the MET++** for C++. Let us consider JMF as a very popular use case.

5.4.1 Software Media Framework Use Case: JMF

JMF (current version can be downloaded from http://java.sun.com/prod-ucts/java-media/jmf/) is a large and versatile API (application program interface) for creating Java programs enabled to play back a wide variety of time-based media formats such as video and audio.

The popularity of JMF comes from vast media support, such as AVI (audio video interlaced), Quicktime, AIFF (Audio Interchange File Format), AU (Audio File Format), WAV (Windows Wave File Format), Real Media, MPEG-1, MPEG-2, and MPEG-4, and protocol support for UDP, RTP, TCP, and so on. In addition, JMF incorporates media capture capabilities as well as playback. By programming to the JMF API, developers can create platform-independent applications and applets that synchronize media playback. JMF can be combined with other software frameworks, such as JavaBean, allowing media playback to be incorporated into component-based pro-grams. JMF can be used to:

- Play multimedia files in a Java application or applet and play stream-ing media format from the Internet
- Capture audio and video with a microphone and video camera, then store the data in a format supported by JMF
- Transmit audio and video on the Internet, broadcast live radio and television programs
- Process time-based media; for example, build a chain of analysis tools that perform content adaptation, video segmentation, render the video for display, and so on

The installation of a JMF Media Player will demonstrate the program-ming paradigm of JMF. A Media Player simply takes a stream of audio or video as input and renders it to the speaker or a screen.

The JMF Media Player has to prepare itself and its data source before it can start playing the media. JMF defines six states in a player (e.g., realiz-ing, prefetching, start). Contained within the com.sun.media.content.video and com.sun.media.content.audio subpackages are classes capable of parsing and handling the variety of content types supported by JMF. All of

---

*http://java.sun.com/products/java-media/jmf/.
**http://www.ifi.unizh.ch/groups/mml/projects/met++/met++.html.

these classes implement the javax.media.Player interface, and an object of the correct type is automatically instantiated to match the type of media being loaded, so the developer only needs to address an object of type player.

For example, assume that a player will display our MPEG-1 video pisa.mpeg file. When this video is loaded using the JMF API, an object of type com.sun.media.content.video.mpeg.Handler is created to deal with this specific content type. Then, a player object is created using a reference to either a local or remote media resource. Player objects have ancestor methods to return the UserInterface components needed to render the media content and also a custom set of controls for that content, which can be added to a standard Java UserInterface.

Exhibit 5.7 shows the standard player application using the default controls and the media property panel for our layer object.

5.5 Content Adaptation

The advances in network technology, together with novel communication protocols and the considerably enhanced throughput bandwidths of networks, attracted more and more consumers to load or stream multimedia data to their PCs. Despite all these technological progresses, to date, nobody can guarantee for an end-to-end QoS over a variety of heterogeneous network domains and devices. For instance, when trying to connect the local network of the University of Klagenfurt (Institute of Information Technology) to that of the University of Krakow (Computer Science Department) we observed at least four different domains having different capacities and characteristics; for example, different link bandwidths and error rates.[19]

One promising solution is to resort to the adaptation principle; for example, dynamic content adaptation of the media quality to the level admitted by the network.[90–93] The requirement for the use of effective content adaptation is accentuated by the client constraints; for example, a user requests for an HDTV quality video object, but the access constraint of the terminal forces the user to view a low-resolution video. In this regard, content must also include personalization and user profile management. These issues are tackled in the MPEG-21[79] DI adaptation part, as described in Chapter 3.4.

Content adaptation is achieved by modifying the quality of a media object so that it can be delivered over the network with the available bandwidth and can then be presented at the terminal satisfying its access and user constraints. The quality of a media object, usually considered adaptable, refers to the resolution of an object and its play rate.[94] Exhibit 5.8 reconsiders the C-S Multimedia System of Exhibit 5.2 for content adaptation.

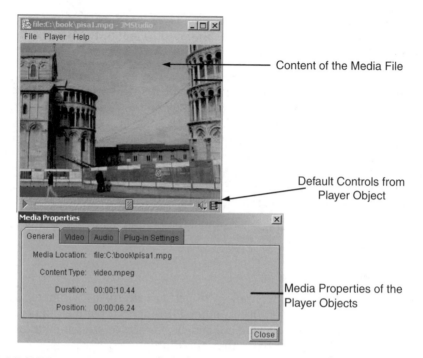

Exhibit 5.7. JMF Standard Player application showing our example video, pisa.mpg.

The server adapts the stored MPEG-4 videos (Main Profile) per request so that they may be displayed on the terminals. For the mobile phone, the video object with the highest priority among the objects compliant to the simple profile will be retained. For the PDA, all video objects not compliant to MPEG-4 Core are removed.

Content adaptation is related to the widely known Universal Multimedia Access (UMA) framework, which means universal access to rich multimedia. This includes methods for scalable coding and content adaptation. Research on UMA is pursued, for example, by projects at EPFL Lausanne (http://ltswww.epfl.ch/~newuma); at NTNU Trondheim (http://www.midgardmedia.net/);[95] at Columbia University, New York (http://www.ctr.columbia.edu/~ywang/Research/UMA/); and at Siemens, Munich (Multimedia Message Box) and in the ADMITS project (http://www-itec.uni-klu.ac.at/~harald/research.html).[96,105,107] These UMA projects provide important results and insights into media adaptation and supply terminal and network capability descriptions as well as user preference descriptions to steer the adaptation process. The latter also holds for the current activities in MPEG-21 DI Adaptation,[79] as described in detail in Chapter 3.4.

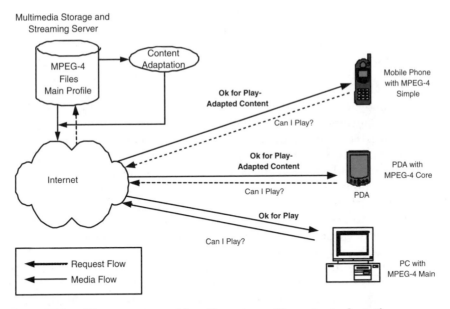

Exhibit 5.8.   Client–server multimedia system with content adaptation.

Content Adaptation is supported by scalable coding. For instance, in MPEG-4,[55] content adaptation can effectively drop video objects (VO) in the MPEG-4 encoded video by attributing priorities to the different VOs and adapting the stream by discarding VOs by their priority information.

Content adaptability depends on the type of media encoding technique employed. In the paragraphs that follow, we will describe content adaptation possibilities for MPEG-4 AV streams. Scalable coding is equally considered for scene descriptions, two- and three-dimensional graphics, and avatars, which are important for distributed games. Research involves here the selection of scalable coding for scene descriptions and vector graphics, focusing on complexity-optimized decoding, composition, and rendering algorithms allowing implementation on terminal devices with low computational power.

Considering MPEG-4 AV streams, content adaptation can be exercised either on single or composed elements of the syntactical structure of an MPEG-4 AV streams by the following means[94,97,98]:

- Translation: Translation involves the conversion from one modality (image, video, text, audio, synthetic model) to another. Examples of translation are text-to-speech, speech-to-text (speech recognition), video-to-image (video mosaicking), image-to-text (embedded caption recognition) conversions, and three-dimensional model rendering.

221

- Summary: This involves the reduction of information details (AV abstract). Examples of summaries include the MPEG-7 summary DS and its subtypes.[99] For example, the subtype SequentialSummary DS can be used for representing multiple key frames extracted from a single Internet streaming video,[100] as it provides the possibility of linking a summary to a VideoSegment.
- Scaling: Scaling involves operations of data transcoding, manipulation, and compression, which result in the reduction of size and quality. Examples of scaling include image, video, and audio transcoding; image size reduction; video frame dropping; color conversion; and Discrete Cosine Transform coefficient scaling.
- Extraction: This involves the extraction of information from the input. Examples of extraction include key frame extraction from video; audio-band and voice extraction from audio; paragraph and key term extraction from text, region, segment, and object; and event extraction from audio and video.
- Substitution: Substitution indicates that one representation can be used to substitute another. Examples of substitution include a text passage that replaces a photographic image when a photographic image cannot be handled by a terminal device, or an audio track that replaces a chart in a presentation.
- Revision: This indicates that the AV program was revised in some way, such as through editing or postprocessing, to achieve the quality adaptation.

Content adaptation can successfully be employed at different levels of the network. For instance, a proxy cache may change the compression ratio of the streamed data to adapt to a changing network bandwidth. An active router may discard an enhancement layer to act against sudden network congestion. A proxy cache can enhance its cache replacement policy by applying filter algorithms to obtain more space instead of replacing an object and, therefore, enhance its cache hit-rate.

There are some initial works considering these issues on proxy caches,[40,101,102] but to the best of our knowledge, there is not any work done for other network components. In this context, our ADMITS project[103–105] proposes to encode the adaptation capability information of multimedia data into MPEG-7 descriptors to provide this information to the components on the delivery path to the client. This information may then be used to improve the performance of these components; for example, they may govern their replacement policies better. MPEG-7 is well suited in this context, as it proposes special descriptors to describe content adaptation (e.g., the Variation DS).

For instance, the following spatialReduction variation of the first frame in our pisa.mpg would lead to the following MPEG-7 fragment (Exhibit 5.9).

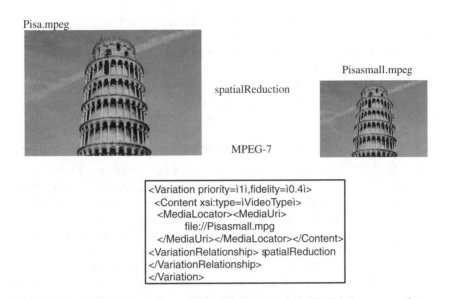

Pisa.mpeg

spatialReduction

Pisasmall.mpeg

MPEG-7

```
<Variation priority=ì1ì,fidelity=ì0.4ì>
  <Content xsi:type=ìVideoTypeì>
  <MediaLocator><MediaUri>
        file://Pisasmall.mpg
    </MediaUri></MediaLocator></Content>
<VariationRelationship> spatialReduction
</VariationRelationship>
</Variation>
```

Exhibit 5.9.   MPEG-7–based content adaptation: spatialReduction example.

In this sense, the ADMITS project aims at global adaptation based on properly distributed individual adaptation measures. This is in accordance with newer approaches in peer-to-peer networking (in comparison to the more C-S-oriented UMA architectures; see also the architectural consideration at the beginning of this Chapter 5), such as the Media Accelerating Peer Services, as described in Lienhart et al.[106] More information on the ADMITS is given below.

Another important issue is the support of the MMDBMS in the content adaptation process. From the point of view of a MMDBMS, the proposed multimedia data models are not able to satisfy the requirements of content adaptation. The implemented data models contain actually only very rudimentary information about the delivery of data, for example, frame rate, but more advanced features such as the quality adaptation capabilities of the streams are not considered. This information would be of interest to the user. For instance, a mobile client is only interested in videos being adaptable to the special requirements of the mobile terminal. Therefore, it is necessary to propose a common framework for modeling and querying content information and quality adaptation capabilities of AV data.[107]

The modeling of the perceptual quality of AV data, with respect to the adaptation possibilities, is the other important issue for effective content adaptation. There have been recent considerable advances in the domain of video quality modeling. Examples are the works of Winkler[108–110] as well as the techniques worked out in the Video Quality Experts Group.[111] The proposed methods focus on the effect of variable bit rates on perceptual quality. For instance, the ITU-R Recommendation 500[112] proposes several standards for perceptual quality testing, including viewing conditions, criteria for observer selection, assessment procedures, and analysis methods. However, conceptualizing and validating models for the perceptual quality of a video with respect to the content adaptation on single or composed elements, as described above, is an open research issue.

5.5.1 Use Case: Metadata-Driven Adaptation in the ADMITS Project

The ADMITS project[103–105],* realizes an end-to-end multimedia delivery chain as shown in Exhibit 5.10. The exhibit gives a walkthrough of the metadata-driven adaptation in the end-to-end multimedia scenario. The numbers in the shaded circles indicate the sequence of events in the adaptation process. The individual components play different roles in the adaptation process. They are connected physically by the network and semantically by MPEG-7 metadata that flow over the network in conjunction with the media data. The major components, together with the metadata life cycle, are discussed in the sequel.

5.5.2 Metadatabase

The metadatabase supports all kinds of adaptations by supplying metadata. Queries formulated by the clients are forwarded to the metadatabase, containing data about the AV data stored on the media server. The metadata enables multiple functionality:

- Support of content-based queries, based on low- or high-level indexing information
- Support of adaptation based on metainformation, such as the definition of transcoding procedures with the help of MPEG-7 variation descriptors

5.5.3 Adaptive Virtual Video Server

The adaptive virtual video server provides a means for component adaptation. The video server stores the raw AV data. It has a distributed architecture containing a number of nodes. In particular, it is composed of a media storage server and a metadatabase (Exhibit 5.10). Content indexing for obtaining relevant metadata is done in two ways: the media is analyzed for semantic and structural content (Step 1a) and for its adaptation capabilities (Step 1b). Therefore, we extract two categories of metadata in two steps:

*This research project is funded in part by FWF (Fonds zur Förderung der wissenschaftlichen Forschung), under the project numbers P14788 and P14789, and KWF (Kärntner Wirtschaftsförderungsfonds). http://www-itec.uni-klu.ac.at/~harald/research.html.

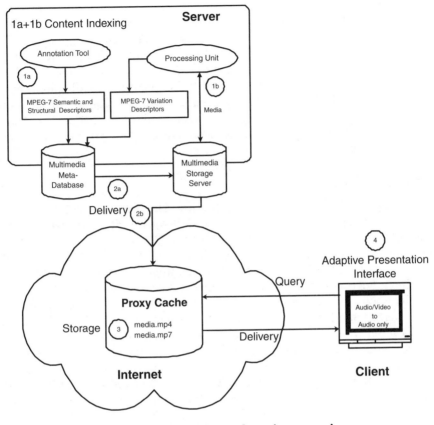

Exhibit 5.10. End-to-end metadata-driven adaptation scenario.

- Step 1a: In this step, video segmentation is carried out, and semantically meaningful information is extracted; for example, which events, persons, and objects are the important entities of a segment. Furthermore, low-level descriptors are extracted; for instance, the MPEG-7 DominantColor and the ScalableColorType. MPEG-7 Semantic and structural Descriptors enable content-based queries.[107]
- Step 1b: In this step, MPEG-7 Variation Descriptors are produced. These descriptors express the relationship between the available variations of the media and their characteristics in terms of media information (e.g., file size and frame rate) and quality.

The ADMITS server provides delivery functionality for media and its descriptive metadata. Therefore, on a media request, the media server contacts the metadatabase for descriptions (Step 2a). These descriptions are attached to the media stream and delivered to the client (Step 2b).

The server is called virtual because it is able to change the set of actually allocated physical nodes on demand. The infrastructure recommends nodes to be allocated to implement adaptation. For example, in a specific scenario, a component called the host recommender might notice that a client is "far" from the nodes storing the stripe units (e.g., because of a slow connection) and that, therefore, it would be desirable to allocate a new node near the client to act as a data collector and streaming proxy. The proxy functionality is loaded by the so-called application loader. After that, the other nodes of the server push their stripe units to the new node, which collects and streams them to the client.

5.5.4 Adaptive Proxy Cache

This component supports media adaptation. The proxy cache implements improved, quality-aware versions of the well-known LRU and greedy dual-size algorithms. The cache initially stores full videos with their respective metadata descriptions in the form of MPEG-7 variation descriptors, and it reduces their quality (and thus their size) in integral steps before fully deleting them. Fortunately, the relation between size and quality reduction is usually nonlinear up to a certain limit, and hence, large size reduction usually causes a moderate quality loss. Thus, the cache can offer both short start-up delay and acceptable quality. The essential new idea is that the quality reduction process is driven by metadata in a standardized format (MPEG-7) that is readily provided in ADMITS by the metadatabase (Step 3 of Exhibit 5.10). For each adaptable video, the cache expects just the simple triple parameter (transcoding operation, resulting size, resulting quality).

5.5.5 Adaptive Routers

Routers with enriched functionality may support media adaptation as well. In contrast to a proxy cache, the operations that a router can perform on a media stream are fairly limited, as the forwarding speed must not be compromised significantly. In contrast, a router is best positioned, for example, to cope judiciously with dynamically varying network load (most importantly, congestion) or to multicast media streams along heterogeneous links or toward clients with different capabilities. Typical adaptation operations of routers would be dropping of video frames, of certain enhancement layers, or of entire MPEG-4 elementary streams. The challenge in this context is to provide and efficiently encode and communicate metadata for routers that convey this information and enable them to perform effective media adaptations.

5.5.6 Adaptive Query and Presentation Interface

The adaptive query and presentation interface supports the specification of search criteria for media resources, displays results from the database (metadata), proposes means for selecting the media from the database results, and opens players for the selected media. It is the final adaptation level in the end-to-end scenario as depicted in Exhibit 5.10, Step 4. It is adaptive in the sense that all interface components adjust dynamically to the usage environment. The usage environment comprises the client's terminal capabilities (e.g., hardware, software) and the usage preferences (e.g., user prefers only audio files).

5.6 Summary

Distributed multimedia database technologies involve network technology, distributed control, multimedia security, multimedia computing, and multimedia content adaptation. This chapter discussed fundamental concepts and introduced VoD systems including video streaming server technology (Section 5.1), multimedia communication and synchronization (Section 5.2), client-design issues—mainly hardware and software requirements and implementations (Section 5.3), and finally, multimedia content adaptation in Section 5.4. With the maturity of these technologies, we are today experiencing multimedia communication such as video conferencing, digital television, distance education, online games, and so forth. Because of the original focus and design of network communication protocol (i.e., TCP/IP), real-time broadband communication is not yet feasible on the current Internet; however we also experience good quality videos on the Internet. This is because of encoding efficiency that has been considerably improved (e.g., with the new MPEG-4 codec available). In addition, scalable coding techniques will provide us in the near future with richer multimedia access than today, access that will be adapted to resource constraints and usage profiles. Moreover, advanced communication protocols, mainly IPv6, are under investigation, which will enable sufficient QoS for multimedia applications, including mobile applications. Finally, in a more general context, content adaptation tools will supply us with universal multimedia access from anywhere at anytime. A major player in the domain of multimedia communication is surely MPEG-21, which proposes an open multimedia framework for interoperable usage of multimedia data, including scalable coding as well as content adaptation.

Universal Multimedia Access (UMA) implies an improved availability of media, often realized through distributed Web spaces. In this context, intellectual properties have to be managed. That means that a distributed multimedia database system has to provide the means to enable content to be persistently and reliably managed and protected across networks and devices. In particular, protection of copyright has to be guaranteed. A promising technology under investigation is the watermark technology. The purpose of such a technology is to embed copyright information into multimedia clips. MPEG-21 integrates intellectual property management and protection, as well as persistence management (watermarking and related technologies to protect the copyright) in one framework. The combination of multimedia communication management together with intellectual property management is one of the main topics of MPEG-21 standardization activities in 2003, and International Standards will be delivered in spring 2004. Such an integrated framework is crucial to multimedia applications. Communication management can no longer be separated from intellectual property and session mobility management for an effective use of multimedia data in today's applications. For instance, consider a person sitting in an international train and downloading the newest Madonna AV clip from a server in the U.S. to her mobile handheld computer. During the download, the train crosses the boarder from Germany to France. Obviously, it is undesirable to have to restart the download in the new network (the France mobile network) and to reauthenticate and renegotiate the rights for download again. The solution to this problem is the employment of session mobility management tools that allow transferring a session to a new network and resolving rights and authentication such that in our case, the download can smoothly continue.

References

1. de Vries, A.P., van Doorn, M.G.L.M., Blanken, H.M., and Apers, P.M.G., The MIRROR MMDBMS architecture, in Proceedings of the International Conference on Very Large Databases, Edinburgh, 1999, pp. 758–761.
2. Oria, V., Özsu, M.T., Iglinski, P., Lin, S., and Ya, B., DISIMA: a distributed and interoperable image database system, in *Proceedings of the ACM SIGMOD International Conference of Management of Data*, Dallas, May 2000, p. 600.
3. Mühlhäuser, M. and Gecsei, J., Services, frameworks, and paradigms for distributed multimedia applications, *IEEE MultiMedia*, 3, 48–61, 1996.
4. Böszörményi, L., Stary, C., Kosch, H., and Becker, C., Distributed multimedia object/component systems (DMMOS'2001), in *Workshop Reader of the 15th European Conference for Object-Oriented Programming*, LNCS 2323, Budapest, June 2001, Springer-Verlag, New York, pp. 7–29.
5. Goldschmidt, B., Tusch, R., and Böszörmenyi, L., A mobile agent-based infrastructure for an adaptive multimedia server, in *Proceedings of the International Conference on Distributed and Parallel Systems DAPSYS'2002*, Linz, September–October 2002, pp. 141–148.
6. Chan, S. and Tobagi, F., Distributed servers architecture for networked video services, *IEEE Trans. Networking*, 9, 125–136, 2001.
7. Xu, D., Hefeeda, M., Hambrush, S., and Bhargava, B., On peer-to-peer media streaming, in *Proceedings of IEEE International Conference on Distributed Computing Systems (ICDCS'02)*, Vienna, July 2002, pp. 363-373.
8. Nguyen, T. and Zakhor, A., Distributed video streaming over Internet, *SPIE Conference on Multimedia Computing and Networking 2002 (MMCN 2002)*, San Jose, January 2002.
9. Guedes, L.A., Oliveres, P.G., Paina, L.F., and Cordozo, E., An agent based approach for supporting quality of service, *Comput. Comm.*, 21, 1269–1278, 1998.
10. Manvi, S. and Venkataram, P., QoS management by mobile agents in multimedia communication, in *Proceedings of the International DEXA 2000 Workshops*, Greenwich, London, September 2000, IEEE CS Press, pp. 407–411.

11. Kosch, H., Döller, M., and Böszörményi, L., Content-based indexing and retrieval supported by mobile agent technology, in *2nd International Workshop on Multimedia Databases and Image Communications (MDIC)*, Amalfi, September 2001, pp. 152–166.
12. Özsu, M.T. and Valdueriez, P., *Principles of Distributed Database Systems*, Prentice-Hall, Englewood Cliffs, NJ, 1999.
13. Lu, G., *Multimedia Database Management Systems*, Artech House, 1999.
14. Oracle9i InterMedia audio, image, and video user's guide and reference, http://technet.oracle.com.
15. Senna, J., Oracle Video Server delivers, *InfoWorld*, 20, June 1998.
16. Sullivan, S.C., Winzeler, L., Deagen, J., and Brown, D., *Programming With the Java Media Framework*, John Wiley & Sons, Wiley Computer Books, New York, 1998.
17. Gemmell, D.J., Vin, H.M., Kandlur, D.D., Rangan, P.V., and Rowe, L.A., Multimedia storage servers: a tutorial, *IEEE Comput.*, 28, 40–49, 1995.
18. Buddhikot, M.M., Parulkar, G.M., and Cox, J.R., Jr., Design of a large scale multimedia storage server, *Comput. Networks ISDN Syst.*, 27, 503–517, 1994.
19. Kosch, H., Sota, R., Kitowski, J., Nikolow, D., Podlipnig, S., and Breidler, K., MMSRS—multimedia storage and retrieval system for a distributed medical information system, in *High Performance Computing and Networking (HPCN) 2000 Conference*, Amsterdam, May 2000, LNCS 1823, Springer-Verlag, New York, pp. 517–524.
20. Kim, K.H. and Park, S., Storage system for supporting more video streams in video server, *Multimedia Tools Appl.*, 13, 177–196, 2001.
21. Ghose, D. and Kim, H.J., Scheduling video streams in video-on-demand systems: a survey, *Multimedia Tools Appl.*, 11, 167–195, 2000.
22. Dan, A., Feldman, S.I., and Serpanos, D.N., Evolution and challenges in multimedia, *IBM J. Res. Dev.*, 24, 177–184, 1998.
23. Tsao, S.L., Chen, M.C., Ko, M.T., Ho, J.M., and Huang, Y.M., Data allocation and dynamic load balancing for distributed video storage server, *J. Visual Comm. Image Representation*, 10, 197–218, 1999.
24. Wu, C.-S., Ma, G.-K., and Liu, M.-C., A scalable storage supporting multistream real-time data retrieval, *ACM Multimedia Syst.*, 7, 458–466, 1999.
25. Dan, A. and Sitaram, D., An online video placement policy based on bandwidth to space ratio (bsr), in *Proceedings of the International ACM SIGMOD Conference*, San Jose, May 1995, pp. 376–385.
26. Serpanos, D., Georgiadis, L., and Bouloutas, A., Mmpacking: a load and storage balancing algorithm for distributed multimedia servers, *IEEE Trans. Circuits Syst. Video Technol.*, 8, 13–17, 1998.
27. Dan, A., Kienzle, M., and Sitaram, D., Dynamic policy of segment replication for load-balancing in video-on-demand servers, *ACM Multimedia Syst.*, 3, 93–103, 1995.
28. Chou, C., Golubchik, L., and Lui, J., A performance study of dynamic replication techniques in continuous media servers, in *Proceedings of the ACM SIGMETRICS International Conference on Measurement and Modeling of Computing Systems*, New York, May 1–4, 1999, Vol. 27.1, SIGMETRICS Performance Evaluation Review, ACM Press, pp. 202-203.
29. Chou, C., Golubchik, L., and Lui, J., Striping doesn't scale: how to achieve scalability for continuous media servers with replication, in *20th International Conference on Distributed Computing Systems (ICDCS '00)*, Washington, D.C., April 2000, IEEE, pp. 64–71.
30. Boral, H., Alexander, W., Clay, L., Copeland, G., Danforth, S., Franklin, M., Hart, B., Smith, M., and Valduriez, P., Prototyping Bubba, a highly parallel database system, *IEEE Trans. Knowl. Data Eng.*, 2, 5–24, June 1990.
31. Balkir, N.H. and Özsoyoglu, G., Delivering presentations from multimedia servers, *VLDB J.*, 7, 294–307, 1998.

32. Balkir, N.H. and Özsoyoglu, G., Multimedia presentation servers: buffer management and admission control, in *Proceedings of the International Workshop on Multimedia Database Management Systems*, Dayton, August 1998, IEEE CS Press, pp. 154–161.
33. Dengler, J., Bernhardt, C., and Biersack, E., Deterministic admission control strategies in video servers with variable bit rate streams, in *Workshop on Interactive Distributed Multimedia Systems and Services (IDMS)*, Heidelberg, March 1996, LNCS 2045, Springer-Verlag, Heidelberg, pp. 245–264.
34. Nagy, S. and Bestavros, A., Admission control for soft-deadline transactions in AC-CORD, in *Proceedings of the 3rd IEEE Real-Time Technology and Applications Symposium (RTAS)*, Washington, D.C., June 1997, IEEE, pp. 160–165.
35. Dan, A., Sitaram, D., and Shahabuddin, P., Dynamic batching policies for an on-demand video server, *ACM Multimedia Syst.*, 4, 112–121, 1996.
36. Lau, S.-W., Lui, C.S., and Golubchik, L., Merging video streams in Multimedia Storage Server: complexity and heuristics, *Multimedia Syst.*, 6, 29–42, 1998.
37. Dan, A. and Sitaram, D., Multimedia caching strategies for heterogeneous application and server environments, *Multimedia Tools Appl.*, 4, 279–312, 1997.
38. Tsai, W.-J. and Lee, S.-Y., Dynamic buffer management for near video-on-demand systems, *Multimedia Tools Appl.*, 6, 61–83, 1998.
39. Tsai, W.-J. and Lee, S.-Y., Buffer-sharing techniques in service-guaranteed video servers. *Multimedia Tools Appl.*, 9, 121–145, 1999.
40. Rejaie, R., Yu, H., Handley, M., and Estrin, D., Multimedia proxy caching mechanism for quality adaptive streaming applications in the Internet, in *Proceedings of the 2000 IEEE Computer and Communications Societies Conference on Computer Communications (INFOCOM-00)*, Los Alamitos, March 26–30, 2000, IEEE CS Press, pp. 980–989.
41. Yeung, K.H. and Ng, K.W., An optimal cache replacement algorithm for Internet systems, in *Proceedings, 22nd annual Conference on Local Computer Networks: LCN '97*, Minneapolis, November 1997, IEEE CS Press.
42. Wang, J., A survey of Web caching schemes for the Internet, *ACM Comput. Comm. Rev.*, 25, 36–46, October 1999.
43. Sen, S., Rexford, J., and Towsley, T., Proxy prefix caching for multimedia streams. Technical Report UM-CS-1998-027, University of Massachusetts, Amherst, August 1998.
44. Kosch, H., Moustefaoui, A., and Brunie, L., Semantic based prefetching in news-on-demand video servers, *Multimedia Tools Appl.*, 18(2), 159–179, 2002.
45. Martínez, J.M., Overview of the MPEG-7 Standard. ISO/IEC JTC1/SC29/WG11 N4980 (Klagenfurt Meeting), July 2002, http://www.chiariglione.org/mpeg/.
46. Bouras, C., Kapoulas, V., Miras, D., Ouzounis, V., Spirakis, P., and Tatakis, A., On-demand hypermedia/mutimedia service using preorcestrated scenarios over the Internet, *Networking Info. Syst. J.*, 2, 741–762, 1999.
47. Raymond, T.N. and Paul, S., Optimal clip ordering for multi-clip queries, *VLDB J.*, 7, 239–252, 1998.
48. Zhang, A. and Gollapudi, S., QoS management in educational digital library environments, *Multimedia Tools Appl.*, 10, 133–156, 2000.
49. Anderson, D.P., Device reservation in audio/video editing systems, *ACM Trans. Comput. Syst.*, 15, 111–133, 1997.
50. Shahabi, C., Dashti, A.I., and Ghandeharizadeh, S., Continuous media retrieval optimizer and hierarchical storage structures, in *3rd International Conference on Integrated Design and Process Technology IADT'98*, Berlin, 1998, pp. 360–367.
51. Garofalakis, M. and Ioannidis, Y., Resource scheduling for composite multimedia objects, in *Proceedings of the International Conference on Very Large Databases*, New York, August 1998, pp. 74–85.
52. Kosch, H., Moustefaoui, A., Böszörményi, L., and Brunie, L., Multi-clip query optimization in video databases, in *IEEE Multimedia and Expo Conference 2000*, New York, July 2000, pp. 363–366.

53. Kosch, H., Böszörményi, L., Moustefaoui, A., and Brunie, L., Heuristics for optimizing multi-clip queries in video databases, *Multimedia Tools Appl.*, to appear.
54. Jiang, H., Montesi, D., and Elmagarmid, A.K., Integrated video and text for content-based access to video databases. *Multimedia Tools Appl.*, 9, 227–249, 1999.
55. Koenen, R., MPEG-4 overview. ISO/IEC JTC1/SC29/WG11 N4668 (Jeju Meeting), March 2002, http://www.chiariglione.org/mpeg/.
56. Asrar Haghighi, K., Pourmohammdi, Y., and Alnuweiri, H.M., Realizing MPEG-4 streaming over the Internet: a client/server architecture using DMIF, in *International Conference on Information Technology: Coding and Computing*, Las Vegas, April 2001, IEEE CS Press.
57. Haghighi, A., Mohamed, A., and Alnuweiri, H.M., Streaming MPEG-4 over IP and broadcast networks: DMIF based architectures, in *Proceedings of the International Packet Video Workshop (PV2001)*, April 2001.
58. Feamster, N., Bansal, D., and Balakrishnan, H., On the interactions between layered quality adaptation and congestion control for streaming video, in *Proceedings of the International Packet Video Workshop (PV2001)*, April 2001.
59. Rejaie, R., Handley, M., and Estrin, D., Layered quality adaptation for Internet video streaming, *IEEE J Selected Areas Comm.*, 18, 2530–2544, 2000.
60. Steinmetz, R., *Multimedia Technology*, 2nd ed., Springer-Verlag, New York, 2000.
61. Paek, S. and Chang, S.F., Video-server retrieval scheduling and resource reservation for variable bit rate scalable video, *IEEE Trans. Circuits Syst. Analog Digital Signal Process.*, 10, 460–474, 2000.
62. Du, D.H-G. and Lee, Y.-J., Scalable server and storage architectures for video streaming, in *International Conference on Multimedia Computing and Systems (ICMCS)*, Vol. 1, Florence, 1999, IEEE CS Press, pp. 62–67.
63. Pietro, G.D. and Lerro, M., The split-proxy approach: a new architecture for parallel video servers, in *International ACPC Conference*, Salzburg, February 1999, LNCS 1557, Springer-Verlag, New York, pp. 327–336.
64. Lin, C.-S. and Wu, M.-Y., Performance study of synchronization schemes on parallel cbr video servers, in *International ACM Multimedia Conference*, Orlando, FL, November 1999, pp. 143–146.
65. Lee, J.Y.B., Parallel video servers: a tutorial, *IEEE MultiMedia*, 5, 20–28, 1998.
66. Bolosky, W.J., Barrera, S., Draves, P., Fitzgerald, P., Gibson, A., Jones, B., Levi, P., Myhrvold, P., and Rashid, F., The Tiger Video Fileserver. Technical report, Microsoft Research, Advanced Technology Division, Microsoft Corporation, 1996. MSR-TR96-09.
67. Hjelsvold, R., Langørgen, S., Midtstraum, R., and Sandstå, O., *Searching and Browsing a Shared Video Database*, Kluwer Academic Publishers, Dordrecht, 1996, pp. 89–122.
68. Kosch, H., Breidler, K., and Böszörményi, L., The Parallel Video Server SESAME-KB, in *Distributed and Parallel Systems: From Concepts to Architectures*, Kacsuk, P., and Kotsis, G., eds., Kluwer Press, Balaton, Hungary, 2000, pp. 151–154.
69. Bougé, L., Méhaut, J.-F., and Namyst, R., Efficient communications in multithreaded runtime systems, in *Proceedings of the Workshop on Runtime Systems for Parallel Programming*, San Juan, Puerto Rico, April 1999, LNCS 1586, Springer-Verlag, New York.
70. Shahabi, C. and Alshayeji, M.H., Super-streaming: a new object delivery paradigm for continuous media servers. *Multimedia Tools Appl.*, 11, 129–155, 2000.
71. Bolosky, W.J., Fitzgerald, P.R., and Douceur, J., Distributed schedule management in the Tiger video fileserver, in *ACM Symposium on Operating System Principles*, October 1997, pp. 212–223.
72. Granville, L.Z., Fleischmann, R.U., Tarouco, L.M.R., and Almeida, M.J.B., Management of networks with end-to-end differentiated service QoS capabilities, in *International Workshop on Advances in Information System*, Izmir, October 2000, LNCS 1909, Springer-Verlag, New York, pp. 147–158.
73. Braden, R., Zhang, L., Berson, S., Herzog, S., and Jamin, S., Resource reservation protocol (RSVP)—version 1 functional specification, *Internet RFC 2205*, 1997.

74. Goncalves, M. and Niles, K., *IPv6 Networks*, McGraw-Hill, New York, 1998.
75. Basturk, E., Birman, A., Delp, G., Guérin, R., Haas, R., Kamat, S., Kandlur, D., Pan, P., Pendarakis, D., Peris, V., Rajan, R., Saha, D., and Williams, D., Design and implementation of a QoS capable switch-router. *Comput. Networks*, 31, 19–32, 1999.
76. Zheng, H. and Boyce, J., An improved UDP protocol for video transmission over internet-to-wireless networks, *IEEE Trans. Multimedia*, 3, 356–365, 2001.
77. Stadler, J., Miladinovic, I., and Pospischil, G., SIP for Unified Data Exchange (SIP4UDE), in *Proceedings of the 1st IEEE Workshop for Applications and Services in Wireless Networks 2002 (ASWN2002)*, Paris, France.
78. Guo, G.D., Li, S.Z., and Zhang, H.J., Distance-from-boundary as a metric for texture image retrieval, in *Proceedings of the International Conference on Acoustics, Speech, and Signal Processing (ICASSP)*, Salt Lake City, May 2001, IEEE CS Press.
79. Hill, K. and Bormans, J., Overview of the MPEG-21 Standard. ISO/IECJTC1/SC29/WG11 N4041 (Shanghai Meeting), October 2002, http://www.chiariglione.org/mpeg/.
80. Shi, C. and Bhargava, B., A fast MPEG video encryption algorithm, in *6th ACM International Multimedia Conference (ACM Multimedia'98)*, Bristol, September 1998, pp. 81-88.
81. Tang, L., Methods for encrypting and decrypting MPEG video data efficiently, in Proceedings of the Fourth ACM Multimedia Conference (MULTIMEDIA'96), New York, November 1996, ACM Press, pp. 219–230.
82. Zhao, J. and Koch, E., A digital watermarking system for multimedia copyright protection, in *Proceedings of the 4th ACM International Multimedia Conference (MULTIMEDIA'96)*, Boston, November 18–22, 1996, pp. 443–444.
83. Voyatzis, G., Nikolaidis, N., and Pitas, I., Digital watermarking: an overview, in *9th European Signal Processing Conference (EUSIPCO'98)*, Island of Rhodes, September 8–11, 1998, pp. 9–12.
84. Dittmann, J., Stabenau, M., and Steinmetz, R., Robust MPEG video watermarking technologies, in *Proceedings of the 6th ACM International Multimedia Conference (ACM Multimedia'98)*, Bristol, September 1998.
85. Liu, H., Ma, H., El Zarki, M., and Gupta, S., Error control schemes for networks: an overview, *Mobile Networks Appl.*, 2, 167–182, 1997.
86. Crysandt, H. and Wellhausen, J., Music classification with MPEG-7, in *Proceedings of the SPIE International Conference on Electronic Imaging—Storage and Retrieval for Media Databases*, Santa Clara, January 2003.
87. Lauff, M. and Gellersen, H.-W., Multimedia client implementation on personal digital assistants, in *Proceedings of the Interactive Distributed Multimedia Systems and Telecommunication Services Workshop*, Darmstadt, September 1997, LNCS 1309, Springer-Verlag, New York.
88. Hu, M.J., Wang, T.F., Boon, T.C., and Lian, C.W., Distributed multimedia database: configuration and application, in *Proceedings of the International Conference on Information, Communications and Signal Processing (ICICS)*, Sydney, November 1999, LNCS 1726, Springer-Verlag, New York.
89. Frankewitsch, T. and Prokosch, H.U., Image database, image proxy-server and search-engine, *Proc.Int. Am.Med.Inf. Assn.*, pp. 765–769, 1999.
90. Gecsei, J., Adaptation in distributed multimedia systems, *Proc. IEEE MultiMedia*, 4, 58–66, 1997.
91. Rejaie, R., On design of Internet multimedia streaming applications: an architectural perspective, in *Proceedings of the IEEE International Conference on Multimedia and Exhibition*, New York, July 2000, pp. 327–330.
92. Mohan, R., Smith, J.R., and Li, C.-S., Adapting multimedia internet content for universal access, *IEEE Trans. Multimedia*, 1, 104–114, 1999.
93. Naghshineh, M. and Willebeek-LeMair, M., End-to-end QoS provisioning in multimedia wireless/mobile networks using an adaptive framework," *IEEE Comm. Mag.*, 35, 72–81, 1997.

94. Prabhakaran, B., Adaptive multimedia presentation strategies, *Multimedia Tools and Appl.*, 12, 281–298, 2000.
95. Perkis, A., Abeljaoued, Y., Cristopoulos, C., Ebrahimi, T., and Chicaro, J.F., Universal multimedia access from wired and wireless systems, *Transact. Circuits Syst.Signal Process., Special Issue on Multimedia Commun,*, 20, 387–402, 2001.
96. Heuer, J., Casas, J.L., and Kaup, A., Adaptive multimedia messaging based on MPEG-7—the M3 box, in *Proceedings of the Second International Symposium on Mobile Multimedia Systems and Applications*, Delft, November 2000.
97. Ramanujan, R.S., Newhouse, J.A., Ahamad, A., Kaddoura, M.N., Chartier, E.R., and Thurber, K.J., Adaptive streaming of MPEG video over IP networks, in *Proceedings of the 22nd IEEE Conference on Computer Networks*, November 1997.
98. Rejaie, R., Handley, M., and Estrin, D., Quality adaptation for congestion controlled video playback over the Internet, in *Proceedings of ACM SIGCOMM 99*, Cambridge, MA, September 1999, pp. 189–200.
99. van Beek, P., Benitez, A.B., Heuer, J., Martinez, J., Salembier, P., Smith, J., and Walker, T., MPEG-7: multimedia description schemes, ISO/IEC FDIS 15938-5:2001, October 2001.
100. Rehm, E., Representing internet streaming media with MPEG-7, in *Proceedings of the ACM Multimedia 2000 Workshop Standards, Interoperability and Practice: Who Needs Standards Anyway?*, New York, November 4, 2000, ACM Press, pp. 93–106.
101. Rejaie, R., Yu, H., Handely, M., and Estrin, D., Multimedia proxy caching mechanism for quality adaptive streaming applications in the Internet, in *Proceedings of IEEE Infocom'2000*, Tel-Aviv, March 2000, pp. 980–989.
102. Podlipnig, S. and Böszörményi, L., Quality-aware proxy caching for web videos, in *Proceedings of the 3rd Austrian-Hungarian Workshop on Distributed and Parallel Systems DAPSYS'2000*, Balatonfüred, September 2000.
103. Kosch, H., Böszörményi, L., and Hellwagner, H., Modeling quality adaptation capabilities of audio-visual data, in *Proceedings of the International DEXA'2001 Workshops*, Munich, September 2001, pp. 141–145.
104. Böszörményi, L., Döller, M., Hellwagner, H., Kosch, H., Libsie, M., and Schojer, P., Comprehensive Treatment of Adaptation in Distributed Mul-timedia Systems in the ADMITS Project, in *Proceedings of the 10th ACM International Conference on Multimedia*, Antibes, November–December 2002, ACM Press.
105. Böszörményi, L., Hellwagner, H., Kosch, H., Libsie, M., and Podlipnig, S., Metadata driven adaptation in the ADMITS Project, *Image Comm.*, 18(8), 749–766, 2003.
106. Lienhart, R., Holliman, M., Chen, Y.-K., Kozintsev, I., and Yeung, M., Improving media services on P2P networks, *IEEE Internet Comput.*, 6, 73–77, 2002.
107. Döller, M. and Kosch, H., An MPEG-7 multimedia data cartridge, in *SPIE Conference on Multimedia Computing and Networking 2003 (MMCN 2003)*, Santa Clara, January 2003.
108. Winkler, S., Visual fidelity and perceived quality: towards comprehensive metrics, in *SPIE Human Vision and Electronic Imaging Conference,*Vol. 4299, San Jose, January 21–26, 2001.
109. Winkler, S., van den Branden Lambrecht, C.J., and Kunt, M., Vision and video: models and applications, in *Vision Models and Applications to Image and Video Processing*, van den Branden Lambrecht, C.J., Ed., Kluwer Academic Publishers, Dordrecht, 2001, chap. 10.
110. Winkler, S., Issues in vision modeling for perceptual video quality assessment, *Signal Process.*, 78, 231–252, 1999.

111. Rohaly, A.M., Corriveau, P., Libert, J., Webster, A., Baroncini, V., Beerends, J., Blin, J.-L., Contin, L., Hamada, T., Harrison, D., Hekstra, A., Lubin, J., Nishida, Y., Nishihara, R., Pearson, J., Pessoa, A.F., Pickford, N., Schertz, A., Visca, M., Watson, A., and Winkler, S., Video Quality Experts Group: current results and future directions, in *Proceedings of SPIE Visual Communications and Image Processing*, Perth, June 21–23, 2000, pp. 742–753.
112. Switzerland ITU, Methodology for the Subjective Assessment of the Quality of Television Pictures, Geneva, 1998.

Chapter 6
Concluding Remarks

Users of future distributed Multimedia Database Management Systems (MMDBMSs) will be heavily mobile and require ubiquitous access to, and satisfactory presentation of, multimedia data, regardless of the actual connectivity and the specific presentation terminal they are currently using. Moreover, users will expect to find information and multimedia content faster and more easily (e.g., query by semantics), and will interact with the content much more intensively than they do today. Finally, users will expect to make avail of more sophisticated multimedia services, such as location-aware services, multimedia billing services, or advanced observation services, that go beyond the simple database searches (e.g., query by color similarity) of today.

This concluding chapter is organized as follows: Section 6.1 summarizes the major contributions of the book. We then focus on semantics in multimedia databases (Section 6.2). The challenge of mobility for MMDBMSs is discussed in Section 6.3. Finally, Section 6.4 draws on the idea of multimedia middleware to bridge the gap between multimedia applications and the network.

6.1 Summary of the Book

The book introduced distributed multimedia database technologies. Its contents were compiled from review of relevant literature, assessment of ongoing projects, and discussion with researchers in the field.

It has been shown in Chapter 4 that broadly used content-based indexing and retrieval methods based on primitive features (such as color, texture, and shape) that can be extracted from the data themselves are not sufficient to meet the requirements of widely used multimedia applications for semantic multimedia indexing and retrieval. However, with the newly emerging MPEG-7 standard, uniform description schemes have been proposed that allow one to build an integrated indexing and retrieval system both for primitive features and semantics. This is why a detailed description of MPEG-7, including a guide on how to build MPEG-7 documents, was given in Chapter 2. Building on the concepts and examples introduced in Chapter 2, we showed in Chapter 4 how a MPEG-7-supported MMDBMS can be realized.

The book was not limited to indexing but also discussed techniques for processing and optimizing queries and for storing, accessing, and finally delivering media data as well as their respective metadata. We introduced the new ISO/IEC SQL/MM standard for querying multimedia data in object-relational databases and compared the data models beyond SQL/MM with that of MPEG-7. A useful collaboration of SQL and MPEG-7 in a MMDBMS was presented that has been applied, for instance, in Kosch.[1]

The distributive aspect of an MMDBMS has so far been neglected, and the research was mostly conducted in isolation from other systems' issues. Therefore, one major contribution of this book was the linking of distributed processing issues to processing and modeling issues in MMDBMSs. We focused here on the effect of MPEG-21, the newly emerging multimedia framework standard, and gave a detailed introduction in Chapter 3. We discussed the effect of MPEG-21 on distributed MMDBMSs with respect to its integration capacity for related coding and metadata standards in Chapter 5. The cooperation of MPEG-21 and MMDBMSs naturally leads to a distributed multimedia system, which enables the augmented use (by rights, intellectual properties, etc.) of multimedia resources across a wide range of networks, devices, and communities.

6.2   Semantics in Multimedia Databases

The management of semantics in multimedia databases is an important concern. To this end, an important contribution of this book the demonstration that it is worthwhile to use semantic information at different levels of abstraction for querying a multimedia database. Examples of high-level abstraction queries are, "give me all sport news from the available TV channels about a penalty caused by a severe foul committed to Ronaldo," or, "give me all videos where Arnold Schwarzenegger is laughing." An example of a low-level semantic abstraction query is, "give me all scores by Klose where he wore the traditional German black and white dress" (match on color feature).

Semantics querying attracted much more attention with the emerging ISO/IEC MPEG-7 Standard. MPEG-7 (see Chapter 2) provides a standardized means of describing audiovisual data content in multimedia environments. Its scope is to facilitate the description of the content of multimedia data so that these data can be searched in a database and browsed, filtered, or interpreted by search engines, filter agents, or any other program. Integrating the semantic descriptors introduced in MPEG-7 into current retrieval tools is an important task.[2]

Semantic querying presupposes efficient semantic indexing. The best technique is a clever combination of manual and automatic indexing methods. We have shown that in many domains (e.g., sports), event detection methods are good enough to make a rough predetermination of the multimedia content and to render manual adaptation simpler.[3]

Using semantics in a MMDBMS is, however, difficult, as the semantics of multimedia data depend on the context in which it is used. Here the meaning of context is twofold. On the one hand, it represents the use of multimedia data in the current application, and on the other hand, it represents the overall placement of the content in the domain to which the application is applied.

Using semantic information equally enhances the performance of distributed multimedia database systems. For instance, in Kosch et al.,[4] the efficiency of prefetching in a multimedia streaming server was improved by using semantic information on the contextual correlations of clips.

However, extracting semantic information cannot be done for free and, hence, involves annotation cost. Therefore, one has to balance the costs of extracting semantic information with the benefits to be obtained from using them. This balance should be determined by qualitative and quantitative analyses. For instance, the contextual information can easily be obtained during the annotation process through video shot detection and by considering the metadata of the already stored and annotated clips, and thus, it is nearly free.

Describing the semantics of multimedia is a complex problem. MPEG-7 provides a solution for generic multimedia content description. Describing the semantics of content is also domain dependent. For instance, the semantic entities differ if we consider a basketball clip (where persons are players and referees) and a political news clip (where persons are politicians, journalists, etc.). As a consequence, the definition of semantic entities should be left to the industrial bodies standardizing domain metadata; for example, NewsML (http://www.newsml.org) for multimedia content used in the news domain. To permit interoperability between the various domains where multimedia is used as the major exchange material, we have to supply a syntactical framework to integrate the different multimedia data models. MPEG-21 provides such a container with the Digital Item Model and enhances descriptions with their digital rights and intellectual properties. An example of this integration is given in Section 4.3. Related to this is the generic ontology by Hunter,[5] which is able to integrate information from multiple genres of multimedia content.

6.3 Mobility

An important factor for the design of a distributed MMDBMS is today's mobile society, where access to multimedia services "anytime, anywhere" is becoming increasingly important. Relevant for determining service requirements are the environmental aspects, such as the user's contextual situation (user preferences), available bandwidth of wireless networks, battery power, and other characteristics of mobile devices.[6]

Let us consider a typical mobile MMDBMS application. A mobile user is walking in the streets of Munich. She would like to check what movies are playing tonight. Her location information is used to select the closest cinema. She connects to the Munich Cinema Database Server, and her user preferences specify what type of movies interest her. Derived from her user preferences and her location, a database query is formulated. As a result of this query, a selection of movies is returned to her. The result presentation is adapted to the user preferences. Different forms are possible, including having a quick look at 5 or 10 seconds of key actions or seeing a number of key frames. Finally, she selects a film and buys the tickets electronically.

This simple mobile MMDBMS application requires a lot of metadata to be searched and exchanged. The multimedia database must contain semantic information on the movies, such as the name of the actors playing in the movie, the movie genre, and so on. It must provide a video summarization that matches the user preferences in terms of content as well as delivery format. Finally, the MMDBMS must resolve issues related to terminal capabilities in terms of memory, bandwidth, display capabilities, and so on. From this application scenario, we identify three main information processes that are crucial.

First, the user's contextual information is crucial, as the query conditions vary depending on the user's situation (location, time, etc.). This contextual information has to be attached to the query for efficient query processing. MPEG-21 defines context information for mobile databases. For instance, the factors on which the media needs of a consumer depend (location, time, etc.) are defined; that is, mapping from user factors to media factors is proposed. In mobile environments, various kinds of situations affect the Users request and also terminals are expected to adaptively control the way media and communication processing are handled. These conditions, such as place, time, surrounding, desirable cost, influence retrieval performance and the way how to deliver the media.

Second, content adaptation in a mobile multimedia database system is crucial. Content adaptation is becoming the key technique to guarantee that a user receives only the information that he or she needs. Content adaptation also means that the delivered content is dynamically adapted to the resource availability (e.g., through transcoding). This book demonstrated that content adaptation may be effectively supported by MPEG-7, which offers metadata for describing the different variations of the audiovisual material (see Chapter 2), and by MPEG-21, which, proposes a framework for distributed adaptation through Digital Item Adaptation (see Chapter 3).

Third, real-time retrieval in mobile environments requires the compact and scalable representation of media and metadata. Thus, new scalable media coding standards are under study within MPEG-21 and shall improve the efficiency of the content delivery and simplify considerably the content adaptation process. Moreover, metadata must be compactly packed. In this context, MPEG-7 proposes the BiM (Binary Format for MPEG-7) for efficiently streaming large Extensible Marketing Language (XML)-based data (see Section 2.7).

Finally, let us remark that true peer-to-peer delivery in mobile environments becomes current practice. Thus, the content delivery chain is no longer one-way, but may change direction in one single database session. To illustrate this, let us return to the first use case example of Chapter 1, which was reconsidered on several occasions further along in the book. A mobile and music-interested user records 10 seconds of a song melody she remembers. To identify the content, she sends the recorded audio piece to an audio recognition service (e.g., the "Music Scout" service from net mobile). If the connection is not lost, she will get a prompt and hopefully positive content identification via SMS (Short Message Service), including the title, the songwriter, and a handle to download the complete version. Let us further assume that the user agrees to download the full version at a low price. Then she will receive an MPEG-1 Audio layer-3 (MP3) file at her mobile phone and is provided with a secure link for downloading the song in a better-quality version later on her desktop at home.

The audio material in this use case is once recorded on the mobile phone and is sent to the recognition database for query and later storage and, once the audio material is downloaded from a music provider server, for local use. Thus, the media delivery in the same session is bidirectional. This example also shows another direction of research that is crucial for future applications. It is the development of persistent storage and management of multimedia resources and metadata in mobile devices; thus, the development of solutions to the question, How can multimedia data be stored persistently, organized and indexed on mobile terminals, and retrieved later?

6.4 Multimedia Middleware

In the age of proliferating information and communication systems, information is becoming a vital production and service provision factor. The interaction between different categories of users is thoroughly supported by multimedia, and without intensive communication and cooperation, this interaction is hardly manageable. To accomplish this level of interaction, an efficient information, communication, and cooperation environment is crucial.[7] The realization of such an environment requires a middleware that provides the necessary multimedia services for the cooperative applications and that also abstracts network and delivery details.

For instance, consider the following cooperative application scenario: In an established working group, participants are exchanging e-mails, phone calls, and several types of multimedia documents. The exchange relies on a multimedia middleware that informs participants, based on their preferences and via their mobile phones, of each new message exchanged on the reflector. In addition, the middleware provides services to search multimedia documents by semantics, to receive multimedia presentations, and to establish peer-to-peer connections between participants.

In this context, a multimedia middleware based on the MPEG-21 framework is a promising technology. MPEG-21 provides for this purpose, in one framework, the low-level functionality that a multimedia middleware must supply: provision of Quality of Service Management, Digital Rights Management (DRM), and XML Data and Streaming Management. MPEG-21 also guarantees efficiency through the use of codecs for XML streams, the capacity of integrating other codecs (e.g., for MPEG-4), and an efficient security and trust management. Furthermore, MPEG-21 smoothly integrates older standards used in cooperative multimedia applications for content negotiations, such as CONNEG from Internet Engineering Task Force (IETF)[8] and Composite Capability and Preference Profiles (CC-PP) from W3C.[9]

Related standard middleware such as CORBA, Java-RMI, Jini, .NET, and so forth, support different subsets of the required features of a multimedia middleware; but none of them supports all requirements.[6] Especially missing are satisfactory support for Quality of Service, for adaptation, and for intellectual property management and protection. Thus, MPEG-21 seems a good candidate to bridge the gap between multimedia applications and the network.

Finally, let us note that MPEG-21 is not limited to the management of multimedia material but may also integrate nonmultimedia shared objects in cooperative applications; for example, courseware material in learning applications, registration information of a new community member, digital signatures, and so forth.

References

1. Kosch, H., MPEG-7 and multimedia database systems, *SIGMOD Rec.*, 31, June 2002.
2. Lux, M. and Becker, J., XML and MPEG-7 for interactive annotation and retrieval using semantic meta-data, *J. Universal Comput. Sci.*, 8, 965–985, 2003.
3. Kosch, H., Tusch, R., Böszörményi, L., Bachlechner, A., Dörflinger, B., Hofbauer, C., Riedler, C., Lang, M., and Hanin, C., SMOOTH—a distributed multimedia database system, in *Proceedings of the International VLDB Conference*, Rome, September 2001, pp. 713–714.
4. Kosch, H., Moustefaoui, A., and Brunie, L., Semantic based prefetching in news-on-demand video servers, *Multimedia Tools Appl.*, 18, 169–179, 2002.

5. Hunter, J., Towards a core ontology for information integration, *J. Digital Inf.*, 4(1), 2003.
6. Perry, M., O'Hara, K., Sellen, A., Brown, B.A.T., and Harper, R., Dealing with mobility: understanding access anytime, anywhere, *ACM Trans. Comput. Hum. Interact.*, 8, 323–347, 2001.
7. Kosch, H., Böszörményi, L., Stary, C., and Becker, C., Distributed multimedia object/component systems and qos in distributed object systems, in *Proceedings of the Workshops held at the 15th European Conference for Object-Oriented Programming (ECOOP) 2001*, Budapest, June 2001, LNCS 2323, Springer-Verlag, New York, pp. 7–29.
8. Protocol-Independent Content Negotiation Framework. IETF-RFC 2703, September 1999.
9. Composite Capability/Preference Profiles (CC/PP): Structure and Vocabularies, W3C Working Draft, March 25, 2003, http://www.w3.org/TR/CCPP-struct-vocab/.

Appendix A
Abbreviations and Acronyms

2D:	Two dimensional
2G:	Second-generation wireless networks
3D:	Three dimensional
3G:	Third-generation wireless networks
AAC:	Advanced audio coding
ACTS:	Advanced communications technology and services
ADMITS:	Adaptation in distributed multimedia information technology systems
ADSL:	Asymmetric Digital Subscriber Line
AIFF:	Audio interchange file format
AMR:	Adaptive multirate
API:	Application program(ming) interface
ARQ:	Automatic repeat request
ASX:	Active streaming XML format
ATM:	Asynchronous transfer mode
AU:	Sun audio file format
AV:	Audiovisual
AVC:	Advanced video coding
AVI:	Audio video interlaced
BFILE:	Binary FILE
BIFS:	Binary format for scene description
BiM:	Binary format for MPEG-7
BLOB:	Binary large object
BR:	Bounding region
BSD:	Bitstream syntax description
CBIR:	Content-based image retrieval
CBR:	Content-based retrieval
CD-ROM:	Compact disk—read only memory
CORBA:	Common object request broker architecture
CODAC:	Modeling and querying content description and quality adaptation capabilities of audiovisual data
CONNEG:	Protocol-independent content negotiation protocol
CC/PP:	Composite capabilities/preferences profile

CS :	Classification Schema
C–S:	Client–server system
CSD:	Color structure descriptor
CTI:	Compression Technologies, Inc.
D:	Descriptor
DB:	Database
DBMS:	Database management system
DCT:	Discrete cosine transform
DDL:	Description definition language
DI:	Digital item
DIA:	Digital item adaptation
DID:	Digital item declaration
DIDL:	Digital item declaration language
DII:	Digital item identification
DMIF:	Delivery multimedia integration framework
DP:	Data-partioning
DRM:	Digital rights management
DS:	Description scheme
DSS:	Digital subscriber service
DTD:	Document type definition
DVB:	Digital video broadcasting
DVB-MHPDVB:	DVB-Multimedia Home Platform
DVD:	Digital video disk
EDF:	Early deadline first
ER:	Entity-Relationship model
FEC:	Forward error correction
gBSD:	Generic bitstream syntax description
GC-tree:	Grid Cell-tree
GMT:	Greenwich Mean Time
GoF:	Group of frames
GoP:	Group of pictures
GPRS:	General packet radio service
GSM:	Global system for mobile communications
GSS:	Group sweeping scheduling
HDTV:	High-definition television
HMMD:	Hue-Max-Min-Diff
HSV:	Hue saturation value
HTML:	Hyper text markup language
ICRA:	Internet Content Rating Association
IEC:	International Electrotechnical Commission
IETF:	Internet Engineering Task Force
IEEE:	Institute of Electrical and Electronic Engineers
I/O:	Input/output
IP:	Internet protocol
IPA:	Intelligent physical agents

IPMP:	Intellectual property management and protection
IR:	Information retrieval
IS:	International standard
ISDN:	Integrated Services Digital Network
ISO:	International Organization for Standardization
IST:	Information Society Technologies
ITU:	International Telecommunications Union
ITU-R:	ITU–Radiocommunication cector
ITU-T:	ITU–Telecommunications standardization sector
JDBC:	Java database connectivity
JMF:	Java Media Framework
JPEG:	Photographic Experts Group
JVT:	Joint Video Team
LAN:	Local Area Network
LCN-R:	Least normalized cost replacement
LFU:	Least frequently used
LPC:	Local polar coordinate-file
LRU:	Least recently used
M3U:	MP3 URL
Mbs:	Mega bits per second
MDS:	Multimedia description schemes
MHMM:	Multiresolution hidden Markov models
MMDBMS:	Multimedia Database Management System
MPEG:	Moving Picture Experts Group
NIST:	U.S. National Institute of Standards and Technology
NFU:	Not frequently used
NN:	Nearest neighbor
ODBC:	Open database connectivity
OODBMS:	Object-oriented database management system
ORDBMS:	Object-relational database management system
PC:	Personal computer
PDA:	Personal digital assistant
PSNR:	Peak signal-to-noise ratio
QBH :	Query by humming
QBIC:	Query by image content
QCIF:	Quarter common intermediate format
QoS:	Quality of services
RDD:	Rights data dictionary
RDF:	Resource description framework
REL:	Rights expression language
RGB:	Red, green, and blue
RSVP:	Resource reservation protocol
RTCP:	Real-time control protocol
RTP:	Real-time transport protocol
RTSP:	Real-time streaming protocol

SCD :	Scalable color descriptor
SIP:	Section initiation protocol
SMIL:	Synchronized multimedia integration language
SMPTE:	Society of Motion Picture and Television Engineers
SMS:	Short message service
SNR:	Signal to noise ratio
SP:	Space partitioning
SPIO:	Spitzenorganisation der Filmwirtschaft e.V.
SQL:	Structured query language
SQL/MM:	SQL multimedia
STB:	Set top box
TETRA:	Terrestrial trunked radio
ToC:	Table of contents
TCP:	Transmission control protocol
TREC:	Text retrieval conferences
TTS:	Text-to-speech
TV:	Television
TZ:	Time zone
UA:	User agents
UAProf:	User agent profile
UDP:	User datagram protocol
UMA:	Universal multimedia access
UML:	Unified Modelling Language
UMTS:	Universal Mobile Telecommunications System
URI:	Uniform resource identifier
URL:	Uniform resource locator
URN:	Uniform resource name
UTF:	Unicode transformation format
VA:	Vector approximation file
VBI:	Vertical blanking interval
VCEG:	Video Coding Experts Group
VCR:	Video cassette recorder
VDSL:	Very high bit rate Digital Subscriber Line
VO:	Video object
VoD:	Video on demand
VoIP:	Voice over IP
WAP:	Wireless application protocol
WAV:	Windows wave file format
W3C:	World Wide Web Consortium
XDSL:	x Digital Subscriber Line (of any type)
XML:	Extensible markup language
XPATH:	XML path language
XSL:	Extensible stylesheet language
XSLT:	Extensible stylesheet language transformations
XSU:	XML SQL utility

Index

NetShow Theater Server, 211
Network(s)
    characteristics, 117
    mobile, 205
NewsML, 237
NIST, *see* U.S. National Institute of
        Standards and Technology
NN search, *see* Nearest-neighbor search
Nonprefecthing strategy, 208
N-tier architecture, 2

O

Object
    coding, 13
    -Oriented DBMSs (OODBMSs), 168, 177
    recognition, semantic indexing and, 139
    -Relational DBMSs (ORDBMSs), 166
    tracking algorithms, 146
Online games, 227
OODBMSs, *see* Object-Oriented DBMSs
Oracle
    Cartridge ORDImage, 171
    Enhancement, 185
    ORDBMS, 168
    video server, 203, 204
    Visual Information Retrieval system, 168
ORDBMSs, *see* Object-Relational DBMSs
ORDImageIndex, 169
ORDImage query, 170
ORION, 185

P

PAMLink, *see* Personal Access over Mobile
        Link
Parfait Olé Melody Search Engine, 162
Path-query expression, 155
PDA, *see* Personal digital assistant
Peak signal-to-noise ratio (PSNR), 118
Peer-to-Peer (P2P) systems, 1, 199, 239
Persistence management, 227
Personal Access over Mobile Link
        (PAMLink), 127
Personal digital assistant (PDA), 155, 198,
        200
Phoneme recognition rates, 94
Photographic libraries, video on demand, 6
Pisa City Web homepage, 62
PointOfView element, 52
P2P systems, *see* Peer-to-Peer systems
Presentation(s)
    clip sharing between, 210
    management, 209

Production description tools, 59
Proxy cache, adaptive, 226
Psychoacoustics block, 11
Pull applications, 129
Push scenario, 29

Q

QBH, *see* Query by Humming
QBIC queries, 175
QCIF, *see* Quarter common intermediate
        format
QoS, *see* Quality of service
QT, *see* Quicktime
Quality of service (QoS), 4
    -aware protocols, classes of, 214
    end-to-end, 219
    guaranteed, 7
    management, coding schemes, 205
    negotiation, 200
    support, 6, 203
Quarter common intermediate format
        (QCIF), 15
Query
    by color similarity, 235
    by Humming (QBH), 161
    by Image Content, IBM, 158, 159
    interface, adaptive, 226
    optimization, 131
    processing techniques, 142
    refinement processing, 177
    by semantics, 235
    song, 29
    vector, lower bound of, 143
Quicktime (QT), 108

R

RDD, *see* Rights data dictionary
RDF, *see* Resource Description Framework
Real Media, 218
RealNetworks, 17
Real-Time Transport Protocol (RTP), 178,
        214
Recognition process, user feedback and,
        140
ReferenceType, 48
REL, *see* Rights expression language
RelIncrTimePoint, 38
Research consortia, industry-supported,
        138
Reservation-based protocols, 214
Reservationless protocols, 214